April 1987.

PRENTICE-HALL INTERNATIONAL

Language Teaching Methodology Series

Applied Linguistics
General Editor: Christopher N. Candlin

Second Language Acquisition in Context

Other titles in this series include

ALDERSON, Charles
Evaluation

BRUMFIT, Christopher J.
Problems and principles in English teaching

BRUMFIT, Christopher J.
Language and literature teaching

CANDLIN, Christopher and MURRAY, Dermot
Language learning tasks

CARROLL, Brendan J.
Testing communicative performance: an interim study

CARROLL, Brendan J. and HALL, Patrick
Make your own language tests

COOK, Vivian
Experimental approaches to second language learning

ELLIS, Rod
Classroom second language development

ELLIS, Rod
Second language acquisition in context

FISIAK, Jacek (ed.)
Contrastive linguistics and the language teacher

JOHNSON, Keith
Communicative syllabus design and methodology

JANICKI, Karol
The foreigner's language: a sociolinguistic perspective

KELLERMAN, Eric and SHARWOOD SMITH, Michael
Cross-linguistic influence in second language acquisition

KRASHEN, Stephen
Second language acquisition and second language learning

KRASHEN, Stephen
Principles and practice in second language acquisition

KRASHEN, Stephen and TERRELL, Tracy
The natural approach

LEE, Y. P. et al.
New directions in language testing

LEONTIEV, Alexei
Psychology and the language learning process

LOVEDAY, Leo
The sociolinguistics of learning and using a non-native language

McKAY, Sandra
Teaching grammar

PECK, Anthony
Language teachers at work

ROBINSON, Gail
Crosscultural understanding

STREVENS, Peter
Teaching English as an international language

SWALES, John
Episodes in ESP

TOSI, Arturo
Immigration and bilingual education

WALLACE, Catherine
Learning to read in a multicultural society

WATERS, Alan
Issues in ESP

YALDEN, Janice
The communicative syllabus

Second Language Acquisition in Context

Edited by

ROD ELLIS
Ealing College of Higher Education

ENGLISH LANGUAGE TEACHING

Prentice-Hall International
Englewood Cliffs, NJ · London
Mexico · New Delhi
Rio de Janeiro · Singapore · Sydney
Tokyo · Toronto

Library of Congress Cataloging in Publication Data

Second language acquisition in context.

(Language teaching methodology series)
Bibliography: p.
1. Language and languages – Study and teaching.
2. Language and languages–Variation.   3. Interlanguage
(Language learning) I. Ellis, Rod. II. Series.
P53.S37 1987   407   86–16928
ISBN 0–13–797895–2 (soft)

British Library Cataloguing in Publication Data

Second language acquisition in context.–
  (Language teaching methodology series)
  1. Language and languages–Study and
  teaching   2. Language acquisition
  I. Ellis, Rod II. Series
  401'.9   P53

  ISBN 0–13–797895–2

© 1987 Prentice-Hall International (UK) Ltd

All rights reserved. No part of this publication may be reproduced,
stored in a retrieval system, or transmitted, in any form or by
any means, electronic, mechanical, photocopying, recording or
otherwise, without the prior permission of Prentice-Hall International (UK) Ltd. For permission within the United States of
America contact Prentice-Hall Inc., Englewood Cliffs, NJ 07632.

Prentice-Hall Inc., Englewood Cliffs, New Jersey
Prentice-Hall International (UK) Ltd, London
Prentice-Hall of Australia Pty Ltd, Sydney
Prentice-Hall Canada Inc., Toronto
Prentice-Hall Hispanoamericana S.A., Mexico
Prectice-Hall of India Private Ltd, New Delhi
Prentice-Hall of Japan Inc., Tokyo
Prentice-Hall of Southeast Asia Pte Ltd, Singapore
Editora Prentice-Hall do Brasil Ltda, Rio de Janeiro

Printed and bound in Great Britain for
Prentice-Hall International (UK) Ltd,
66 Wood Lane End, Hemel Hempstead,
Hertfordshire, HP2 4RG
at the University Press, Cambridge

1 2 3 4 5   91 90 89 88 87

Contents

Preface   vii
CHRISTOPHER CANDLIN

SECTION ONE: INTRODUCTION   1

**Two Approaches for Investigating Second Language Acquisition
in Context**   3
ROD ELLIS AND CELIA ROBERTS

SECTION TWO: THEORETICAL AND METHODOLOGICAL ISSUES   31

**Methodologies for Studying Variability in Second Language
Acquisition**   35
ELAINE TARONE

**Stylistic Variability and Not Speaking 'Normal' English: some Post-
Labovian approaches and their implications for the study of
interlanguage**   47
BEN RAMPTON

Non-systematic Variability: a self-inflicted conundrum?   59
MICHAEL SWAN

SECTION THREE: VARIABILITY IN INTERLANGUAGE SYSTEMS   67

**Variability and Systematicity in the Acquisition of Spatial
Prepositions**   73
MARIA PAVESI

**Processes in Classroom Second Language Development: the
acquisition of negation in German**   83
REGINA WEINERT

Strategy and System in L2 Referential Communication   100
ERIC KELLERMAN, THEO BONGAERTS AND NANDA POULISSE

Variability and Progress in the Language Development of Advanced Learners of a Foreign Language   113
RICHARD TOWELL

SECTION FOUR: VARIABILITY AND SOCIAL CONTEXT   129

'This is My Life': how language acquisition is interactionally accomplished   133
CELIA ROBERTS AND MARGARET SIMONOT

The Notion of 'Competence' and the Patois Speaker   149
VIVIAN EDWARDS

SECTION FIVE: VARIABILITY AND PEDAGOGIC ISSUES   159

Variability and the Reading Behaviour of L2 Readers   165
CATHERINE WALLACE

Contextual Variability in Second Language Acquisition and the Relevancy of Language Teaching   179
ROD ELLIS

Variability and Language Testing   195
PETER SKEHAN

SECTION SIX: CONCLUSION   207

Concluding Comments   209
RICHARD ALLWRIGHT

Bibliography   213

Index   223

Preface

Rod Ellis and his colleagues at the Ealing College of Higher Education are to be warmly thanked for having mounted, with the support of the British Association of Applied Linguistics and Pergamon Press, the seminar on *Contextual Variability and Second Language Acquisition* which has given rise to this innovative collection of papers. The seminar had four aims:

* to examine methods for investigating interlanguage variability;
* to examine the linguistic and situational determinants of interlanguage variability;
* to examine the role of variability in second language acquisition;
* to examine the significance of interlanguage variability studies for language teaching and testing

These aims have naturally enough been refocused in the course of producing this present book, but we still retain in the sections devoted to *Theoretical and Methodological issues; Variability in Interlanguage Systems; Variability and Social Context* and *Variability and Pedagogic Issues*, the essence of what motivated the seminar itself, the urgent need to maintain (and in some cases to establish) the connection between social context and acquisition. There will not be one way in which such a connection will be interpreted or drawn. That much is clear from the lucid and well-argued positions of Celia Roberts and Rod Ellis in their Introduction. They have much in common; nevertheless they represent distinct paths to the study of discourse in context, not merely of interlanguage, but of language *per se*. These paths, one more descriptive the other more critical, point up the hidden significance of this collection of papers, namely its message for those working with language in use albeit outside the domain of second language acquisition.

Perhaps this is the additional perspective to highlight in this Preface, since the papers, with their helpful commentaries, may be expected to speak clearly for themselves. For workers concerned with understanding language in context, this collection offers insights into a range of conditioning variables. Different papers emphasize the significance of setting, topic, asymmetry in attempting an explanation of interlanguage variation. In that we are all in some sense interlingual speakers (if one accepts the crucial stress on *style* made by the authors of the Introduction), the charting of variation in interlanguage development according to domain has consequences for all students of language. What is novel for those students, however, is the need to accommodate the psychological and processing dimension, axiomatic in SLA research. It is that, linked to judgements about the relative volatility of particular domains as moments of linguistic change, which may be of greatest general relevance to students of language.

Pursuing this extendability beyond the field of acquisition, what general conclusions can be drawn? We might put forward five:

  (i) that communication patterns are constitutive of particular cultural environments and are ways of inferring particular values;

  (ii) that there are social psychological as well as ideological constraints on what
is perceived by participants and what is attended to for interpretation;

(iii) that understanding talk requires an understanding of goals, both linguistic and
social, and the prototypical notions of what, say, 'doing X' consists of, the
frames we 'discover' do not exist separately from our own ideologies;

(iv) that the features we selectively attend to as analysts depend on knowledge
passed to us through social relationships and in part on our awareness of
linguistic convention and pragmatic principle;

  (v) that in our understanding of interlanguage (and language in general) in terms
of communicative and cognitive strategy, we need to distinguish between the
knowledge that the participants make use of in constructing their discourse
and the ulterior knowledge of the analyst. In particular, we need to uncover
our hidden presuppositions which derive in part from our social science methodologies, in part from the social objectives of the institutions from which data
are taken, in part from the commonsense knowledge of the participants.

These conclusions of one reader of the papers collected here are, of course, not
unproblematic. They raise questions about the conduct of SLA research once it has
sought a link with social context, which could be conveniently ignored in the regular-
ized and asocial world of laboratory experiment. What are these questions? Firstly,
to ask at what moments researchers should, in Cicourel's terms, 'appeal to higher
levels of predication', and what kinds of socio-cultural information to invoke in the
accounting and explaining of data? Secondly, in steering a course between a stereo-
typing positivism and a free-for-all qualitativism, what bounds to set upon the apparently endless search for motives? Thirdly, what ways can be found to bring to
practitioners and consumers of SLA research an understanding of the links between
text and context which does not merely propagandize but involves them reflexively
in 'owning' the data?

To conclude, the papers collected and introduced in this book do not present a
packaged and always coherent face. They are explorations, and as such, untidy, both
in their different methodologies and their assumptions. What holds them together
and makes them important is that they have tried to come out of the closet of the
controlled environment and take their chance in a world where language is variably
performed and perceived under the influence of context.

Christopher N. Candlin
University of Lancaster
May 1986

Section One:

INTRODUCTION

Two Approaches for Investigating Second Language Acquisition

ROD ELLIS
CELIA ROBERTS
Ealing College of Higher Education

One of the changes that has taken place in the study of second language acquisition (SLA) has been the increasing attention that researchers pay to the role of *context*. Early research typically consisted of the collection of isolated learner utterances which were then subjected to various kinds of analysis. Little attention was paid to either the language that was addressed to the learner (i.e. the input) or to the situation in which the data arose. This study of SLA took place within a theoretical framework which posited an ideal speaker–listener in a homogeneous speech community and was directed at describing and explaining the learner's linguistic competence (cf. Chomsky, 1965).

Some of the later research has operated within a different framework – one that acknowledges the role of context. On the one hand researchers have recognized that we need to examine not only the language produced by the learner but also the language addressed to her. This is because the properties of the input may be reflected in the properties of the output in various ways. On the other hand researchers have recognized that the situational context in which the learner is attempting to communicate will influence her output, and furthermore, that this influence will occur in systematic ways. Whom the learner is speaking to, where and when she is speaking, why she is speaking and what she is speaking about are all seen as potential variables effecting the choice of language. So, the study of SLA has begun to pay attention to sociolinguistic models predicated on the social use of language in a heterogeneous speech community.

The purpose of this introduction is to describe two rather different approaches to the study of SLA in context. The first approach seeks to answer the question, 'How can the study of the context of SLA throw light on the acquisition of the linguistic code?'. Its focus, therefore, is still how linguistic competence is developed. Attention is paid to context because it has become clear that both the use and the acquisition of the code are sensitive to this. The second approach seeks to answer the question, 'What can the social context tell us about how learners develop communicative competence in an L2?'. Here the concern is with more than just the linguistic code. It embraces the competence the learner develops for using the second language (L2) in social interaction.

The study of the relationship between context and acquisition of the linguistic code can be undertaken in two ways. First, it is possible to compare to what extent differences in broad situational contexts lead to differences in the route of acquisition. For example, a comparison can be made between the route of grammatical development evident in naturalistic contexts with that evident in classroom contexts. Second,

3

more detailed studies can be undertaken of how contextual variables such as addressee, topic, or task affect both the use and the acquisition of linguistic knowledge. The aim of such studies is to explain *variability*. The learner performs differently on different occasions. Therefore, the study of SLA in context is also the study of the learner's variable output. By identifying how the learner varies in the use of L2 and by relating the patterns of observed variation to contextual variables, the researcher is able to study how different aspects of the context affect SLA. This research tends to be quantitative in nature, involving counting the frequency with which linguistic forms occur in different contexts.

The study of how the learner develops a capacity to communicate in social contexts and also of how these contexts facilitate or impede this development has followed a rather different path. The approach owes its perspective to many of the methods of anthropology and sociology. When it draws on more linguistic approaches, it is those of discourse analysis and pragmatics. It has two, not easily compatible, concerns. One is to describe interactions from a participant perspective. The other is to relate these interactions to the social structure which they help to maintain, and involves taking a critical stance in order to understand the relationship between language and power and how this affects the L2 learner. In this approach, then, 'context' is explored through the study of interactions. The methodology is essentially qualitative and interpretative. It involves both the detailed study of representative samples of learner discourse, as far as possible from the actors' point of view, and, the social and cultural knowledge which the interactants use in communications. Interpretation is necessary in order to relate the local with the non-local and so to understand how people create contexts together.

This Introduction falls into two major parts. The first deals with the relationship between context and the linguistic code. The second is concerned with social context and interactional competence. The main focus of both sections is the development of a second language – whether viewed narrowly as linguistic competence or broadly as communicative competence. However, we feel it will assist the reader if we first give an account of a number of key sociolinguistic concepts. Each section, therefore, starts with a description of language use in general, before turning to SLA.

Part one: context and the linguistic code

The main aim of this section is to consider how the study of SLA in context can contribute to an understanding of the process of interlanguage development. We will be concerned with the acquisition of linguistic competence. In order to provide a thorough grounding in the sociologistic methods of enquiry which have been used to investigate this we will look first at context and variability in native speaker language use. Then we will turn to SLA.

Context and variability: a sociolinguistic viewpoint

We begin this section by introducing the reader to how the sociolinguist views the effects of context on language use. The basic premise of the sociolinguist's approach to the study of language is that language use involves *choice*, so we start with this. We then consider what is meant by the term *context*, considering both the extra-linguistic and linguistic factors that influence language choice. Finally,we review what sociologists have had to say about language change.

Language use and choice

Language use involves choice. Just as getting dressed involves deciding which clothes to wear, so communicating involves decisions about which words to use. Each time we construct an utterance we have to select from our available resources in such a way as to convey what we want to say. Furthermore, because each utterance is also an action (i.e. it performs some function) we must select those exponents that most appropriately realize the action. Language is organized in such a way that there is always choice; it is by choosing that we create meaning.

Choice can be shown to exist at different language levels – phonological, lexical and grammatical. For reasons of space, however, we will illustrate it at the gram-matical level only. If we take a sentence frame such as:

I've just met the man ____ you were talking about.

we can see that there is a choice between three forms of relative pronoun which can be used to complete it – 'who', 'that' and zero. There is probably a certain amount of 'free' choice in the sense that any of the three forms might be used on any occasion. However, there is probably a tendency to use 'who' in formal situations and 'that' or zero in informal situations, particularly where speech is involved.

Choice also arises in the way language functions are realized. For example, Ervin-Tripp suggests six distinct ways of realizing *directives*. These can be ordered according to how 'direct' they are. For example, a need statement such as 'I want a cup of coffee' is clearly much more direct than an embedded imperative such as 'Would you make me a cup of coffee?' which in turn is more direct than a hint such as 'It's ten o'clock and I'm thirsty'. Speakers are sensitive to the social conditions prevailing in any situation and respond to these by selecting exponents of a function that convey the right social meanings.

There is also choice at the discourse level. The language user has to decide how to realize an action, as suggested above, but he also has to decide which action to perform. For example, if someone were to give the directive:

Make me a cup of coffee.

you would have a number of choices about what to do next. One possibility would be to agree (e.g. 'Okay'), another to query whether the speaker had the right to make such a request (e.g. 'I made the last one so now it's your turn'), another to put forward a suggestion (e.g. 'What about some tea for a change?'). Yet another possibility would be to keep silent, although this might be thought of as breaking the co-operative principle that governs conversation (Grice, 1975). It is, nevertheless, feasible.

It is possible to classify the kinds of choices that language users make. Choices can involve *categorical* language behaviour. This occurs when there is total predictability in the use of two forms of functions. For example, if *x* is always used in context *a*, while *y* is always used in context *b*, the use of these forms is categorical. In most cases, however, choice leads to *variable* language behaviour. Here it is useful to distinguish between *free variation* and *systematic variation*. Free variation occurs when the use of two forms (*x* and *y*) is entirely unpredictable, such that both *x* and *y* are used randomly in contexts *a* and *b*. Systematic variation arises when choice reveals a probability of *x* being used in context *a* and *y* in context *b*. Sociolinguists disagree over whether there is such a thing as free variation. Some argue that variation is always systematic and that if it appears not to be this is just because the determining factor (i.e. the principle affecting choice) has not been discovered. Other sociolinguists, however, perceive of language as in a constant state of flux and, therefore, argue that free variation is normal.

The principle that language use involves choice can be applied to sociolinguistic analyses in a number of ways. One way is to look at how choice operates within a single code (e.g. in one dialect of a language). This involves the study of what we can call *intralinguistic variation* and is the main focus of this book. It is also possible to study *interlinguistic variation*. For example, multilingual language users can code-switch by selecting which language to use in either different situations or within a single situation. Other language users are multidialectal and so are faced with choices about which dialect to use.

In emphasizing the notion of choice, we do not want to convey the idea that there are no constraints on the kinds of choice that the language user can make. Indeed it is precisely because there are constraints – psychological, social, cultural and even political – that the study of the choices which different language users do make is of so much interest. Language choice is at the heart of all sociolinguistic enquiry. What constrains someone to choose *x* rather than *y*? What is the significance of this choice? To examine how the constraints operate and the meanings created by language choice it is necessary to examine the second major construct – context.

The linguistic and situational context

The term *context* is often defined with reference to the actual situation in which a communicative event takes place. Clearly not everything present in the situation is likely to affect language choice, so from a sociolinguist's point of view the 'context' consists of those aspects of the situation which activate choice. As Lyons (1977:572) puts it, context is:

> a theoretical construct in the postulation of which the linguist abstracts from the actual situation and establishes as contextual all the factors which, by virtue of their influence upon the participants in a language event, systematically determine the form, the appropriacy and the meaning of utterances.

This provides a basis for our initial definition of context.

We need to recognize that 'the actual situation' to which Lyons refers consists of both linguistic and extralinguistic elements. The linguistic elements are generally referred to as the *linguistic context* and the extralinguistic elements as the *situational context*. We will consider each separately.

It can be shown that the choice of one linguistic form rather than another is influenced by the linguistic elements that precede or follow the variable structure in question. For example, Labov (1969) found that whether a speaker uses contracted copula (e.g. 'He's a doctor') or full copula (e.g. 'Simon *is* tall') depends on the linguistic environment. Contraction is much more likely if the word preceding the copula ends in a vowel. Contraction is also more frequent if the word following the copula is a noun phrase than if it is an adjective. Labov's work demonstrates that linguistic context affects choice.

The construct of 'linguistic context' should not be limited to the preceding and following elements in isolated utterances (as in the example above). It can be extended to include the verbal environment of whatever category the linguist chooses to examine. For example, we could talk about the context of a complete utterance. This would lead us to examine how the choice and form of individual speech acts is governed by the discourse in which they occur.

The situational context can be defined at the macro or the micro level. At the macro level we can distinguish prototypical contexts or, as they are sometimes called, *domains*. A domain is a grouping together of recurring situation types. Examples often cited in the literature are the school, the family, the church, government administration, etc. Each domain is associated with the use of either a separate language or a particular variety of a single language. Thus, different choices arise in the domain of the school from the domain of the family. The notion of domain is an important one for SLA studies in several ways. First, it can be used to study when the learner uses his mother tongue and what he uses the L2. This approach is often followed in the sociolinguistic study of bilingualism, but is not used in this book. Second, the notion of domain can be used to explore whether observed variability in the use and acquisition of a second language can be explained by reference to general contexts of use. One way that this has been attempted in SLA research is in global comparisons of SLA in the classroom domain and in the 'naturalistic' domain (cf. the papers by Weinert and Pavesi in this book). A third way in which the effects of domain on L2 use and acquisition have been explored is through the detailed analysis of a specific domain, such as that associated with unequal encounters (cf. the paper by Roberts and Simonot). One of the problems of research based on the notion of domain is that it is not always clear what a particular domain consists of. For example, to categorize the classroom as a domain can be misleading, in that the kind of language behaviour that occurs in such a context can vary enormously from one classroom to another, and also within a single classroom. Ideally, then we need to examine context at the micro level.

To do this we need to examine how individual situational variables affect language choice. There are a number of descriptions of these variables available to choose from. One of the best known is that of Hymes (1974). The one we will briefly outline here is Brown and Fraser's (1979). They begin by classifying 'situation' into 'scene' and 'participants'. 'Scene' is in turn divided into 'setting' and 'purpose'. The former involves such factors as who the bystanders (i.e. non-active participants in the language event) are, and what the locale or time is. Purpose is described in terms of activity type (e.g. buying, lecturing, or playing a game). The 'participants' category of Brown and Fraser's framework is also further subdivided. There are various factors to do with the participants as 'individuals' (e.g. personality, interests, moods, social class, ethnic background) and other factors to do with how the participants interrelate (e.g. their shared knowledge, social status and social power). The general framework is shown in Figure 1.

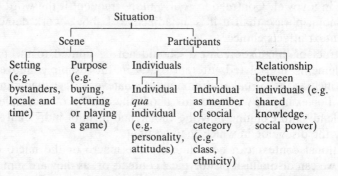

FIGURE 1   *Situational variables (based on Brown and Fraser, 1979)*

Such frameworks must be treated circumspectly, however. As Brown and Fraser point out, there is no consensus on what constitute the criterial variables of the situational context. Also we cannot assume that the variables interrelate in precisely the pattern shown in any one framework. However, a framework such as that of Brown and Fraser does provide a basis for examining how different contextual factors affect language use. The researcher can investigate which linguistic features correlate with which contextual factors. For example, a study could be set up to investigate how the time factor in settings influences language choice. Ochs (1979) has shown that there are systematic differences between planned and unplanned discourse, depending on the amount of time the speaker has to organize what he wants to say and how he wants to say it. It should be noted, however, that these differences are probabilistic and not absolute; situational factors such as the time variable are likely to result in *systematic variability* rather than *categorical language use*.

One type of situational variation which has received considerable attention is *stylistic variation*. This can be defined as variation that results from differing levels of formality. That is, language choice is governed by a cluster of factors relating to both scene and participants. For example, the choice of address terms is affected by the relationship between the speaker and the addressee and also by whether the speech event takes place in an institutional or a more informal setting. Labov (1970) has suggested that stylistic variation occurs on a single dimension according to differences in the degree to which the speaker is attending to the form of his speech. In formal situations the speaker pays a lot of attention to his choice of language in order to avoid the use of socially stigmatized forms and to ensure the use of socially prestigious forms. In informal situations he pays less attention to language choice, and uses those forms that are easily retrieved and which belong to his 'vernacular'.

To summarize, the construct of *context* is used by sociolinguists to explain why language users make the choices they do. A large proportion of language variability is deemed to be systematic because it can be shown that language choice is contextually determined. Both the linguistic context and the situational context affect choice. In the case of the latter this effect can be investigated at the macro level (i.e. by relating language use to situational domains), and at the micro level (i.e. by correlating the use of specific linguistic features with narrowly defined social categories to do with the scene and participants of the situational context).

Variability and language change

So far we have been examining the relationship between language use and context. We have seen that we can explore this relationship by looking at the correlation between language choice and contextual factors. We now turn to the relationship between context and language change. An understanding of this relationship is particularly important for the sociolinguistic study of SLA.

We can draw a distinction between *synchronic variability* and *diachronic variability*. The former refers to variability present in language at any one point in time and is what we have been looking at up to now. Diachronic variability refers to the historical development that takes place in a language between two different points in time. The question which arises is what the relationship is between variability on the horizontal axis (i.e. synchronic variability) and variability on the vertical axis (i.e. diachronic variability).

One way in which the relationship can be examined is by studying what can happen to forms that are used initially in *free variation*. You will recall that this refers to the random use of two or more variants of a structure in the same contexts. Labov (1972) provides a good example of how this kind of variation can be exploited by language users when there is social pressure to do so. Labov examined how a sound change took place in the inhabitants of Martha's Vineyard, an island off the New England coast. This change involved the intensification and exploitation of a feature, (ay), which, was already present in the islanders' linguistic repertoires. It consisted of the gradual centralization of (ay) and was motivated by the islanders' felt need to maintain their own social identity against the influx of outsiders from the mainland. In this way, then, what started as free variation evolved into systematic variation. A second kind of change occurs when there is a shift in the pattern of systematic variability. Table 1 illustrates this. This kind of development can be viewed as the gradual movement towards categoricality. That is, over time, two forms which initially were both used in two contexts, come to be used in complementary distribution, such that each form is restricted to its own context. In this way, changes in the pattern of variability over time constitute interim stages in the long term path of historical development.

An example may help to make this clearer. A good one is the development of the modern English negative structure. The dominant negative structure in Chaucer's day was verb + neg (e.g. 'speak not') – similar to modern German. However, in the *Monk's Tale* there are one or two examples of the modern English negative structure

TABLE 1
The movement towards categoricality

Time	Feature	Context a	Context b
1	x	66%	34%
	y	34%	66%
2	x	80%	20%
	y	20%	80%
3	x	100%	0%
	y	0%	100%

(i.e. aux + neg + verb). Interestingly these occur in the speech of a young child. By Shakespeare's day both forms are in common use, with a tendency for the older form to denote age, conservatism and social authority and the newer form youth, radicalism and social equality. In present-day English, the two forms still exist, but their use has become categorical. The old form is now restricted to encoding 'olde English' (and, except for this rather special function is obsolete), while the new form is used in all other contexts.

So far the language changes we have described – all deriving from horizontal variability – have been the result of external factors (e.g. the language users' desire to maintain their social identity). However, change can also arise as a result of internal factors. Because language works as a system, a change in one part of it, perhaps brought about by some external factor, is likely to lead to changes in other parts. Initial change creates structural pressure inside the language which brings about further changes. Labov shows how this happened in the speech of the Martha's Vineyarders. We have already seen that (ay) was gradually centralized; this led to a similar change in (aw).

Internal linguistic factors are also involved in another way. When change starts, it does so in specific linguistic contexts and only gradually spreads to other linguistic contexts. We may surmise that change is first introduced in 'heavy' contexts because these in some way favour its use, perhaps for psycholinguistic or even physiological reasons. The new form is then systematically introduced into 'lighter contexts', until, finally, categorical use is achieved in all linguistic contexts requiring the new form. Table 2 shows what happens.

TABLE 2
The introduction of a new variant across linguistic contexts

Time	Linguistic contexts		
	a	b	c
1	50%	0%	0%
2	100%	50%	0%
3	100%	100%	50%
4	100%	100%	100%

Ideally sociolinguists would like to investigate language change *longitudinally* but this is hardly practical, as language change is typically a very slow process. For this reason they have developed techniques for investigating change *cross-sectionally*.

This is possible if data are collected from language users of different ages and different social backgrounds. It is then possible to identify the patterns of variability of selected features for this population and establish how these are are hierarchically ordered. For example, if the feature under investigation was contracted and full copula, it might be shown that every language user who employed the contracted copula also employed the full copula, but that the converse was not true. In other words, the presence of one variant (full copula) implies the presence of the other variant (contracted copula). In this way it is possible to establish a hierarchy of features, such that the order in the hierarchy reflects the extent to which each feature is present in the population of language users being studied. Sociolinguists suggest that the route of language change follows this hierarchy – that is, the higher up the hierarchy a form is, the earlier it appeared in the language. This method of analysis – known as *implicational scaling* – has been used in particular by sociolinguists interested in the evolution and development of creoles. It has also been used in SLA research – as we will see later.

Context and interlanguage development

We have now examined how sociolinguists investigate the relationship between context and language use through the study of linguistic variability. We have also seen how the study of variability can be used to make statements about the way language develops historically. We now turn to the relationship between context and variabilty in SLA. We will consider this relationship in two ways. First, we will examine how *domains* of SLA affect development. Second, we will consider how SLA is influenced by the linguistic and situational context. In both cases the discussion will be limited to the acquisition of the L2 linguistic code.

Domain and interlanguage development

Strong claims have been advanced (e.g. Krashen, 1981) that the development of L2 knowledge follows a more or less standard route. This route, it is claimed, is evident in a fixed order of development of grammatical morphemes such as plural -s, past tense -ed, and articles, and also in a fixed sequence of development for transitional structures such as negatives or interrogatives, which involve the acquisition of a series of interim rules before the target language rule can be mastered. It has been suggested that the universality of this route is the result of the way the L2 learner processes input data. The learner is predisposed to construct his interlanguage in fixed ways.

Not all SLA researchers agree with Krashen that there is a 'natural' route of development, and the extent to which interlanguage development can vary is an issue currently receiving much attention. In particular, researchers are interested in whether different learning conditions can affect the order of development. One way of investigating this is by comparing how interlanguage develops in different domains.

One type of comparison that can be made is between SLA in a naturalistic domain and SLA in a classroom domain. There are now a number of reviews of the research which has undertaken this comparison (e.g. Long, 1983; Ellis, 1985c). Where route of development is concerned, the general picture which emerges can be summarized as follows:

(1) In general the route of development is impervious to context. That is, there is general agreement that the order in which a set of morphemes are acquired or the stages through which learners pass in acquiring transitional structures like negatives or interrogatives, is not affected by the learning domain. Also, the error types found in naturalistic and classroom SLA are the same.
(2) Certain structures are influenced by instruction, however. For example, third person -s and plural -s appear to be used more accurately (and, therefore, possibly acquired earlier) by learners who receive instruction.

In addition, the available evidence suggests that instructed learners learn more rapidly than uninstructed learners (cf. Long, 1983b) and also go on to achieve higher levels of proficiency. Instruction may not be able to 'beat' the natural order of development in any significant way, but it may enable the learner to pass along it more rapidly. There are a number of possible explanations for this. One is that if instruction is timed to take place when the learner is developmentally 'ready' to acquire a particular structure, acquisition takes place more easily than if the learner is left to 'discover' the rule for himself. Another explanation is that formal instruction may sensitize the learner to the presence of specific formal features in the input, which otherwise, left to his own resources, he might not attend to. A third explanation is that in the classroom the learner is exposed to a more formal register of language use which provides a different kind of data to work on and facilitates the development of features that are infrequent or insignificant in the kind of informal language use experienced naturalistically.

It is becoming clear that we can expect some differences in interlanguage development according to learning domain. These differences will probably be manifest more in the rate and success of acquisition than in the sequence of development or the central processes of interlanguage rule-formation. However, the effects of learning domain are likely to operate in subtle ways. It is becoming clear, for instance, that the effects of instruction on SLA are very complex. A lot more research will be needed to establish when and how classroom learners differ from naturalistic learners. Also, research is needed to explore how differences in the learning conditions within each of these broad domains affects SLA. We already have evidence to suggest that naturalistic learners experience very different contexts for acquiring the L2 (cf. Schumann, 1978a; Roberts and Simonot, this book) and these affect the level of proficiency attained. We need more finely grained comparisons of learning domain to discover how learner-internal (i.e. innate factors) interact with learner-external (i.e. environmental) factors.

The linguistic and situational context and interlanguage development

It is possible to identify a number of different kinds of rules which comprise the interlanguage of an L2 learner. These are:

(1) *Formulaic structures*

These are linguistic units which have no internal structure and which are acquired and used as unanalyzed wholes. Formulas which figure in the interlanguage of many learners of L2 English are, 'I don't know' and 'Can I have a ____?'. Arguably, formulaic structures do not constitute rules in the normal sense of this term.

(2) *Categorical interlanguage rules*

These are invariable rules which differ from those found in the target language. For example, at any early stage of development, L2 learners may have a single categorical rule for verbs – the unmarked, simple verb form (e.g. 'come') – which is used in all contexts irrespective of how the target language is used.

(3) *Variable interlanguage rules*

These are rules that account for the systematic distribution of two or more variants, one or both of which is/are not found in the target language. For example, learners in the process of acquiring English negative structures may alternate, at some point, between the neg + verb pattern and the aux + neg + verb pattern (cf. the earlier discussion of the historical development of English negatives) in a systematic way.

(4) *Categorical target language rules*

These are invariable rules found in the target language. For example, there is a categorical rule for German that requires the verb to be end-positioned in subordinate clauses. Such rules may not be acquired until late on in SLA. In some learners they may not be acquired at all.

(5) *Variable target language rules*

These are rules that account for the systematic distribution of two or more variants which are also found in the target language grammar. An example is the rule that describes the use of full and contracted copula (cf. Labov, 1970). We know very little about how or whether L2 learners acquire such rules.

With these different types of rules in mind, we can try to specify how the linguistic and situational context affects SLA.

First consider the learner who produces these utterances:

I don't understand.
I no understand.

These utterances might be used as evidence to claim that the learner is operating a variable interlanguage rule. However, such a claim might be ill-founded. It is possible that 'I don't understand' exists as a formulaic utterance, while 'I no understand' is produced in accordance with an underlying interlanguage rule for negative structures. In order to identify true variability in an interlanguage system we need to first identify all utterances which exist as formulaic structures. Unless we do this, we will create a false picture.

Any interlanguage system is likely to manifest a large number of variable rules of type (3). Variability is an inherent property of interlanguage systems. Examples can be found to show that both the linguistic and the situational context determine the distribution of variants in an interlanguage variable rule. For example, Ellis (forthcoming) has shown that one L2 learner of English whose interlanguage contained a variable rule for third person -s (the variants being -s and the simple verb form), distributed these variants according to whether the preceding element was a pronoun or a noun phrase subject, as shown in Table 3. Here, then, is a clear example of how the learner's variable output is governed by linguistic factors.

TABLE 3
*Percentage suppliance of two variants by one L2
learner according to linguistic context*

Linguistic context	Variant	
	-s	simple form
Pronoun subject	81%	19%
Noun phrase subject	39%	61%

There is abundant evidence, too, to show that factors to do with the situational context influence when the L2 user uses one form as opposed to another. For example, Fairbanks (1983) reports that a Japanese learner of English rarely used third person -s in casual speech (using, instead, the simple form) but supplied it consistently in his careful style, even overgeneralizing it to contexts requiring the plural verb form. Third person -s, therefore, constitutes a variable interlanguage structure which is influenced both by the linguistic and the situational context.

Fairbanks' research utilized the methodology developed by Labov to investigate stylistic variability. As we explained earlier, stylistic variability results from the language user's response to the degree of formality in a situation. Labov hypothesized that speakers would show greater attention to their speech in formal situations than in informal ones. He designed studies to investigate stylistic variation in native speakers by selecting different elicitation instruments in order to tap vernacular speech, careful speech and speech in intermediate styles. For example, he got his subjects to read out lists of words (careful style) and recorded naturally-occurring conversations (vernacular style). In choosing these elicitation instruments Labov argued that language users would pay greater attention to speech in careful styles than in vernacular styles. A similar approach has been used by a number of SLA researchers (e.g. Dickerson, 1975; Schmidt, 1977; Tarone, 1985). These studies reveal very similar patterns of variation to those reported by Labov. In general, the more that learners are attending to their speech, the more likely they are to use the target language variant. However, other studies show that the picture is more complicated where L2 behaviour is concerned. For example, it has been shown that speech produced in a careful style can be *less* target-like if attending to form leads the learner to make greater use of a first language variant as opposed to a target language variant. This is likely to occur when the L2 learner associates the first language variant he has 'borrowed' with a formal style.

Nearly all studies of interlanguage variability have been carried out using the

Labovian model. This is perhaps unfortunate, as a number of papers in the book make clear (cf. papers by Rampton, Swan, and Skehan). We need to explore more rigorously which factors in the situational context account for variability. Rampton suggests that variability can arise when the learner feels a need to mitigate the force of certain speech acts, such as boasts and refusals. Rampton argues we need to examine the sociocultural framework in which interaction takes place. This requires a more interpretative analysis to explain the dynamic, moment-by-moment choices which the learner makes during an interaction. The techniques of interactional socio-linguistics and the contribution they can make to the study of SLA are discussed in greater detail in Part Two of this Introduction. We would like to point out that such techniques, while ideally suited to investigating how L2 learners develop communi-cative competence, will also throw light on how they develop linguistic competence, which is our focus here.

One way in which interlanguage development takes place is by the gradual elimin-ation of variability. This is because variable rules are more evident in interlanguage than in the target language. But it is important to realize that variability is never entirely eliminated, even in the learner who proceeds to target language competence, as the target language itself contains a fair number of variable rules. It is a mistake to view SLA as targeted exclusively on the acquisition of categorical rules. It is targeted on those patterns of variability that exist in the target language variety. Thus successful SLA will involve the acquisition of target language variable rules (i.e. type 5). This obvious truth has been neglected, in general, by SLA researchers, and perhaps even more so by teachers. For example, studies which have investigated how learners acquire English copula have treated the copula rule as a categorical one. They have sought to determine whether acquisition has or has not taken place by seeing whether learners supply the copula in obligatory contexts (i.e. in utterances where the presence of the copula is required in native speaker performance). However, as we have seen earlier, the copula is best accounted for by a variable rule, which specifies the probability of the full or contracted copula occurring in different linguistic contexts. Ellis (forthcoming) has shown that a learner can achieve apparent native-like control over the copula, if this is measured in terms of suppliance in obligatory contexts, but not achieve total control if this is measured in terms of native-like variable use. In short, we know very little about how L2 learners acquire variable target language rules.

So far we have been considering how interlanguage variability – viewed synchron-ically – can be accounted for. We will now examine the relationship beween context and interlanguage development by investigating to what extent and in what ways *horizontal* variability predicts *vertical* growth.

One way in which SLA researchers have investigated acquisition is by calculating the *accuracy order* of different linguistic features in a corpus of data collected cross-sectionally and then equating this with the *acquisition order* (cf. Dulay and Burt, 1973). For example, if the accuracy levels for three structures at a single point in time are as follows:

structure *x* 90%
structure *y* 50%
structure *z* 30%

it is claimed that these structures will be acquired in the order *x, y, z*. Such an assumption may be unwarranted, however. Kellerman (1985) has shown that for some structures there is a U-pattern of development. Learners start off using them with more or less target-like accuracy but then, as new forms are introduced into their interlanguage, begin to produce errors, before finally once again producing them correctly. Thus the level of accuracy of a structure at a particular point in time cannot be taken as a measure of whether it has been acquired. It follows that accuracy order may not be a reliable indication of acquisition order.

Another way of plotting the relationship between horizontal variability and inter-language development is by means of *implicational scaling* (see previous section). This exploits the variability evident in a group of learners in cross-sectional data. Acquisition is determined by establishing whether particular structures are absent or present in the interlanguage of individual learners in the group. The subjects are ranked according to the presence or absence of particular rules. This produces a 'staircase order' of the kind reported by Dittmar (1980) for the acquisition of verb forms in L2 German (see Figure 2).

Thus a learner who manifests 'aux + modal + verb' will also manifest all the other forms. Another learner will have acquired only 'verb' and none of the features to

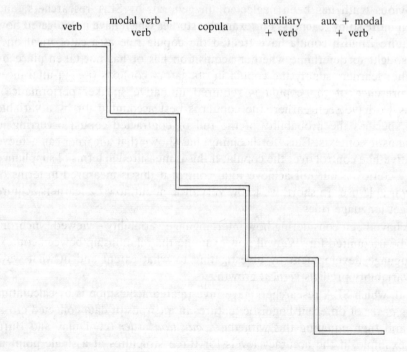

FIGURE 2   *Implicational order for the development of verb forms in L2 German (based on Dittmar, 1980)*

the right. In this way the variable pattern of use in cross-sectional data can be seen to reflect acquisition over time. Development consists of moving down the staircase.

Implicational scaling offers a way of relating variability across learners to interlanguage development. But what of variability to be observed in the speech of a *single* learner? Can this be related to development? You will recall that language change is influenced by contextual factors, both internal and external. There is some evidence to show that this is also the case for interlanguage development.

When a form first appears in an interlanguage, it does so in restricted contexts. As the learner gains greater control over the form its use spreads to other linguistic contexts. Thus, for instance, the rule for third person -s may first be restricted to contexts where the subject of the verb is a pronoun. Later the learner extends the rule to contexts where the subject is a noun phrase. This change occurs as a gradual process in much the same way as historical change (see Table 2). It is possible to identify how the contexts are developmentally ordered by examining the accuracy with which a specific form such as third person -s is used in each context at a single point in time. Thus initially we find that third person -s is used with greater accuracy with pronoun than with noun phrase subjects (see Table 3).

However, the true picture is much more complicated. This is because when a form first appears it is likely to do so in contexts where some previously acquired form is used. Initially this gives rise to *free variation*. Gatbonton (1978) provides a framework for describing what appears to happen. In her *diffusion model* there is an 'acquisition phase' and a 'replacement phase'. In the former the learner first acquires a specific form which he uses in a number of different linguistic contexts. Then he acquires a second form, which is used in the same contexts. By the end of the acquisition phase, therefore, the learner has two forms operating in free variation. In the replacement phase the learner first restricts one of the forms to a specific context, while continuing to use both forms in all other contexts. Later both forms come to be restricted to their respective contexts. Gatbonton shows how her model can be applied to L2 phonological development, but there is no reason why it cannot also be used to describe grammatical development.

Finally, we will consider how variability according to situational context is related to interlanguage development. Tarone (1982) suggests that there is a 'pull effect' from the learner's careful style in the direction of the vernacular style. That is, new forms may enter the learner's interlanguage in the careful style and then gradually spread to other more informal styles. For example, third person -s may first be evident in carefully monitored speech (as Fairbanks' research showed) but later become apparent in unattended speech. Thus the accuracy levels of third person -s in different styles at any one developmental point provide an indication of the degree of control which the learner has achieved over this form at this stage.

The claim that stylistic variability and interlanguage development are related must be treated circumspectly, however. While it appears an entirely plausible claim from what is known about the nature of language use in general, it has not yet received any clear empirical support. Further caveats are in order. It would be wrong to suggest that *all* forms emerge first in the careful style. Some forms may be acquired directly into the vernacular style. Indeed, the spread of forms may work in the opposite direction – from the vernacular style to the careful style. Also it should be recognized that there will be within-style variability, which is also contextually determined. Rampton's discussion of the 'me no . . . ' pattern is evidence of this. The learners he studied varied in their choice of the 'me no . . . ' form as opposed to the target language form (which they had acquired), while communicating in the vernacular style. Rampton suggests this may have been interactionally motivated to mitigate the force of their utterances by taking on 'learner status'.

In general, then, we do not know very much about how synchronic variability brought about by situational factors is related to acquisition. What we know about language change suggests that such a relationship is likely. The stylistic continuum may be related to vertical development in the way that Tarone and others have suggested. But synchronic variability is much more complex than the Labovian model suggests. Learners may revert to an early L2 form if the pragmatic demands of the situation make this appropriate. When this happens a 'horizontal slice' will not necessarily reflect 'vertical development'.

In conclusion, we can say that the study of interlanguage has gained enormously from sociolinguistic approaches which have sought to relate language use to context. In this approach the formal mastery of the L2 is to be seen as embedded in its communicative mastery. Not all researchers are in agreement with such an approach. Some researchers continue to view the learner's competence as homogeneous and to discount variability as performance (see Swan's article in this book). It is our belief, however, that context is of crucial importance for understanding how interlanguage develops and that the study of variability provides a way of observing both what the learner's linguistic competence consists of at any one time and also how this competence changes over time.

Part two: social context and the development of communicative competence

In this section we shall discuss the resources any speaker uses when they engage in meaningful interaction and how the context of that interaction helps to create or inhibit the development of these resources. The focus of this part is how communicative competence is developed in SLA but, as in Part One, we will begin by considering language use in general before turning to SLA. We begin by considering what is included in the notion of communicative competence.

Communicative competence

The notion of *communicative competence* was introduced by Hymes in the mid 1960s. Hymes was interested in what degree of competence speakers needed to give them membership of a particular speech community. In other words, he examined what factors, particularly sociocultural, were necessary – in addition to grammatical competence – for speakers to engage in meaningful interaction.

Hymes set the sociocultural ball rolling. He showed how language variation correlated with social and cultural norms of certain defined public interactions – or speech events. However, he did not look at the specific ways in which interactions work.

This type of detailed, anatomical work has been carried out by the ethnomethodologists examining conversation as an 'ongoing accomplishment' (Schegloff, 1982). They have demonstrated how conversations are systematically organized by speakers and that this organization is fundamental to how interaction is accomplished. This is an important step in understanding how interactions work, but it is only a small part of the totality of processes that are going on when people make sense of each other and accomplish a conversation together.

Gumperz (1984), reviewing the current position on communicative competence, suggests that it should not be defined in terms of rules that speakers must use – as many other sociolinguists have tried to define it. Instead, he argues that communicative competence is about creating conditions that make possible shared interpretation. The knowledge and skills to do this require relating essentially context-free linguistic competence to context-specific discourse processing conventions. As yet, we know little about this relationship.

Canale (1983b) in his pedagogical perspective of communicative competence also admits that we know little about how the different aspects of competence interact. However, Canale and Swain (1980) and Canale (1983b) have proposed a framework for communicative competence which is particularly helpful in attempting to categorize learners' use of language for assessment purposes. They propose four competences:

(1) grammatical competence
(2) discourse competence (i.e. the ability to use grammatical competence to make cohesive and coherent texts)
(3) sociolinguistic competence (i.e. the ability to use language appropriately in different contexts)
(4) strategic competence (i.e. the ability to compensate for difficulties and make the use of language effective).

Whether we argue for a participant perspective on conversation, as Gumperz has, or whether we attempt a modular definition of communicative competence, as suggested by Canale and Swain, it is clear that the study of language use in context is impoverished if it does not include research into interactional knowledge and skills. It is to this view of communicative competence that we now turn.

Context as interaction

In Part One of this Introduction we referred to the situational and linguistic context and considered the correlation between isolated features of situation and linguistic variability. In this section we examine context as interaction.

Context is, more than any particular set of non-linguistic features, used to place or account for the nature of an interaction. Context is created by the interaction itself. As such it consists of the particular beliefs and presuppositions that the interactants bring to the encounter. It is also mutually constructed by them, turn by turn.

In other words, there is a dynamic element to context. Each utterance creates its own context within which the next speaker will respond. For example.

A: Will you be home early today?
B: When do you need the car?
(from Milroy, 1984).

Speaker B's utterance can only be understood if we explore B's inferential processes (i.e. the processes used by a listener to interpret the implied meanings of an interaction). B has constructed a context for A's question on the assumption that it was an indirect request. Of course, this might not have been A's intention but that is now the context B has set. A must either pursue the original negotiation or clear up the misunderstanding.

We make on-the-spot judgements about what is going on in an exchange. We pick up cues from the talk and physical setting which trigger expectations about what the activity is. The cues we give and receive in talk have been described by John Gumperz (1982 a and b) as *contextualization cues*. They help to channel the interpretations that listeners may have, and they help interactants to see how what is being said ties in with the preceding and following utterances. Where speakers share the same mother tongue and the same overall style of communicating, contextualization cues help participants to feel they understand each other – that they are on the same wavelength.

Context is, therefore, created in interaction partly on the basis of particular and individual choices by speakers at a local level and partly by those speakers being able to make inferences about each other on the basis of shared knowledge and assumptions about the world and about how to accomplish things interactionally. In this respect, the study of pragmatics (Levinson, 1983) is useful in helping to explain how the particular and the individual works with the general and the systematic. Meaning can only be interpreted in a particular context but it is only possible to get the meaning across because the processes of inferencing that are required are based on general maxims, principles or assumptions. Cicourel (1974) has indicated what these general ground rules are, such as the 'wait and see' principle and agreement on what needs to be said and what needs to be left out. Levinson, who has related early work on pragmatics by linguistic philosophers to more recent work on interactional analysis, suggests that these inferential processes are systematic. In other words, he suggests that members of the same speech community are likely to make the same sort of inferences and recognize the same sort of pragmatic constraints when asked to analyse a piece of naturally occurring data.

One of the most crucial choices that speakers have to make is deciding how much knowledge has been established during the course of the conversation. They have to decide what to leave out and what to put in, what is given and what is new (cf. Clark and Haviland, 1977, for the given/new contract). Speakers use their linguistic resources to foreground new information and put into the background what they assume the other already knows, either explicitly or by implication (the latter being the case in the example given above). This is just one way in which speakers co-operate together, basing their decisions on the general principle about how much needs to be said and what can be left out.

The following is an example of how the context is negotiated as the interaction proceeds. In a job interview between white managers and an Asian applicant, the following exchange took place:

A: So you eventually did get a job with the assistance of a friend. I was wondering what that meant. Did he recommend you to the employment centre or to the manager. . . ?

B: No – well, he brought me a form. . . .

There is a clear context for the job interview, much of which is retrievable from even this small fragment in terms of sanctioned topics, topic control, and initiation by the interviewer, speakership rights, etc. But it is also a good example of the subtle manipulation of context. *B*'s response, instead of confirming the kind of stereotype about Asians doing favours for each other and getting round the system – which the interviewer appears to assume – sets up an alternative schema. In this the formal selection procedures are referred to and *B*'s response creates a new frame of reference for the interviewer. Also by simply referring to 'a form' the applicant assumes that the interviewer knows about formal selection procedures and that this is given information. So here is an interesting example, where at one level given information is assumed – in the schema that collocates getting a job with a job application form – but at another level speaker assumptions are challenged by the Asian applicant creating a new frame of reference.

This example also, by implication, illustrates the range of choices available to speakers when they interact. Despite the obvious constraints of the interview context, the applicant could still have chosen to respond in many different ways. For example, he could have tackled explicitly the fact that he was not recommended, or he could have talked in more general terms about recruitment practices in his department. Stopping to think about what a speaker did not do, but could have done, makes us realize how each individual interaction has a life of its own.

Context and ideology

A great deal of sociolinguistics has been essentially descriptive and correlational. In other words, sociolinguists have been concerned with correlating variables in language use with situational and social variables, as described in the section above dealing with the linguistic and situational context. Sociolinguistics has also been concerned with describing the links between language and society and, in particular, the influence of social structure on language.

There is, however, an alternative approach, which may be described as *critical sociolinguistics*. This approach owes much to the work in critical sociology – for example that by Giddens (1977) – and also to work on language and social meaning – for example that by Halliday (1978), and Fairclough (1985) who has investigated critical goals in discourse analysis. In this approach language is seen as not only reflecting social structures but as helping to actively create them. So language is used to hold together, control, manipulate and maintain social systems and institutions. A purely descriptive approach to how language does this runs the risk of accepting that the way language is used is normal, natural and neutral. For example, it is taken for granted that the control exercised by the teacher in the classroom through her choice of language is the only way that education can be done, or that the language of the housing officer or of the job interview – typical contexts in multi-ethnic societies in which the adult second language learner has to acquire language – simply reflect, uncritically, the commonsense way of doing things.

Considerable work has been done to show the orderliness and regularity of inter-actions. The concept of conversational cooperation is also fundamental to our under-standing of how meaning is negotiated (Grice, 1975). However, there is a danger in describing the smoothness and co-operativeness of interactions without relating them to the social and, above all, the power structure of any institutional discourse. A conversation may be highly co-operative but ultimately controlling, and maintaining fundamental inequalities.

One of the most obvious settings of inequality is the employment interview where the interviewer has the right to control topic and speaker turn and to manipulate the applicant onto the defensive without being constrained by any ethical considerations. Note the downward spiral in the following example, where A is the interviewer and B the applicant:

A: I see you've had a fairly mixed bag of jobs over your time. Perhaps you could tell me a bit about some of them?

B: My last job, if you could call it that, was a company manager negotiating contracts for electrical alarm systems.

A: What brought you into that particular field? It doesn't seem to tie in with your previous occupations.

B: Well, I had to move from my previous job for personal family reasons. I was offered the opportunity and thought I would do well to take it.

A: I see. Is it family reasons that have often caused you to leave the job you've had?

(Roberts, 1985)

In contexts such as this one, the native speakers are in a privileged position in terms of power status, often the representatives of an institution such as a school, a company or a public service. In their discourse they actively create their institutionalized role. To this extent what they say is determined by their position, however unconsciously. It would be wrong, therefore to only describe interaction in terms of free-wheeling individuals creating decisions about how to pursue their personal goals. Language is a system of choice, as we have already shown, but there are many social constraints on what can be chosen. Appropriate discourse is largely determined by presuppo-sitions about social relationships. As Fairclough (1985) puts it: 'Discourse makes people, as well as people making discourse'.

A critical approach to sociolinguistics is essential to an understanding of how communicative competence is accomplished interactionally. It goes beyond describing what goes on, to an understanding of the effects of interaction on the acquiring of communicative competence. In other words, it helps to account for differences in the communicative power between individuals and groups, depending on the kind of interaction learners are exposed to and the opportunities for acquiring that are available to them in an interaction.

How context creates new resources for the language user

Earlier we have suggested that a context consists both of what is created in the interaction and what is brought to it in the way of presuppositions about the world, interactional knowledge and knowledge of the linguistic code. The language user needs to have developed both his knowledge and also the skills to sustain interaction and maintain involvement in the conversation. These are developed interactionally. In this way, when we describe language use, we are at the same time giving an account of language development.

Although language is acquired interactionally, we cannot say that the users' communicative competence is determined solely by the type and frequency of the interactions they are engaged in. There are cognitive processes at work which affect what language the user tends to develop. In the literature on language acquisition there is conflicting evidence about whether it is the frequency or relative complexity of language items which correlates most closely with what language users acquire, although the most recent research by Wells and his associates (cf. Wells, 1985) suggests that it is relative complexity which is the critical factor. What we can say is that it is only in interactional contexts that users have the opportunity to develop their communicative resources, and that these contexts not only enable specific forms and communicative styles to be developed, but they, in part, determine what is acquired and used.

We now need to discuss what these communicative resources are and to examine briefly the contexts in which they are developed. In our discussion of definitions of communicative competence, we referred to Gumperz's focus on conditions for shared interpretation. We also referred to Canale and Swain's four models of competence. Here we suggest some of the discourse processes that interactants use, and try to show how these help to create the conditions for developing communicative competence. We recognize however, that the relationship between these processes and communicative competence has hardly begun to be researched.

It is helpful to consider the processes as four interlocking dimensions of users' language.

(1) schema
(2) interpretative frame
(3) discourse management
(4) linguistic code

The notion of *schema* originally described by Bartlett (1932) and developed by Schank (1977) and Winograd (1972) in their work on artificial intelligence, accounts for the knowledge structure which interlocutors bring to an encounter. A schema is the set of presuppositions about the knowledge of the world and the way things get done which sets up 'structures of expectation' (Tannen, 1979) in the encounter. Negotiating some basis of sharedness of schema is crucial to effective interaction. Studies of inter-ethnic communication suggest that lack of shared schema in interaction are more likely to lead to communication breakdown than differences and difficulties at the level of linguistic code.

The *interpretative frame* (see particularly the work of Bateson (1972) and Goffman (1974)) establishes speaker intentionality at any point in the interaction. For example, at a given moment the speaker may be defending herself or simply giving an explanation. The extent to which interactants agree on what frame they are in will depend largely on whether they share the same schema. Frame and schema mismatches often represent the cruces in a conversation, where things go wrong and awkward moments arise. To take the job interview example again, a question which an interviewer may assume is a straightforward elicitation of information may be perceived by the interviewee with a different 'job interview schema' as a demand to defend herself. For example:

A: Can you tell me about your past driving experience?
B: I've got a clean driving licence. I don't think I've done anything wrong.

So the mismatch between the schema which the interviewer and interviewee bring to the interaction leads to a wrong interpretation on the part of the interviewee.

Conversations are accomplished because there are rules of *discourse management* which govern speakership rights, turn-taking and ways of holding the floor. These in turn affect topic initiation and control and so the opportunities that speakers have to say what they want to say. As the conversational analysts, Sacks, Schegloff and Jefferson (1978) have shown, there are systematic rules of discourse management in ordinary conversation. The rules of turn-taking, topic control and sanctioning are much more explicit in the formal setting of the classroom (cf. Mehan, 1979) and the courtroom (cf. Atkinson and Drew, 1979). The asymmetry and inequality enacted in these contexts have to be learnt by those on the receiving end – schoolchildren, witnesses, etc. Paradoxically, they are acquiring new interactional knowledge – new resources – but in contexts in which their social role, and so their communicative power, is being controlled.

Finally, language users never stop developing their *linguistic code*. The most obvious way this happens is by acquiring new lexical items, as a glance at the latest edition of a dictionary illustrates, whether we are talking about new words like 'telecast', new meanings for old words such as the 'chip', or new associations for familiar words collocated in a new way, like 'pumping iron'. But changes and developments also occur at the phonological and syntactical levels. Labov's study of phonological change in Martha's Vineyard, which we discussed earlier, is a good example of this.

All four dimensions of user language are interacting together all the time. For example, listeners recognize and interpret *contextualization cues* for the speaker's syntactic, lexical and particularly prosodic messages, and these cues trigger interpretative frames and cultural assumptions about the particular discourse task. Language users are developing their resources in all four dimensions, although we do not know as yet precisely how one aspect of resource development helps the others. What we do know is that the development of communicative resources is a very subtle process since the development arises from interaction which is characterized by a high level of indirectness.

Let us now turn to the contexts themselves. If we look at them developmentally – that is from babyhood to adulthood – or cross-sectionally, in terms of the range and complexity of contexts experienced by the typical adult language user, the same pattern emerges. Broadly, we can describe this pattern as one of overall continuity with significant but often subtle differences in context which can markedly affect the opportunities for language use and development for the language user.

Gordon Wells and his associates (cf. Wells *et al.* 1981; Wells, 1985), in their study of child language acquisition, have compared the home interactions of children's earliest years with the classroom interactions they face when they first move from home to school. Contrary to earlier research their findings suggest a basic continuity between type of interactive sequences created by parent and child in the home and teacher and children in school. For example, the three part sequence of question, answer and evaluation, typical of teacher initiated discourse is also typical of parent–child talk. However, there are some differences within the basic continuity, which in some respects may make the classroom context a less facilitative setting for developing interactional contexts than the home. For example, in the home children have more opportunity to ask questions, initiate topics and make evaluations. Furthermore, Wells suggests, as children in asymmetrical relationships with more powerful parents, they also need specific strategies to get conversations going and topics sanctioned. They have learnt the rules of the game and are beginning to find ways around them. By contrast, in the classroom, there are fewer opportunities to initiate, and breaking the rules of this game is usually severely sanctioned.

In the adult context, knowing and finding ways around the rules are considerably more complicated and, as in school, breaking them is usually heavily sanctioned. Linguists and ethnographers, notably Michael Halliday (1978) and John Gumperz (1982a and b) have described the type of complex human environments which typify our modern, urban, bureaucratic, multi-ethnic society. Unlike young children, adults have to enact and re-enact a variety of social roles in these different environments. New domains of language use require the development of new rules of communicative competence. For example, the shopfloor worker who becomes an active trade unionist will experience and be trained in ways of negotiating with management, hearing grievances from workers and explaining decisions to the shopfloor. Her new role requires her to operate in new contexts and so develop new communicative resources.

However, it would be naive to assume that all new contexts necessarily provide opportunities for access to 'the communicative economy' (Bordieu, 1977), just as it is naive to assume that there is a simple reciprocal relationship between teaching and learning. As suggested above, there are many contexts which are constituted by interactional rules that limit rather than enable the user's language development. There are types of unequal encounter in which topics are initiated, controlled and sanctioned by the more powerful interactant. People learn to co-operate in these encounters and in so doing learn to collude in the inequality of them. Some people discover how the rules are being used by those in power, and once all the rules are known, they are easier to break. However, for most people these encounters reflect and recreate the social position of relative powerlessness that they inhabit. Class, gender and ethnicity are the major determinants of social position and identity, and these are constantly being re-created interactionally. For example, there is considerable evidence to show that we are continually acting out our sex role – that gender is interactionally accomplished (cf. Goffman, 1971, and Fishman, 1983). There are sociolinguistic subcultures bounded by class, ethnic and even gender factors, which mean that different interactional styles develop. Women, Fishman argues, do more of the basic conversational maintenance in female–male communication, and the latter are more likely than women to have their topics responded to positively. The orientations and values developed by particular subcultural groups in interaction will affect the extent to which they can use the range of contexts they encounter as adults to develop new linguistic resources and communicative power.

The second language learner in context

We have now examined in some detail how communicative competence is accomplished interactionally and have emphasized the need for a critical perspective. We shall now consider the L2 learner and discuss how context influences the development of communicative competence in SLA.

There is very little research to show how communicative competence is interactionally accomplished for the second language learner. This is true both of oral interaction and interaction between learners and texts. This is all the more surprising since it is widely accepted that interaction provides the opportunities for communicative competence and that the classroom, however formal and removed from the realities of everyday interaction outside, is essentially an interactive environment. The reason for this unsatisfactory state of the art is the still-limited knowledge that we have about the relationship between learning processes and discourse/inferential processes. Another reason is the difficulties researchers have had in accounting for and controlling the variables in interaction.

The pioneering work of Gordon Wells and his associates in first language acquisition in children, which we briefly referred to earlier, should be an inspiration to those working on interaction and second language development. The ten year project has analysed how child–parent interaction contributes to the development of the child's language (Wells *et al.*, 1981). Wells has identified the kind of collaborative, non-directive and learner-orientated contexts which lead to the most successful language development. In these contexts children are encouraged to choose and progress topics. There is a high level of positive parent feedback so that the children's contribution is valued. These interactions are characterized by considerable cohesion, relevance and equality. So, children learn the interactional knowledge which helps them to collaborate and develop topics, discover cohesion and coherence in discourse and to maintain conversational involvement.

These are not simply rules that are learnt in one interaction and applied in another. In a powerful analogy, Widdowson has illuminated what actually seems to happen;

he likens how rules are used in interaction to the way we play chess. We learn the rules of the game, 'But when we are actually engaging an opponent, we do not merely move one piece in accordance with these rules: we *use* these rules to create openings, to develop a plan of campaign, to make a game of it' (Widdowson, 1979).

Despite some illuminating illustrative material, for example Hester (1985), there is very little research on how L2 learners develop communicative competence. Notable exceptions can be found in the work done by researchers such as Keenan (1974). Research on classroom interaction (for example by Gaies, 1983; Allwright, 1980; Ellis, 1985a) has not yet given us an account of the causal connection between patterns of interaction which have been observed and learner output. Research on inter-ethnic communication among adults, in particular by Gumperz and his associates (1982a and b), Ron and Suzanne Scollon (1981) and Tannen (1982) has described how there are systematic differences in the use and interpretation of discourse conventions between different ethnic groups. However, there has been little systematic work on how L2 learners acquire these conventions. For example, in a major study of natural-istic SLA of German by Turkish workers in Heidelberg (cf. Klein and Dittmar, 1979) only a small part of the project was concerned with communicative competence and the research was based on a limited number of case studies.

In a rather different tradition, Selinker's (1972) work on interlanguage has led to interesting studies of interlanguage strategies from a psycholinguistic perspective (see Faerch and Kasper, 1983a). This has led to a debate concerning communicative and learning strategies which has not yet been resolved. The research has begun to document what strategies learners use in communication but these have not been systematically related to language development or variable language use. In other words, the relationship between *use* and *development* is still poorly understood.

Research is urgently needed on communicative competence in L2 speakers which integrates issues related to the social context, interactional skills and knowledge and the development of all aspects of communicative competence, including the linguistic code. Hatch (1978) in a challenging paper on discourse analysis and SLA relates SLA to the skills required to 'do conversation'. For example, Hatch shows how learners can negotiate a pool of shared information on a particular topic which simultaneously establishes appropriate discourse conventions and encourages linguistic development (lexical and grammatical).

The first major cross-linguistic, longitudinal project on national second language acquisition (cf. Perdue, 1984) is attempting the integration of social and linguistic contexts in researching SLA among minority ethnic workers in five European coun-tries. The project relates interpretative, interactional studies to more quantitative work on the learner's developing lexicon and syntax. It is also gathering in-depth ethnographic data on individual learners. This is the beginning of much needed studies charting the relationship between linguistic and communicative competence; assessing how different interactional outcomes across domains affect the route and rate of acquisition and combining quantitative and qualitative research methods.

In conclusion, we can suggest that the contexts in which L2 learners interact affect – positively and negatively – the development of communicative competence. However, we know very little about how this take place. Considerable work still needs to be done in identifying what kinds of contexts promote development and how the interactions which typically occur in these contexts provide the basis for successful SLA. This work will entail exploring the relationships between the different discourse processes involved and how 'accomplishing conversations' is also 'accomplishing SLA'.

Investigating second language acquisition in context

In this Introduction we have described two different approaches for investigating SLA in context. First, we considered the kind of approach which has been used to examine the effects of context on the use and acquisition of linguistic competence. This approach has relied to a large extent (although not exclusively) on the theoretical framework and methodology developed by Labov to study variability in native speaker language use. In particular this approach explores *stylistic variability* using quantitative research techniques. The second approach involves a more qualitative approach in order to examine how the social context relates to the use and development of communicative competence. This approach draws on a different socio-linguistic tradition, one that is concerned with *interactional variability* and explores this through the study of the discourse processes that enact different social contexts.

These approaches offer different perspectives on SLA in context. Each provides its own picture – drawn, as it were by different artists. Each picture is valid in itself, so it has not been our purpose to evaluate them comparatively. However, we do believe that our understanding of SLA will be advanced if the two pictures can be encompassed on a single canvas – if we can integrate the insights gained from the Labovian tradition with those provided by interactional sociolinguistics. We conclude, therefore, with one way in which this might be accomplished.

The concept of style remains central. The narrow definition of style as those linguistic features which correlate with situational variables, as described in Part One of this Introduction, is too limiting for the kind of integrated approach we have in mind. Style is much more than a set of linguistic features; it includes the discourse processes through which interaction is accomplished, as described in Part Two. In other words, rather than limiting the notion of style to linguistic competence, it needs to be extended to include those aspects of language use that comprise communicative competence. Stylistic analysis provides the means for investigating SLA in context; this analysis must account for the product and the process of interaction by considering both linguistic and interactional variation.

Once this broader view of style is accepted it is clear that the relationship between context and language use cannot be reduced to a single dimension, as proposed by Labov. Instead we envisage a two-dimensional framework. The horizontal dimension consists of a continuum of styles that range from the formal to the informal. The principal extralinguistic factor determining where on this continuum a particular interaction is located is the audience. As Bell (1984) states, 'persons respond mainly to other persons' and 'speakers take most account of hearers in designing their talk'. Thus different styles arise as a result of communicating with different kinds of audience. Speakers assess whom they are addressing and endeavour to make their language appropriate. However, each style, so identified, will be characterized by considerable interactional variability; it is this that constitutes the vertical dimension of our framework. There will always be within-style variability, as speakers shape their discourse according to local factors that arise in the process of interaction.

Thus we can distinguish *between*-style and *within*-style variability. That is context (viewed as a set of extralinguistic factors, as discussed in Part One) determines the choices the learner makes, but also the learner creates context through interaction by means of the kinds of discourse processes discussed in Part Two. We envisage, therefore, that the learner operates (potentially at least) a series of styles in accordance with general situational constraints. However, each style has to be enacted in the sense that it has to be interactionally accomplished. This is a dynamic process, involving much more than simply responding to extralinguistic factors. The learner has to create an interaction, turn-by-turn, using language pragmatically to perform not only those general social meanings that represent the overall style but also a host of more local social meanings that arise from the interaction as it proceeds.

The kind of integrated sociolinguistic analysis of SLA in context which all this would require is:

(1) The study of how SLA varies in different styles.
(2) The study of how each style is enacted on specific occasions of use.

As we have already noted the analysts would need to investigate both linguistic *and* non-linguistic aspects of communicative competence. Also it will make use of both quantitative and qualitative research techniques.

Such an approach offers a framework for examining a number of important questions about SLA. What are the typical styles of interaction experienced by different learners? What effects do the range of styles experienced by learners have on their individual social identities? How does a learner learn to perform in a particular style? Is stylistic variation a relatively late acquisition or is it evident from the beginning? Does SLA proceed faster when learners experience interaction in certain styles? Does SLA follow different routes in different styles? What strategies do learners use to enact discourse in different styles?

To conclude, we maintain that SLA needs to be studied in relation to the social contexts in which it takes place. This study can proceed by comparing how learners perform in different styles (i.e. in communication with different addressees). But also it will require qualitative analyses of how interactions within a given style take place. In this way, the two approaches we have described can be related so that each contributes to the other.

Section Two:

THEORETICAL AND METHODOLOGICAL ISSUES

The articles in Section Two describe different methodological frameworks for investigating variability in second language acquisition (SLA). As the choice of research methodology is dependent upon a theoretical view of the nature of language itself these papers are also statements of theoretical positions. They provide points of reference for interpreting the articles in the subsequent sections.

All three articles see SLA as a process involving variable language use. Two of the articles – those by Tarone and Rampton – seek to explain this process within a sociolinguistic framework. The article by Tarone draws on the Labovian framework; SLA variability is seen as the product of style shifting. Tarone's work on interlanguage as a variable system is now well known and has afforded important insights into how learners construct a second language grammar. On this occasion Tarone draws on her experience as a researcher to describe what factors need to be considered in designing empirical studies of SLA variability. Rampton is concerned with how L2 speakers use their knowledge of the L2 in social interaction. He examines SLA variability from the perspective provided by interactional sociolinguistics, as practised by Gumperz and Levinson. Rampton makes a powerful statement in favour of this alternative model as a basis for SLA research. The third article – by Swan – argues that variability phenomena can best be accounted for within the Chomskyan framework, i.e. by positing a distinction between *competence* and *performance*.

We have considered both the Labovian and Gumperzian models in the Introduction to this book. However, it will probably assist you to read the Tarone and Rampton articles if we briefly review both models here.

Labov views the language user's underlying competence as heterogeneous. It is made up of categorical and variable rules. The latter describe the way the language user selects from a number of linguistic variants in different contexts. All language users possess several styles; that is, they adapt their speech to make it fit the social context. These styles comprise a continuum. They can be ranged along a single dimension according to the amount of attention that is paid to linguistic form. The style where there is minimum attention to form is called the vernacular. The style where maximum attention is paid is referred to as the careful or superordinate style. Style markers are variable structures containing two or more variants, one of which is socially prestigious. Thus, when the language user is performing in the careful style higher frequencies of this variant will be evident, while in other styles, closer to the vernacular, other, socially marked variants will be more frequent. The main point to grasp about the Labovian model is that attention to form is treated as the psycholinguistic mechanism for socially motivated style shifting. That is, variable rules are applied in accordance with how much attention the speaker is paying to what he says.

Gumperz is interested in how social identity is established and maintained through face to face interaction. His work has involved the detailed analysis of conversations between non-native speakers (usually members of ethnic minorities) and native speakers in institutional settings. These are occasions such as interviews or courtroom interrogations, where the non-native speaker is frequently disadvantaged, not only by his lack of linguistic competence but also by his socially subordinate position. Variation arises in these unequal encounters as a result of: (1) different cultural assumptions about the situation and what constitutes appropriate behaviour in it; (2) different ways of structuring information in conversation; and (3) different ways of speaking (i.e. different ways of realizing social meaning through language). Thus, variation will arise between situations as a result of changes in the role relationships of the interactants, and also within a single situation in accordance with the shifting pattern of communicative purposes. Central to this view of variability is that 'we simultaneously signal both content and about content' (Gumperz 1982a). The speaker varies the use of his linguistic resources to create social meanings which he considers appropriate at any one point in a conversation.

There are several important differences between the Labovian and the Gumperzian frameworks. One is that, whereas Labov draws on a psycholinguistic construct (i.e. 'attention to speech') in order to explain how linguistic choice creates social meaning, Gumperz works within a framework that is more completely sociolinguistic (i.e. he is not concerned with the internal mechanisms responsible for language choice). Another important difference concerns the range of extralinguistic factors for which the two models try to account. Labov is interested only in those factors responsible for stylistic variation; Gumperz is concerned with both *between-* style and *within-* style variability and hence considers those factors which contribute to non-stylistic as well as stylistic variability. In particular, Gumperz investigates how pragmatic factors influence language choice in the course of a single conversation. Interactional socio-linguistics is concerned, among other things, with the attempts of language users to regulate their speech in accordance with their understanding of what is appropriate language behaviour for expressing speech acts under different social conditions (e.g. changes in addressee). Thus, whereas Labov explains variability in terms of a single dimension, interactional sociolinguists see it as a multi-dimensional phenomenon.

Swan also attacks accounts of SLA based on the Labovian notion of a stylistic continuum. He is critical of the elicitation devices used in studies of stylistic varia-bility, pointing out that tasks such as grammaticality judgement tests, imitation and minimal pair production reveal little about the competence to engage in anything he would want to call 'language use'. More importantly, he questions whether the notion of 'style' is really appropriate for describing the shifting level of accuracy with which individual linguistic features are performed. For Swan 'style' would only be appropriate if it could be shown that 'a significant number of features all varied together.' Swan argues that interlanguage performance is influenced by a host of factors (he lists eighteen) and suggests that we cannot expect to predict variable behaviour in a precise way. For this reason he prefers a model which makes a clear distinction between competence (what the learner knows) and performance (what the learner does). Swan does not claim that competence is entirely homogeneous, only that much of the variability evident in the learner's production is the result of performance factors such as fatigue, state of mind, frequency of use, etc. Swan, then, unlike both Tarone and Rampton envisages variability that is *not* related to context, not socially significant at all. His article is a timely reminder of the dangers of 'over-interpreting' variability phenomena.

As was pointed out in the Introduction, most of the research which has investigated variability in SLA has been conducted within a Labovian framework. One reason for this is doubtlessly the methodological convenience which the model affords. It enables the researcher to examine the effects of context by means of experimental studies of SLA variability. Data can be collected cross-sectionally using a variety of tasks designed to produce different levels of attention to form and hence to elicit a range of styles. In addition, it is possible to investigate variability in the use of particular structures, which would probably not be sufficiently represented in data collected naturalistically. As Tarone points out, such research can be designed in order to 'tease out' the contribution of individual factors to interlanguage variability. We can discover, for instance, to what extent interlocutor factors as opposed to task factors affect stylistic choice.

In contrast, the interactional model has not been widely used in SLA research. Rampton's article is a plea for more research using the techniques of interactional sociolinguistics. Rampton argues that 'the continuing influence of Labov in SLA is not a good thing', and he then advances a number of criticisms of the 'attention to form' construct. In contrast to Tarone, who emphasizes the importance of exper-imental manipulations of the context, Rampton is sceptical of such research. Instead he recommends research that investigates naturally occurring language behaviour in order to find out more about the sociocultural world of the learner and how this influences language choice. He emphasizes that 'being a language learner can itself constitute a particular status'.

The Chomskyan tradition has figured strongly in SLA research, justifying the study of learner utterances in isolation from both their linguistic and situational context. In this tradition linguistic knowledge is separated from its use in interaction, so that no attention needs to be paid to how context affects the way it is organized. The central issue is whether language use determines the structure of the linguistic code itself. If the answer is 'yes' – and this is emphatically the position adopted by sociologists such as Labov and Gumperz – then it will be necessary to widen the scope of enquiry to investigate communicative competence. However, investigating communicative competence does not mean that *all* sources of variability must be included. Some sources, e.g. those associated with processing constraints, can still be left to 'performance'. The problem is that processing factors are inextricably linked to social factors, so that it is theoretically and empirically very difficult to separate them. The question arises, then, as to whether we should treat all instances of variability as of *potential* social significance and seek to account for them in terms of communicative competence, or whether we should delimit the competence construct so as to exclude at least some instances as performance. If we take the former course of action we are left with the horrendous task of trying to explain (and, therefore, to predict) variability derived from a host of sources (which almost certainly interact on each other). Swan argues that we are not likely to be successful and, therefore, should not try. If we take the latter course of action, we are faced with the problem of determining which sources to include as competence and which to exclude as performance. It is this problem which sociolinguists grapple with.

These articles, then, stake out different theoretical positions, each with its own associated research methodology. The papers that make up the rest of the book take a sociolinguistic perspective; that is, they view linguistic knowledge as heterogeneous and they consider that language use is instrumental in shaping it. This does not mean to say that Swan's arguments are to be easily dismissed. Indeed the current resurgence of interest in how *universal grammar* constrains the development of interlanguages is indicative of renewed interest in purely linguistic explanations of SLA. This book, however, is an exploration of the alternative paradigm, one that owes more to Halliday than to Chomsky in seeing language (and, therefore, language learning) as both creating and created by the wider context of language use.

With regard to the alternative models proposed by Tarone and Rampton the reader would do well not to see them as 'either–or' theories. There definitely is style shifting in SLA and this can be investigated in the ways Tarone suggests. She points out, quite correctly, that attention to form should be seen as a mediating variable not as a primary causal variable. We need to discover what social factors cause the learner's attention to vary. We also need to acknowledge that not all variability is the result of attention to form. There can be variation within a single style (e.g. the vernacular). Interactional sociolinguistics provides us with a way of exploring how 'impression management' leads to variable language use. The qualitative research that this requires will both complement and extend the more quantitative investigations of style-shifting.

Methodologies for Studying Variability in Second Language Acquisition

ELAINE TARONE
University of Minnesota

There may be considerable variability in formal accuracy when an individual learner of a second language produces that language in various situations. The occurrence of this sort of variability is of interest to teachers and researchers alike. Teachers who need to assess the accuracy with which their students produce or perceive particular features of the target language must concern themselves with the effect the method of assessment has on these accuracy rates. Researchers who are attempting to establish the general characteristics of learner language and to construct a theory of second language acquisition must also concern themselves not only with this sort of situational variability, but also with contextual variability: the way in which the accuracy of any given form may vary when produced or perceived in different linguistic contexts.

Methodologies for studying these sorts of variability are themselves extremely varied, differing in terms of the design of the elicitation tasks used, the language forms selected for study, and the method of data analysis. In this paper, we review some factors to be considered in designing an elicitation task for this sort of study, consider some problems involved in selecting the language forms to be studied, and review some methods of data analysis which have been used. It is the author's contention that the issues involved in designing a study on situational variability must also be involved in the design of a study on contextual variability: care must be given to the design of elicitation tasks, as well as to selection of forms for study and method of data analysis. Further, these factors must be clearly specified when we report our research, so that accurate replication of our studies can take place.

Elicitation task

Perhaps the single most important issue affecting the design of elicitation tasks in studies on variability in interlanguage relates to claims about the cause of such variability. The primary cause which researchers have postulated to account for situational variability is that different elicitation tasks cause the individual to pay greater or lesser degrees of attention to language form, thus producing and perceiving language forms with greater or lesser accuracy.

Following Labov's (1969) work on variability in production of one's native language, attention to language form which is related to task, has been posited as the primary causal factor (Dickerson, 1974; Krashen, 1981; Tarone, 1983) in second language production. Proponents of this position have observed that accuracy of production of some grammatical forms varies depending upon the task which any given speaker performs: reading word lists, reading connected discourse, speaking formally with an interviewer, or narrating an involving story. The cause of this variability has been claimed to be that different tasks require (or allow) different degrees of attention to language form; if tasks are ordered in terms of degree of attention to language form required, the language produced by any given learner in response to those tasks may be ranged on a continuum of grammatical accuracy. For native speakers, as tasks require more attention to language form, grammatical accuracy improves (i.e., more standard variants occur). The work of Dickerson (1974) shows a parallel pattern for second-language learners; phonological variants produced by Japanese learners of English are less 'Japanese' and more 'English' on tasks like reading minimal pairs than on tasks like 'casual conversation'. Most foreign language teachers seem to make the assumption that accuracy of production of grammatical forms is best on exercises where learners must focus on language form, and lowest on exercises where learners focus upon 'communication'. Krashen's (1981) Monitor Model has formalized these assumptions to some degree, postulating that learners will monitor, or consciously apply grammar rules, when three conditions are present: knowledge of the rule in question, adequate time to apply the rule, and *a focus on language form*.

While it seems to be clearly established that different tasks elicit different degrees of grammatical accuracy in interlanguage (IL), Bell (1984) has pointed out that there are a number of difficulties with focus on form as a cause of situational variability. Most seriously, attention to form can at best be only an intermediary, not an explanatory, factor: we are still left with establishing *what it is in the task and in the situation* that causes learners to pay attention to form. For purposes of experimental design, we are still left with specifying factors in the elicitation situation which will cause variability to occur in the language production of second language learners (SLLs) – whether or not those factors directly cause variability, or whether they cause attention to form which in turn causes variability. In many studies which have considered 'attention to form' as a causal variable, my own included, too little attention has been paid to specifying exactly what it is in the elicitation task which ultimately causes variability in IL production.

For purposes of selecting an appropriate methodology for eliciation of variable data, therefore, it is valuable to consider all the task-related factors which have been set forth as possible causes of situational variability, so that we may select some for study and hold the others constant in designing our elicitation task. All of the following factors may vary in different elicitation tasks used in our studies, and each of them may cause a learner to produce language forms variably; these factors break down, I believe, into factors relating to the identity of the interlocutor, the topic, or content, of the language, and the procedures required by the task itself.

Interlocutor

In normal communication, a learner does not speak in a vacuum; there is some audience for her to speak to. A good elicitation task must provide an interlocutor who has some reason for listening to the speaker (cf. Yule and Tarone, forthcoming).

Decisions we make about the identity and role of the interlocutor may affect the grammatical accuracy of the speaker.

According to accommodation theorists like Bell (1984), Beebe (1980) and Giles (1980), the learner shifts styles in response to his perception of the interlocutor, either attempting to *converge*, making his productions more congruent with those of the interlocutor, or to *diverge*, making productions congruent with those of some other group of speakers. Thus, for example, a learner speaking to a teacher of the target language (TL) might be expected to produce language forms which were more TL-like than when speaking to another learner from his own country; such a learner would then be said to converge (linguistically) with his teacher. However, it is also possible, as Rampton points out (this volume), for a learner to deliberately produce language forms which diverge from those produced by his teacher, and converge with forms produced by some other reference group.

Bell (1984) argues that the monolingual individual shifts style in order to sound like speakers in other groups, to move from one part of the speech community into another. Social variation comes first, and individuals shift styles to 'fit in' with their perception of this social dimension. Surely it is reasonable to expect multilingual individuals to shift styles within a language for the same reasons.

But what is the speech community of the second language learner? Where all learners speak the same native language and share the same culture, this may be clear. But what about the case of the ESL classroom where nearly every learner may come from a different native language background? With what speech community(ies) does a learner in this situation identify? In a global sense, Bell's claim fits the SLL; s/he is learning the L2 in order to fit into the society of L2 speakers. But in order to explain style-shift at a micro-level, we must deal with more complex issues. In an ESL classroom composed of twenty learners from seven different native-language backgrounds, can we really speak of speech communities and shared qualitative norms in the way we can speak of these for monolingual speakers? Can we expect learners from different native-language (NL) backgrounds to share the same perceptions of the social dimensions of English language use, and to adjust their own speech styles in the same way? This is obviously an empirical question, one which we need clear data on, and do not have, because our studies have not been designed to answer such questions.

What is needed is clear data on the ways in which speakers from different NL backgrounds style-shift in communicating with different interlocutors, when all other factors are carefully controlled. Minimally, even in studies which aim to examine contextual variability and to hold situational variables constant, we need at least to be informed as to the identity and social role of the interlocutor. To whom was the learner speaking in this study? If we are interested in replicating one another's studies, and generalizing our findings beyond our own sample, we need to specify the identity of the interlocutor. We need to know more, for example, than that the interlocutor was a native speaker of English: we need to know what the social role of the interlocutor was *vis-à-vis* the learner. For example, Beebe (1980a) showed that Thai learners of English produced R variably in different contexts, using an R variant which was socially prestigious in Thai in word-initial position in English. In this case we know more than usual about the characteristics of the interviewer, but we do not know how the learners perceived him. How was this contextual variability related to the learners' perception of the social role of the interviewer? Would this pattern of contextual variability have occurred with another interviewer – one who, perhaps, was not learning Thai, or one who was more (or less) professional in appearance?

If we can be clearer in controlling and specifying the identity of the interlocutor in our studies, and we find that the style-shifting patterns are the same for different NL groups, then possibly we can speak of all learners in a classroom being members of the same speech community. If not, then we have an additional complicating factor in our model. In either case, we will have important information about the effect of the identity of the interlocutor upon the variability of interlanguage.

Topic

In normal communication, learners do not just direct language at some interlocutor; there is content and purpose to their communications. And, there is considerable evidence that topic will affect grammatical accuracy in complex ways. Labov (1969) showed that, where the interlocutor remained the same, shifts of topic in a conversation, from, say, evaluation of local politics to a description of a situation in which the speaker's life was in danger, correlated highly with styleshifts. Bell (1984) argues that the effect of topic is related to the interlocutor effect, in that topics which are normally dealt with in conversation with intimates produce the speech style normally used with intimates. An additional topic-related factor which must also be considered is the relative familiarity or complexity of the topic: Felix and others have convincingly shown that a learner who is forced to talk about an unfamiliar or complex topic in the L2 may produce disjointed language and more inaccurate grammatical forms than when conversing about more familiar or simpler topics. (In fact, such language has even been described as lacking in systematicity altogether, though this remains to be empirically verified.)

If our studies are to approximate normal communicative behaviour, and yet also allow us to compare the performance of different speaker/writers, we must control topic. We cannot allow different subjects to ramble on with general topics like 'tell me what you did on your summer holiday', because then different individuals will end up talking about different topics, and possibly providing different discourse types: one will *describe* his garden, another *complain* about his summer job, and yet another *narrate* a close brush with death while sky-diving. Learners need to be provided with tightly-controlled, narrow topics. The researcher needs to decide whether, for example, s/he wants a description of a concrete object or abstract concept, instructions on how to assemble an apparatus or draw a picture, or a narrative of a particular series of events and then provide the same stimulus material to all the subjects. Simple elicitation prompts which have provided effective topics for communication are photographs, pictures, and non-verbal videotapes; such prompts can be held constant for all subjects, so that inter-subject comparisons can ultimately be made.

In addition, the ability to hold topic constant in this way makes it possible to obtain *baseline data* – something which will be dealt with below as all-too-often missing in our interpretation of results – baseline data from native speakers of the TL, and NL data from the subjects themselves, for purposes of further comparison. And, factors such as familiarity of the topic, or complexity of the topic, may also be systematically varied in an attempt to determine whether, and how, these factors affect variable language forms.

Task

A wide variety of tasks have been used to elicit data on variability in IL: 'tasks' ranging from rating the grammaticality of TL sentences, to correcting TL sentences with errors in them, to reading minimal pairs and word lists (in the study of pronunciation), to telling stories in response to tightly controlled visual stimuli, to talking aimlessly over a beer at one's own kitchen table. In addition to the problem of maintaining topic constant, which we have just discussed, there are other task factors which vary wildly just in the brief list I have just provided, any of which may have had an effect upon the formal accuracy of the subjects' language.

The first point to consider is that these different tasks elicit different amounts of discourse – from single sentences to long monologues. On grammaticality judgement tasks, subjects may not produce language at all, but rather perceive language which is given to them and judge its correctness, or conformity to the TL norm. Some grammaticality judgement tasks may ask subjects to rewrite or correct, incorrect sentences, but often these rewritings may consist only of a single word or two. Accuracy scores on these tasks are then compared to accuracy scores on tasks where the subjects are asked to produce the TL. In addition to differences in sheer volume of data produced on these different tasks, the amount of connectedness of the discourse may vary considerably, from single, unconnected sentences to long, extended pieces of connected prose. It seems reasonable to suppose that certain kinds of language form, like cohesive devices, for example, will be more frequent, and possibly more 'monitored', in the more-connected sorts of discourse.

Second, the mode of discourse may vary, from descriptions and instructions to narratives and persuasive pieces. In the example cited above, the topic of 'summer holidays' could easily have produced a description from one subject, a complaint from another and a narration from another, thereby confounding subject identity with discourse mode. And the language forms which we have selected to study (see below) may occur with different degrees of frequency in different types of discourse. For example, past tense forms are not likely to occur in the description of an apparatus; past tense forms are more likely (but certainly not obligatory) in narratives. Furthermore, some evidence has now been accumulated to show that different modes of discourse place different demands upon the language system, so that a subject may find it easier to be grammatically accurate within one discourse type than in another. For just one example, Yule and Tarone (forthcoming) found that their NNS subjects were more fluent and seemed to show less hesitancy in performing narratives than in describing objects or giving instructions. Tarone's (1985) study on style-shifting, which compared learner performance on grammaticality judgement tasks, oral descriptions of their field of study, and oral narratives, showed that grammatical accuracy of some language forms seemed to improve on narrative tasks while others simultaneously decreased in accuracy on the same task. Thus, the discourse mode elicited by a task may have a very complex effect upon the grammatical accuracy of the language forms produced. And, so, discourse mode needs to be tightly controlled in studies on variability. Using carefully designed elicitation prompts such as those I have just described will go a long way towards controlling discourse mode.

A task factor related to the issue of mode of discourse elicited has to do with the nature of the operations the individual is being asked to perform. It is not only that the medium differs on different tasks: it seems clear that *writing* a narrative is a different operation from *orally* relating a narrative. It is also that judging grammatical accuracy is a different operation from correcting TL sentences, and this in turn demands different mental processes from those involved in producing discourse. In a recent study, Lund (1985) asked English-speaking learners of German to perform two different types of metalinguistic judgement task. He found that accuracy rates on both the syntax and morphology of German verbs could vary markedly between a task requiring learners to judge the correctness of sentences, and a task requiring them to write in correct versions of erroneous sentences. Thus, even different metalinguistic tasks which require different operations on the part of the learner may affect formal accuracy. And, although this has not been shown, it is also conceivable that tasks which demand that learners perform different sorts of mental operation may provide very different pictures of contextual variability as well. Keeping the nature of the operations required by any task explicitly in mind is important in experimental design in this area.

Another task factor relates to the nature of the instructions given for the task: a learner may be told to be careful to be grammatically accurate, or may be told that grammatical accuracy is important. While the identity of the interlocutor, and other factors such as setting may affect the subjects' willingness to follow such instructions, we must assume that differing instructions have different effects upon the language forms produced.

A related task factor has to do with the subjects' perception of the purpose of your study. If the subjects believe that their performance on your study will in any way affect their grade in their ESL class, we must assume that their grammatical accuracy will be affected, one way or another. Studies on contextual variability must be especially well-designed here as learners may have studied the target variant more in one linguistic context than another, and therefore 'monitor' more in one context than another if they believe your study is related to their coursework.

Another factor relates to the physical setting in which the task is given. One might expect different rates of formal accuracy on the same task, when that task is administered first in an academic office, possibly with a prominently displayed tape recorder going – and again at the subject's own kitchen table.

A final task factor, and one which Krashen has often pointed out, has to do with the amount of time allotted for the task. The accuracy with which learners produce certain language forms seems to vary systematically in relation to the amount of time they have to perform the task. Krashen has argued that some morphemes are produced with less accuracy when learners are given less time to 'monitor', or adjust their production in the direction of the TL. Learners provided with a lot of time in producing their utterances may produce more 'grammatically accurate' variants of these morphemes. Clearly, this factor of time must be related to the question of medium outlined above: writing allows one more time than speaking for modifications of language form. What has not been established is the way in which this time factor affects patterns of contextual variability; does it affect all contextual environments equally, or do variants improve in accuracy more in some environments than in others as more time is allowed?

Each of these features of the elicitation situation should be clearly specified and if possible controlled. For example, learners might be asked to perform the same tasks but with different interlocutors and their language examined for variation under these different conditions. Or, the identity of the interlocutor and the other factors might be held constant, and only the operations required by the task changed, and so on. Clearly, a variety of factors may interact in complex ways to produce situationally and contextually variable interlanguage production, and it is only by designing our elicitation tasks very carefully that we will ever be able to begin to tease those factors apart.

Selecting language forms for study

One factor which we have already mentioned has to do with the selection of language forms to study. Labov (1969) pointed out that not all language forms are variable; as his subjects produced language in different elicitation situations, some language forms shifted and others did not. Clearly, we may expect the same to be true in studies of interlanguage variability, and in designing our studies, we want to determine: (a) which language forms are variable, and (b) the pattern of styleshifting for each language form.

In beginning a research study, we must have some way of deciding which forms we anticipate will show variability. This is because we will want to design the elicitation tasks accordingly; we will want to design our tasks in such a way that all the tasks will be likely to demand the production of all the language forms we are interested in looking at.

Clearly, some language forms will be more amenable to variability studies than others. Simple, frequently occurring forms (like phonemes, or certain morphemes – like articles, past tense markers, or object pronouns) will be easier to elicit and study than more complex and/or less frequently occurring forms (like relative clauses, or subject pronouns). The logistical problems involved in designing elicitation tasks which will demand that subjects will spontaneously and naturally produce the same sorts of relative clauses on two or more tasks are mind-boggling. So frequency of occurrence of the forms in natural language production is an important factor for consideration.

There are at least two ways for a researcher to proceed here. The first way, and the one which I have used in my own research, has been to begin with a collection of (usually unrelated) language forms which in casual observation of a large number of language learners seem to evidence situational variability. Every ESL teacher, if put to it, could identify seven or eight language forms which her students seem to be able to produce accurately in certain kinds of classroom activities and unable to produce accurately in conversations outside of class. Such a collection of language forms might provide a reasonable set for more systematic study. The advantage of this approach is that one has begun with a set of clear and troublesome (at least to the teacher) 'learning problems' and is therefore likely to obtain information about those problems which will prove helpful to the classroom practitioner. The problem with this approach is that the set of language forms being researched is usually linguistically unrelated and therefore possibly less interesting to the theoretician.

Another possibility would be to begin with some single semantic or grammatical system; one might for example look at tense and aspect, or some subset thereof. Or one might examine Valdman's (personal correspondence) suggestion that morpho-phonemic forms are likely to improve on grammaticality judgement tasks and more complex forms are not. One would then end up with more theoretically interesting results to one's study. Certainly, as results begin to come in from the 'scatter-shot' types of study such as those described in the last paragraph, questions about such patterns of style-shifting are most likely to arise and to lead to a more systematic approach to the selection of language forms for study.

Methods of data analysis

In addition to deciding which language forms to study and what sort of elicitation task to provide, one must decide how the data are to be analysed.

The first point to be made here relates to the use of 'obligatory context' which has typically been used to analyse the occurrence of a TL form in 'natural' language data, that is extended discourse over which the learner has had some control. Briefly, an 'obligatory context' for any language form is a linguistic context in which NSs of the TL would be obliged to supply that language form in order to produce a grammatically correct utterance. An example might be:

Yesterday John walk__ on the old trail.

Here, an 'obligatory context' for a past tense morpheme -ed is created. For any subject, the number of obligatory contexts for any TL form may be counted up, and the number of times the form was supplied in such obligatory contexts may be calculated.

Now there are innumerable problems with the use of obligatory context in analysing the occurrence of forms in natural discourse. It seems increasingly clear, for example, that many learners are quite adept at avoiding the production of some obligatory contexts for problematic TL forms; so not all linguistic contexts for the target form may be supplied by the learner in natural data. This will mean that the researcher will have 'holes' in the data, where one subject may have produced all the linguistic contexts of interest in large numbers, and another subject may not have produced any of one particular linguistic context. This will present massive problems for interpretation and for quantitative analysis, because we do not know whether such holes in the data are accidental or due to avoidance on the part of the learner. Another problem is that analysis by means of occurrence in obligatory context does not permit the researcher to identify cases of overgeneralization in the data – that is, cases where the target form was supplied in other contexts than the obligatory contexts. For example, the -ed marker might be observed to occur in all the obligatory contexts for the past tense marker – but the learner's one hundred per cent accuracy in obligatory context may not mean that the form has been acquired; it may also occur whenever a verb is used by the learner, in contexts where no NS of English would use such a marker. Analysis in terms of obligatory context would be unable to capture this pattern in the data. Alternative methods of analysis to analysis by means of obligatory context are needed and have been proposed by a variety of researchers (such as Huebner, 1983; Pica, 1984; Parrish, 1985) and should be drawn upon when we analyse our data.

The second point to be made here has been alluded to earlier, and this is the importance of establishing good baseline data for the purposes of comparison. Far too many studies on variability in interlanguage elicit data only from second language learners. Researchers then go on to analyse those data and to suggest causes for the IL patterns observed by comparing those patterns either with idealized patterns of some ideal native speaker of the TL, or to discuss patterns which supposedly derive from the NL. The point here is that real IL performance data are being compared to idealized TL or NL competence, and not to real performance on the same tasks by speakers of the TL or the NL. Surely we know enough about variability in language performance in general to know better. In a recent study (Gundel and Tarone, 1983) which attempted to elicit production of direct object pronouns on several tasks, we asked SLLs to describe a series of pictures which we supposed would force production of direct object pronouns in referring over and over to the same entity. Our subjects, however, did not use direct object pronouns; they repeated the full noun phrase:

> The boy sees a ball, and he picks up the ball, and throws the ball, and he sits on the ball, and he puts the ball in a mailbox.

Since the NL of these subjects did not require direct object pronouns, but rather allowed zero anaphora, we thought that NL transfer might indirectly be causing some hypercorrection, since of course we knew that native speakers of English would not produce such a stilted piece of discourse. Fortunately, we decided to also ask native speakers of English to perform the same task – and we found the same pattern, possibly due to something in the design of our task. In order to make valid assessments of the patterns in our data, then, we need to ask native speakers of the TL to perform the same tasks which our SLLs perform, in order to establish a valid target baseline. And, if we wish to make claims about NL transfer in analysing our data, we may also need to ask the SLLs to perform those tasks in the NL as well. Then our analysis will be based upon more solid and less speculative, ground.

Provided that we have such valid baselines for purposes of comparison, we may analyse our data using either quantitative (that is, comparative) or qualitative (descriptive) methods of analysis. The purpose of qualitative methods of analysis is to describe the pattern of variability one has found in that data: essentially, 'my subjects did this on the tasks presented'. Qualitative methods are useful in summarizing the behaviour of the group, or of the individual. It is very useful to have detailed information on the performance of individuals on the tasks in a variability study, in that individuals do perform differently from one another; there may be certain *types* of learner who can be identified in this way. There are many different methods for displaying the data obtained in a qualitative analysis: implicational scaling, Labovian rules, charts and graphs. A typical, and very useful, qualitative method of analysis has been to calculate individual subjects' scores in terms of percentage of correct forms produced on each task, or in each linguistic context on each task, and then to either display those individual scores in the form of graphs, like that in Figure 1, or to sum up *all* these percentage scores for the group, and to display these group scores in a similar graph, like that in Figure 2.

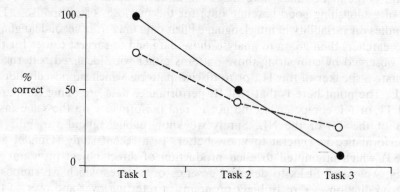

FIGURE 1   *Two learners' accuracy rates on three tasks*

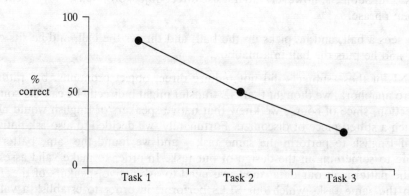

FIGURE 2   *Group B's accuracy rates on three tasks*

Note that it is best to calculate the group scores on the basis of the individuals' *percentage* scores, and not on the basis of the individuals' *raw* scores. This is because when tasks require individuals to produce communicative discourse, some individuals within the group will produce a great deal of data and others less. If we calculate group scores based on the raw scores of individuals, those who produce a great deal of data might have a greater influence upon the group score than those who produce little. Hence it is best to base group scores upon the percentage scores of the individuals in order to equalize the influence of all the individuals in the study. The purpose of qualitative methods, then, is to establish that learners do style-shift in particular ways in response to the tasks assigned, and to establish the general pattern of that style-shifting. Qualitative methods can be used by teachers, for example, who want to learn something useful about their own students' performance on a variety of tasks. For example, one might want to know whether, and how, the accuracy of a feature like the form of the imperfect verb varies on two different types of classroom grammar tests, and in oral narratives. A qualitative analysis, displayed in graphs like those just provided, will provide a useful answer to this sort of question. However, one cannot ever claim 'significance', or generality, of one's findings using qualitative methods, nor should one go on to suggest that one's findings have significance for other learners or other people's classrooms based on qualitative analysis alone. It is surprising how often researchers do go on to claim such generality and significance, even on the basis of a single subject's performance!

An even more detailed qualitative analysis of the performance of individuals on the various tasks may be quite useful in studies on situational variability. For example, if we are studying learner accuracy on verb forms, by listing the particular verbs used by individual learners in narrating the same story, one may discover that Learner *A*, who has a high formal accuracy rate, also seems to have told the story using very few verbs, and all of these had simple conjugations, while Learner *B*, who has a lower formal accuracy rate on this task, told the story using a wider variety of verbs, many of them requiring difficult conjugations. Our conclusions about the competence of these two learners, and the causes of their variability in formal accuracy on this task, may be tempered by such a detailed qualitative analysis.

Qualitative analysis may also include observations of limited data sets, and discussion of their possible significance, such as those made by Rampton (this volume). Such observations, and the careful consideration of their significance, must also be considered data, of interest in the building of theory. However, we must be extremely careful to avoid *over*interpreting such data: all we can say is that a phenomenon has occurred in a particular context at a particular time, and that that phenomenon had interesting implications. But we cannot say whether that phenomenon is at all frequent in similar contexts, nor can we say whether it will occur in other sorts of learning contexts. More systematic collection of wider sets of data in a variety of contexts are required in order to obtain the latter information.

Another sort of qualitative analysis, and one which may precede quantitative measurement, involves assessing the influence of the surrounding linguistic environment upon the formal accuracy of a particular form. For example, Dickerson (1975) found that when Japanese learners of English produced the phoneme /z/, the phonetic environment of this sound was related to these learners' accuracy of production. Here, the investigator must not only record the accuracy of the target form, but also the nature of the surrounding linguistic environment; some system must be found to categorize different *types* of surrounding environment; and the relation between formal accuracy and context must be evaluated, both qualitatively and quantitatively. One of the difficulties here involves specifying the system used to categorize types of surrounding environment; surprisingly few studies are clear on this point. For example, what constitutes the environment for an initial C? is this a word-initial, or a syllable-initial C? And what procedures were used to decide in cases where it was difficult to categorize the relevant linguistic environment? Again, if we are interested in having our studies replicated and in finding significant patterns across studies, we must be clear as to the procedures used in qualitative data analysis.

The purpose of quantitative methods of data analysis is to establish that the patterns one has found in the data are 'significant' – that is, that they are not due to chance – and therefore that similar groups of subjects would show simpler patterns of variability in their language, should the study be replicated. It is only when one has used quantitative methods to show 'significance' that one can categorically make claims about other learners, or make recommendations for pedagogy which go beyond the particular group of subjects one has studied. The statistical measure which has proven itself most useful in studies of language variability has been the ANOVA (analysis of variance) which measures the interactions of two or more sets of variables. So, for example in Figure 2 above, an analysis of variance can tell us whether the three different accuracy rates achieved by the learners in our study on our three different tasks could have been due to chance, or whether the odds are that they were really related to the tasks themselves. This in turn would suggest that, if these same tasks were provided to a similar group of learners, similar patterns of language variability would occur. Again, while most researchers in our field would say that the distinction between qualitative and quantitative research is an elementary one, and one they are well aware of, it is surprising how often these same researchers claim generality and significance for their findings without having performed any kind of quantitative analysis of their data.

Stylistic Variability and Not Speaking 'Normal' English: some post-Labovian approaches and their implications for the study of interlanguage[1]

BEN RAMPTON

Institute of Education, University of London

In this paper, I propose to look briefly at some methodological and theoretical criticisms of Labovian approaches to style, and I will extend these to their use in the study of IL variability. I shall then consider some alternative sociolinguistic models of style and consider a little ESL data in the light of one or two of these. I shall state my preference and end by giving a few social and academic reasons why I think the continuing influence of Labov in SLA is not a good thing.

Perhaps I should preface this by saying that my own research is of a sociolinguistic nature, and that my fieldwork (from which none of the data in this paper has been drawn) has been with monolinguals and highly proficient bilinguals, not anyone one might call an ESL learner. For reasons given at the end I don't think this disqualifies what I have to say. However, I am aware that my reading in this field is not as extensive as it might be and I am conscious that I may fall into the trap of overgeneralizing.

Problems with attention-to-speech as an explanation of style

Labov's theory of stylistic variability holds that 'styles can be ranged along a single dimension, measured by the amount of attention paid to speech'; the more attention paid to it, the more formal and less systematic it becomes (1972: 208).

This has been referred to as being the 'received wisdom' within variationist socio-linguistics until quite recently (Bell, 1984: 147), and it has had, and continues to have, a good deal of influence within second language acquisition research (e.g. Dickerson, 1975; Widdowson, 1975; Krashen, 1977; Tarone, 1979, 1982, 1983; Beebe, 1980a; Ellis, 1985b; Sato, 1985).

Despite this, however, there has been a feeling within sociolinguistics that this model does not account for style adequately (Gal, 1979; Brown and Levinson, 1978: 287; 1979; Coupland, 1981; Bell, 1984) and this has grown to the extent that, in my view anyway, attention-to-speech is no longer really viable as an explanation of style. Gal (1979) and Bell (1984) contain very cogent criticisms of Labov's theory, which may be worth briefly reiterating here:

> (i) The results of the white noise experiments on which Labov bases his theory are in fact ambiguous.[2] Bell (1984: 148) reanalyses George Mahl's data, and shows that (a) the (*th*) variable behaves differently from the (*dh*) Labov cites;

(b) loss of aural monitoring is on balance less important than loss of visual attention to the person of the interviewer.

(ii) Secondly, the empirical difficulties involved in measuring attention to speech have been considerably underestimated (see Dressler and Wodak, 1982: 353–4; Bell, 1984: 149; Beebe, 1980a: 443; McLaughlin, 1980; Skehan (this volume)).

(iii) It is not hard to imagine situations in which people attend to their speech in order to sound more *informal* and more colloquial (Wolfson 1976: 203; Gal, 1979; even Ochs, 1979: 77, 78) and there is some 'empirical' evidence (quite loosely defined of course – see ii above!) to suggest that this can be the case (Milroy, 1980: 106; Rickford and Wolfram, cited in Bell, 1984: 149).

(iv) The attention-to-speech model is deficient in focusing only on the private states of the speaker (Gal, 1979: 9); it ignores the addressee (Giles and Powesland, 1975; Bell, 1984; Beebe, 1981), and overlooks the social interaction between them.

(v) In line with this, it ignores the speaker's communicative intentions and de-emphasizes the rhetorical, symbolic and expressive functions of stylistic variation. It takes no cognisance of impression-management (Gal, 1979: 8; Brown and Levinson, 1978: 287).

To summarize these five criticisms, I can say that the validity of using attention-to-speech as a construct in dealing with interview and other data looks increasingly questionable, and more importantly, if you believe that the purpose of language is to communicate meaning, the most that one may want to claim about attention-to-speech is that it is a correlated, maybe mediating variable, not a causal factor in stylistic variability. What really *motivates* intra-individual/stylistic variability is the speaker's relationship with the hearer, the meanings he wants to express and the impressions he wants to create.

Attention-to-speech, Labov, and second language acquisition research

It seems to me that there is quite a powerful strand within SLA research that would not accept this view of what motivates variability. The basic postulate of Krashen's Monitor theory is obviously that attention-to-speech and meaningful communication are diametrical opposites (Krashen, 1981: 1), and elsewhere in SLA unattended, non-conscious speech is regarded as 'real', 'natural communication', 'use', whereas monitored speech is merely 'citation', 'usage', 'language like' (see e.g. Widdowson, 1975: 195; Tarone, 1982: 82, 1983: 143, 146; Ellis, 1984a: 169; 1985b: 119). This school would, I think, reject the view that impression-management and the expression of meaning are the superordinate, determining variables in stylistic variability, and that attention-to-speech is merely subordinate (if that); the drift of SLA is to suggest that meaning and monitoring exist complementarily at the same explanatory level, and that stylistic variability results from the (greater or lesser) influence of one or the other. Where meaning leaves off, monitoring takes over and vice versa.

My own preference is to give due recognition to the importance of the indexical/ associative significance of form (as does Labov) and to opt for Gumperz' view that two alternative formal realizations of the same propositional message produce different final meanings (Gumperz, 1982a: 84). When people concentrate on form, maybe they are trying to get it 'right', to say it 'correctly', but the crucial issues for both participants and analysts are for example: Which are the norms providing the standard of correctness towards which the speaker is orientating himself? Why is he selecting these in particular and with such and such a degree of effort? And how does this choice affect the way we should interpret the utterance as a whole? (For a fuller account, see Le Page, 1980.) When people attend to linguistic form at the expense of propositional meaning, they are thinking about, say, social impressions, and when L_2 learners become more target-like in their behaviour in grammatical intuition tasks than in casual speech, this is not because of attention to speech which is making their rule systems more permeable, or upsetting the operation of some interlanguage vernacular. Their speech becomes more target-like because grammatical intuition tasks are simply more teacherly: and in teacherly settings you try and talk like the teacher if you are keen to make a good impression (this also explains why prestige NL variants are transferred in the so-called careful style cf. Tarone, 1983). (For a similar line of argument, see Gal, 1979: 92.)

The drift of my argument is that at one of the points where IL scholarship draws closest to sociolinguistics – namely in the study of contextual variability – it runs the risk of remaining restrictively preoccupied with the space between the speaker and his grammar, rather than with the relationship between speakers and the world around them. In picking attention-to-speech as its explanatory variable, researchers into IL variability cut out systematic relationships between language and social structure. Indeed in setting itself an a-social agenda, the study of IL variability maybe runs the risk of bias and erroneous overgeneralization. I shall return to this issue at the end, but in the meantime it is worth briefly mentioning at least one more (quite) frequently noted shortcoming in the Labovian model and this relates to the notion of a continuum.

(vi) A single bipolar continuum may adequately represent speech variation in New York, where social stratification might just be portrayable along a single dimension. But in other societies, social stratification may be multidimensional and an adequate account of linguistic variability would need to recognize continua deriving from several points, if indeed, it is appropriate to speak of continua at all (see, for example, Giles and Powesland, 1975: 171; Hudson, 1980: 187; for very empirically based arguments, Milroy, 1980: 106, 107 and above all Le Page, 1980; Le Page and Tabouret-Keller, 1982). In adopting the Labovian bipolar model, IL study risks falsely reconstruing as psychological and universal what is social and merely local.

All in all, Labovian assumptions and methods have undoubtedly proved very handy, but it is no longer reasonable to assume that they capture universal laws, and if this is what Selinker and Douglas are thinking of, I can sympathize with them when they tell SLA researchers to be wary of sociolinguistics (1985: 197). But the trouble is, of course, that sociolinguistics is not just Labov and in taking this line Selinker and Douglas potentially overlook sociolinguistic/socio-psychological accounts of language that should serve as an *essential* adjunct to psycholinguistic perspectives. The work of Giles *et al.*, on speech accommodation is obviously already quite well known within SLA (cf. Beebe, 1981; Zuengler, 1982; Beebe and Zuengler, 1983); one might also mention Le Page's acts of identity theory (e.g. 1980); or alternatively anthropological/'interactional' sociolinguistics as propounded by Gumperz, Brown and Levinson. In contrast to Labov, all of these take cognisance both of the addressee (Le Page perhaps to a lesser degree) and of the social structure in which interaction occurs. With greater or lesser degrees of specificity, all are concerned with the cognitive processes involved in orienting oneself linguistically to the world around, and in all of them, again defined with greater or lesser degrees of delicacy, meaning and intentionality hold a central place.[3] Furthermore they offer explanations of both interactional variability *and* of language acquisition and change (see Beebe and Zuengler, 1983: 200 on this distinction).

I would like now to explore the relevance of one of these (interactional socio-linguistics) to a small 'error' analysis. I shall start with the 'error' analysis.

'Me no like it', 'me too clever'

The data presented in the Appendix at the end of this paper were collected while I was an ESL teacher in a Local Education Authority language unit. Having heard quite a few similar constructions around, I prepared a data protocol which allowed me to record what was said where, by whom to whom, when, about what and in what mood (I used a very rough approximation to Hymes' *Speaking*). I carried this protocol in my school diary and jotted down '*me*' constructions whenever I heard them. As you can see, the data is fairly sparse: I obviously could not record full details of the linguistic and dialogical environment of these utterances and representing as they do, several months' listening, occurrences of this construction were fairly infrequent. Also, I never discussed it with any of these speakers (though I did with others) so that, strictly speaking, the analysis that follows is not based on 'authoritative reconstructions' (cf. Kasper, 1979b: 396; Gumperz, 1982a: 87). The data does however have the advantage of being non-experimental (cf. other IL studies of politeness), the informants had no reason to feel that they were being observed, and the researcher was a fully ratified participant. Even so, I am presenting these data speculatively, to illustrate a point rather than prove a case.

The children who produced these utterances were all post-beginners and had generally been learning English for between at least one and three years. They were aged between 9 and 14, and all of them normally used '*I*' – the SE first person singular pronoun – as well as fairly standard pre-verbal negation (auxiliary + neg + verb (see e.g. 5 and 24, page 57)). For all of them, these *me/me no* constructions are very unusual, so what is going on?

It would, I think, be inappropriate to pursue a grammatical analysis here, though an explanation in terms of transfer or TL overgeneralization might well be worthwhile if the speakers had been really basic ESL beginners and if this *me* construction was used by them more regularly and in a greater variety of contexts (cf. below). As it is however, I think it would be fairly inept to treat this data as if it had anything specific to say about these particular speakers' 'core' competences and the IL processes centrally shaping them.

In contrast, an analysis which considers indexical and pragmatic meaning suggests one or two more fruitful lines of enquiry, and it is worth continuing a little with the data description.

Considering indexicality first, this *me* construction might conceivably be intended to connote West Indian creole, in which one also finds this structure and of which there are plenty of speakers in the neighbourhood. While a creole resonance may be at work in 4, by and large this seems unlikely since (i) on occasions, these utterances were clearly accompanied by very Punjabized pronunciation (or references to the subcontinent); (ii) in many cases, the youngsters were still relatively early learners of English and may thus have been unaware of West Indian English speakers (B and TL being the exceptions): (iii) *me* generally had a quite close, front, longish vowel (/i:/) in contrast to the shorter, half-close, more central /I/ stereotypical of West Indian *me* (Sutcliffe, 1982: 187). I cannot rule out this creole possibility but I prefer the alternative interpretation that the association being conjured here is with the language spoken by people who cannot speak much English (see data items 8, 9, 14, 24?),[4] by ESL beginners.

Looking sideways at the settings and topics connected with these utterances, we can go further and speculate about the social evaluations attached to this broken (Asian?) English. The topics covered are uniform in so far as they are nearly all related to school and school activities; the setting is also invariably in lessons or around the school, and the speaker–addressee relationship is either pupil–pupil, or pupil–teacher. In this context, what with the continual institutional pressure towards better and more standard English, it may very well be that these *me* constructions are generally recognized as being low status and institutionally stigmatized.

Switching our attention to the illocutionary function enacted by these utterances, it emerges that a substantial proportion of the data falls into one of two broad illocutionary categories – on the one hand something like rejection/refusal, and on the other, boasting. (I take 1, 2, 3, 4, 5, 7, 12 and 23 to be cases of refusal and rejection; 6, 8, 9, 13, 15, 16, 19, 21, 22 to exemplify boasting; which leaves 10, 11, 14, 17, 18, 20, 24 more uncertain.) In view of this, one may proceed to argue that many of the interactions have entailed unequal status relations in one of two ways: either the listener was in a position of permanent superiority (i.e. the teacher), or the speakers, through the act of boasting, were claiming for themselves a temporary superiority over their peers. Even so, the 'key' for nearly all these interactions was, I think, amicable.

To sum up this description, I consider the important 'product level' components in the use of *me no* to be its association with low status Broken English, its realization of the illocutionary functions of refusal and boasting, and its connection with asymmetrical status relations in a friendly atmosphere. What can the sociolinguistic models I have mentioned offer in terms of an explanation of the process underlying the use of this construction? Let me take the Labovian and interactionalist accounts in turn.

Two sociolinguistic perspectives on 'me no like it' and 'me too clever'

I do not think the Labovian attention-to-speech/formality model is very helpful with this data, since

(i) it has nothing specific to say about speaker-hearer relations or speech act type;

(ii) it will not countenance the possibility of *me no* being an approximation of West Indian speech, as this would entail the continuum being more than bipolar;

(iii) in my view it is impossible to say whether these *me* constructions represent monitored speech or not: it seems to me perfectly possible that attention has been paid to planning at a relatively abstract, prelinguistic stage, and that *me no* has flowed with complete automaticity from the higher level decision to, for example, act like an incompetent (see Faerch and Kasper, 1983c: 35);

(iv) however, because it is highly irregular grammatically (in the sense of being infrequent and unpredictable), because it is certainly salient to this and other addressees, and because it is recognized and remarked upon elsewhere in the community, we might feel justified in identifying it as a Labovian 'stereotype', and as such, on Labovian logic, take it as a symptom of speech monitoring. But even if we did accept this rather dubious reasoning, a fourth problem would have to be faced. According to IL and other variationists, attention to speech leads to the occurrence of prestige NL and TL variants, not to the 'basilectal' forms in evidence here (see e.g. Ellis, 1985b: 120, even Richards, 1979: 10, though cf. Sato, 1985: 195).

A better and fuller explanation of my data lies, I think, within interactional sociolinguistics.

In Gumperz' framework, different linguistic forms are seen as linking up with underlying assumptions about social categories, and the use of these forms as symbols is held to play an important role in rhetorical effectiveness and persuasion (1982a: 99). I have already implied that in connoting the social category 'people who don't know much English', *me no* probably carries further implications of more general cultural and social incompetence (some empirical support for this is in Rampton (forthcoming)). And as such *me no* is maybe operating strategically as a 'plea of insanity', a way of justifying the fact that the speaker isn't going to do what's been asked of him. The grammar of *me no* may be mimetically enacting the speaker's excuse, at least in the case of rejections and refusals.

That doesn't cover boasting of course, and I think a more comprehensive and more elegant account however lies in Brown and Levinson's theory of politeness (which is by no means new in SLA research but has been rather differently applied). As speech acts, both boasting and rejection/refusal threaten the hearer's face, and *me no*, it seems to me, may very well be functioning as what Brown and Levinson call a self-humiliative honorific (Brown & Levinson, 1978: 183 ff). What I think it is doing is toning down the force of speech acts which either challenge the authority of a superior or claim superiority over an equal, and it achieves this again because the construction connotes linguistic and general incompetence, low status, harmlessness even. If you reject something the teacher says, you make the challenge to his authority much less grave if your syntax is also saying 'but look, I'm only little' or 'I can't do much'. Equally, you are less likely to offend a mate when you tell him that you are seven sums ahead if the grammar of your utterance signals, 'But never mind, I'm still a fool'.

This seems to me to be quite a coherent and comprehensive account of this data, and it might not be too hard to devise elicitation experiments to investigate it further. In the meantime however, it is apparent that the interactionalists offer a richer model than that of Labovian or interlanguage variationists.

Interactional sociolinguistics and SLA generally

In fact, interactional sociolinguistics may very well have wider implications for SLA, and the kinds of pragmatic processes I have described here may account for other types of IL data as well.

The kind of politeness strategy that I have outlined in relation to *me no* may account for 'backsliding' quite generally. Rather than trying to explain backsliding exclusively in terms of task difficulty, anxiety, excitement and extreme relaxation (Selinker 1972: 36; note the similarity of these terms to the idiom of the attention-to-speech variationists, for example Tarone 1982: 80), surely it is worth exploring the extent to which backsliding is motivated by deference.

More generally interactional sociolinguistics (and indeed accommodation theory) provides a process model which may account not merely for interactional variability. It may also add an important additional dimension to explanation of the shape of proficiencies developed in the long term. For example, Brown and Levinson (1978: 262) suggest that 'there will be correlations between overall levels and kinds of face redress in a culture and the special elaboration of grammatical devices for achieving that redress'. On this basis, we might very speculatively suggest that learners from for example dominant cultures disposed to positive politeness (1978: 250) might be predisposed to develop ellipsis and contraction in their L2s (1978: 116) whereas negatively polite groups would be oriented more to impersonalization techniques and passivization (1978: 196–203).

Certainly, politeness phenomena have been invoked in quite a number of IL studies, and indeed some have considered the relationship of politeness to long-term development. But these particular studies have focused mainly on the ways in which face considerations affect conversational repair and access to 'comprehensible input' (e.g. Scarcella and Higa, 1981 [though see p 414]; Varonis and Gass, 1985; Selinker and Douglas, 1985). In these studies, it seems to me, politeness considerations play a subsidiary role in relation to what is held to be the 'real' motor of grammatical development: the expression of propositional meaning. Certainly the case has been made elsewhere for the impact of interactional process on language structure (see Hatch, 1978) but the point being made here is that aspects of social structural positioning – power, distance and face – may additionally directly influence the shape of learner grammar – social factors may well do much more in linguistic development than merely influence the stage that learners get to in some universal path of SLA (see Gregg, 1984: 85).

IL study in a social context

This line of enquiry has some important implications for SLA research: trying to identify grammatically influential aspects of social meaning requires a complex emic comprehension of social structure. If you are looking for the impact on linguistic development of social meaning, you have to try and gain understanding of the roles and relationships in which a learner habitually participates, and you certainly also have to recognize that elicitation tests and indeed laboratory role plays are on their own inadequate means (see for example Tajfel, 1981; Wetherell, 1982). Even if your claims about the intersection of social structure and linguistic form are weaker, like mine relating only to interactional behaviour rather than long-term development, you need to understand more about the socio-cultural world of the learner than maybe IL variationists acknowledge. There is apparently a consensus, at least among British linguists, that pronunciation is especially closely associated with social groupings (Hudson, 1981: 340), and this being the case, fairly detailed socio–cultural awareness is probably particularly important to the study of IL phonology, though of course it may affect other areas as well. With *me no*, for example, relatively close and sustained investigation of learners' social environments has been important in intimating to me the low status of these children's school in the eyes of their peers, the types of speech act occasioning the use of *me no* and the currency of this kind of (self-directed?) rhetorical foreigner talk elsewhere in the bilingual community.

I mentioned bias earlier on and I would finally like to amplify this a little. It seems to me that without a fair degree of background understanding, there is a danger of regarding language learners as social entities only to the extent to which they conform to the norms of some notional and notionally singular (cf. Rosen and Burgess, 1980: 36; Beebe and Zuengler, 1983: 198) target language group. Thus in another group of IL politeness studies (not concerned with the facilitation of propositional meaning), theories of tact have fairly often been used simply to provide product level accounts of the ways in which language learners fail to meet TL pragmatic norms (Kasper, 1979a, 1979b; Tanaka and Kawade, 1982; Frazer, Rintell and Walters 1980; Scarcella and Brunak 1981). The important points of reference have only been the TL and the NL. In contrast, I have tried to show how being a language learner can itself constitute a particular status, how this status is a potentially active element in inter-action, and how linguistic form can be used to strategically allude to this for politeness (and other) purposes. A most important point is that not only are *me no* utterances non-erroneous, but that it would be wrong – systematically distorting (Habermas, 1970a, 1970b; Wuthnow, 1984: 224)[5] – to see them as developmental, as a 'phase' (in partial mitigation of Kasper here, see Kasper, 1979b: 395). These *me* utterances are effective in down-toning face-threatening acts: they are successful in their appeal to shared perceptions of social reality; they are honest in their recognition of linguistic inability/prejudice; they need to be taken seriously as maybe being mechanisms for transcending linguistic stigmatization (see perhaps Hinnenkamp, 1980: 194), and as I said before, they may be in line with a rhetorical foreigner talk widespread in the bilingual community.

In saying that *me* constructions are non-erroneous, I do not think I am just repeating the orthodox avowals about linguistic integrity and systematicity that have both inspired and served as the guiding methodological premise for interlanguage research for a decade and a half. My gist is in fact to criticise the traditional IL research stance, quite generally, I think. IL not only entails new and distinctive linguistic forms, but also, new and distinctive sociolinguistic statuses. These statuses are *relational*, derived from and sensitive to the relationship between Native and Non-native Speaker (among other things) (cf. Candlin 1983b: x, xi). In their concern with 'natural IL vernaculars' and with overcoming the observer paradox, IL variationists in particular take very little notice of this, and they try to eliminate the influence of the researcher from their most highly prized data. Of course, the observer's influence is recognized, but this influence is only a source of technical interference – noise – not as a cultural force codetermining the shape of verbal behaviour.

In essence IL is still seen only as a psycholinguistic property immanent in the speaker, and in taking this view, researchers do two things I think they should avoid: (a) they ignore the relevance of this status to their informants and in doing so miss out on the linguistic acts (like '*me no*') symbolically reflecting its situationally variable salience; (b) they risk taking a rather conservative tack, and are liable to bestow stigmatized language learner status where this is not due. By failing to investigate the addressee as a socio–cultural presence in their data, IL variationists of a Labovian bent cut out consideration of target language speakers, and shut down on any critical awareness of themselves as 'true', competent or legitimate representatives of the group the learner aspires to. The idiosyncrasy of their own linguistic and cultural positions is not a matter for examination, and the usual cross-cultural research injunctions concerning the need to try and enter the participants' own meaning systems don't apply. In this idiom, Subcontinental Indian English remains simply a dialectal aggregation of fossilized competences (see Selinker 1972: 38; cf. Kachru (ed.) 1982 which in my view does not go nearly far enough); and instead of trying to acquire the subcultural knowledge that would enable valid inferences to be made about the implicatures generated by incipient bilinguals (Grice, 1975; Gumperz 1982a: 94–96; Richards and Sukwiwat 1983), perhaps too many IL researchers prefer to look out for breakdowns and repairs, prematurely operating what Faerch and Kasper (1983c) call the co-operative principle for learner–native speaker interaction – 'if the learner signals that he has problems formulating himself, help out' (1983: 229; contrast Candlin, 1983b: *xi*; Widdowson, 1983: 142; Thomas, 1983: 96). Unintentionally this creates 'learners' where people may be very happily getting on with interpersonal (Candlin, 1983: 130) or subcultural communicative conventions of their own (see Dorian, 1982: 30 for a graphic illustration); it ends up with the learner being held responsible for the perlocutionary failure of his utterances (e.g. Kasper, 1979b: 395) and ultimately, with the non-patrials getting the instruction, not the native speakers (cf. Furnborough *et al.* 1982; Smith (ed.) 1983). Codeswitching in sociolinguistics winds up as interference in SLA.

Conclusion

It seems to me that IL variationists are looking backwards too much to the issues and methodologies of the morpheme studies and in doing so failing to connect properly with SLA research concerned with discourse and IL (as per Larry Smith).[6] This is not to deny them credit for a very vital function: Labovian approaches within IL study have added considerable force to the argument that interlanguage is qualitatively just like any other (Tarone, 1983). But if one accepts that premise however, there is an important consequence. If IL is like other languages, then sociolinguistic accounts of IL are just sociolinguistics pure and simple. I have tried in this paper to outline some of the dangers to IL study if it allows a private version of sociolinguistics to develop. But equally, I think, the loss would be to sociolinguistics. Generating as it does a particular status with linguistic interactional and socio-cultural implications, foreign language learning entails a social position that sociolinguistics ought to account for; and at a broader level, as Corder (1967) underlines, accounts of deviance help to define the ordinary. On this principle, widening the scope of sociolinguistics to encompass the foreign language learner would benefit our understanding of speech communities in general.

Notes

1. I am grateful to Jill Bourne, Ahmed Chaudhri, Tutiaz Chaudhri, Dick Hudson and Peter Skehan for comments on an earlier draft and for other pertinent discussions.
2. Labov describes the white noise experiments as follows:

   Mahl has conducted a series of studies on the effect of removing subjects' ability to monitor speech. . . . This was done by feeding random noise through earphones at a volume high enough to prevent the subject from hearing his own speech. In addition, the subject was sometimes facing away from the interviewer so that he could not see the interviewer's face. The speech of each subject was then studied during three interviews under four conditions: with white noise, facing or not facing; and without white noise, facing or not facing. (1972: 97)

3. In addition, all of them are geared to empirical work in fluid multilingual settings much better than Labov, and are better suited to handling the diverse linguistic pulls operating within heterogeneous societies.
4. Although I cannot be sure with regard to these particular speakers who may be untypical to quite a degree, I do have evidence elsewhere that broken English is a recognized variety within the local community, and that *me* constructions are instantiations of this. (See Rampton, forthcoming.)
5. Wuthnow's (1983: 224) summary of systematically distorted communication may point to some challenging questions with regard to IL study generally:

   Systematically distorted communication is for Habermas (1970a) what false consciousness was for Marx: it prevents the resolution of major social crises. *Systematically* distorted communication is to be distinguished from simple breakdowns of communication stemming from misused rules of language. These are easily recognized by participants themselves, who simply fail to comprehend what others are attempting to communicate. A *systematic* distortion is more serious in that participants assume they have understood one another and have arrived at some consensus, but because of unacknowledged interests they have engaged only in pseudo-communication, and have failed to achieve genuine consensus. Pre-existing patterns of thought have prevented them from communicating fully and effectively. These pre-existing patterns of thought are not distinguishable in terms of content, but by the level of complexity or sophistication they embody. Because of the importance of communication to the functioning of advanced capitalist societies, high levels of sophistication and self-awareness concerning communication are necessary; values and facts cannot be accepted uncritically as 'givens'; attention must be paid to the effects of communication on values and facts and to their expression in discourse. Any failure to question the nature of values and facts can lead to systematically distorted communication.

Habermas . . . regards science and technology as sources of systematically distorted communication. Because of their sheer pervasiveness, they are a serious form of ideology, reflecting rational-purposive action, and conflicting with communication oriented toward social solidarity and the attainment of consensus. While promoting economic growth through manipulation of the physical and social environment, they pay no attention to promoting self-conscious reflection about values. Advances of science and technology substitute manipulative rules and context-free knowledge for norms of solidarity and reciprocity, and lead to an emphasis on technical skills at the expense of roles and values defining moral obligations.

6. Underlying quite a lot of my criticisms can be seen the tension between nomothetic and hermeneutic science outlined by Ochsner (1979). My drift is obviously towards the hermeneutic, which is also in line with the social criticism implied in note 5. On connections between democracy and e.g. ethnography, see also Hymes, 1980.

Appendix: *me* constructions used by children in test related settings

Utterance	Addresser	Addressee	Setting	Topic
1. me no shower } 2. me no like it }	3 or 4, 11–13-year-old Pakistani boys	teacher [M white]	cold football touchline	teacher's instruction to watch a football game, and the necessity to have a shower afterwards
3. me got pencil already	B [aged 9, M Pakistani]	teacher	lesson	instruction to get a pencil
4. me no want to draw myself, man	B	teacher	lesson	self-portraits requested by the teacher
5. me no do it – I won't be able to do it	B	teacher	lesson	maths
6. me just done it	KH [aged 9, F Sikh]	TL [9 years, F Sikh]	lesson	dictionary work
7. me no do it	KH	teacher	lesson	classroom task
8. me too clever (Punjabized pronunciation)	TL	KH	lesson	dictionary work
9. me going to London (Punjabized pronunciation)	TL	teacher	lesson	weekend plans
10. me no lose it	Ba [aged 14, M Pakistani]	T [aged 14, M Bengali]	lesson	
11. me new there	Ba	teacher	lesson	referring to time when first came to an L centre in England
12. me no play gym	G [aged 12, M Pakistani]	teacher	after school	voluntary 5-a-side soccer game
13. me go to Biddenham	G	teacher	classroom after school	showing letter of acceptance to Upper School
14. me got it (Punjabized pronunciation)	KL [aged 13, F Sikh]	teacher	lesson	
15. me on nineteen	N [11 yrs, M]	Bo [12, M Bengali]	lesson	maths textbook work

Utterance	Addresser	Addressee	Setting	Topic
16. me lucky	Z [9 yrs, F Pakistani]	KH	lesson	
17. me got it	Z	KH	lesson	
18. Sir, me no pencil, sir	Nc [11 yrs, M Bengali]	teacher	lesson	teacher's question about where his pencil was
19. me finished	Nc	Na [11 yrs, M Bengali]	lesson	classwork
20. me know nothing	Nc	Na	lesson	classwork
21. me know everything	Nc	Na	lesson	classwork
22. me finished	Nc & Na	Na & Nc	lesson	reading-books
21. no, sir, me not out	Nc	teacher	lesson	teacher's instruction to get out of the classroom
24. me no like Pakistan . . . see I can't speak English language	Nc	Bc [12 yrs, F Pakistani]	lesson	

M = male, F = female

Non-systematic Variability: a self-inflicted conundrum?

MICHAEL SWAN

Introduction

When people use a foreign language, there are generally some things that they always get right and some things that they always get wrong. Much of a learner's[1] vocabulary, for instance, is likely to fall into the first category, while a good deal of his or her pronunciation may come in the second. More intriguingly, there are also things which fall between the two extremes. An item may be produced correctly and appropriately on one occasion, but misused or replaced by an inappropriate item on another occasion.

This variation can be systematic. That is to say, there are cases where a learner's use of an item varies with the linguistic or non-linguistic context, in accordance with a distinction not made by native speakers. For instance, learner A might pronounce the English phoneme /v/ correctly in general, but always replace it by /f/ at the ends of words. Learner B might use whispered vowels systematically when anxious to appear deferential, but not in other circumstances. Learner C might regularly use *big* inappropriately before uncountable nouns, while otherwise distinguishing correctly between *big*, *large* and *great*. And learner D might tend to drop *-s* from the plurals of words ending in *-en* and *-er*, but not from other words. (In a sense it is perhaps misleading – though it is common practice – to describe cases like these as examples of variability: the learner is simply doing what the native speaker does – matching forms systematically with functions and contexts. He or she may not make the same matchings as the native speaker, but that simply makes his or her interlanguage different from the target language; it does not really make it 'variable' in any very useful sense of the word.)

In other cases, there seems to be no such systematic basis for the learner's choice of forms. He or she may alternate between correct and incorrect negative structures in apparently identical contexts, for instance; or talk indiscriminately about 'doing' and 'making' a mistake; or drop the plural ending from a certain word 30% of the time. This kind of variability has attracted a good deal of attention from linguists, and has been seen by many writers as raising a cluster of theoretical questions. How can we integrate such non-systematic variability into our model of interlanguage? Should we posit the existence of variable rules, and if so, what is the psycholinguistic status of such rules? How do they square with other aspects of interlanguage competence? What about the fact that the ratio of correct to incorrect usage can sometimes be shown to vary in proportion to the amount of attention paid by the learner to formal accuracy (so that the non-systematic variability is itself variable – systematically)? What are the implications of this for our view of interlanguage competence? And should we be talking anyway about 'competences' rather than 'competence'?

Attempts to deal with such questions have led to substantial theorizing, and to some rather heavyweight model-building. In what follows, I shall argue that much of this is unnecessary. I believe that the type of non-systematic variability under discussion does not in fact raise any additional conceptual problems beyond those that we already have to grapple with when we try to understand interlanguage in general, and that it can be handled perfectly well using existing models of competence and performance.

Permeable systems, continua and the like

Discussion about language acquisition is frequently highly metaphorical. In particular, writers often find it convenient to account for observed phenomena by attributing them to the operation of non-observed psychological entities such as 'the language acquisition device', 'the affective filter', 'variable rules', 'interlanguage competence' and so on. This is often helpful – perhaps it is even necessary – but it has its dangers. While such labels no doubt often correspond to psychological realities of one kind or another, one can sometimes be misled into taking one's own use of language too literally, assuming unconsciously, for instance, that because one is using a singular countable abstract noun such as *system*, one must necessarily be referring thereby to something singular, unitary, 'thing-like'.

Writers on variability use their share of metaphor. Adjemian talks about interlanguage being 'permeable' to outside forms (Adjemian, 1976.). For Ellis, too, interlanguage 'constitutes an unstable system, and as such is permeable to invasion by new linguistic forms' (Ellis, 1985b). And later in the same paper, discussing his 'multiple competence paradigm', Ellis posits that the learner possesses not 'a single interlanguage system, but a number of separate and overlapping systems'. Tarone, accounting for the fact that learners get things right more often when they are paying attention, talks in terms of a 'capability continuum' or a 'continuum of styles', along which a newly learnt target language structure can move 'from right to left' until it is assimilated into a learner's 'vernacular style' (Tarone, 1983).

Language of this kind makes me uneasy. It often looks as if the principle of Occam's razor is being flouted – as if such models introduce more than is necessary in order to explain the phenomena under consideration. Take the fact that language learners modify their rules, acquire new words, and so on. How realistic is it to account for this by describing a learner's language as, for instance, 'an unstable system, permeable to invasion by new linguistic forms'? People keep building new houses in my village, but I would not readily describe the place as 'an unstable system, permeable to invasion by new architectural forms'. Perhaps interlanguages are sufficiently different from villages to make such a mode of discourse appropriate in one case and not in the other. I would feel more comfortable, though, if I could see more clearly why. What exactly is meant by using the word *system* to describe the whole of a learner's language? Are questions being begged here? Is it realistic to describe the whole of a learner's language as *unstable* or *permeable* because new items can be added and some items can change? Or are some parts of the language actually stable and waterproof? The word *invasion* has powerful overtones, implying an attack on the autonomy and integrity of an organism or society. Are these connotations justified by the nature of interlanguage change? Or – in short – are we getting more out of our metaphors than we put in?

Multiple competences: Tarone's continuum model

Several writers have handled aspects of variability by constructing models which attribute more than one interlanguage competence to the learner. Krashen and others distinguish 'acquired' and 'learned' knowledge of a language (Krashen, 1981). Ellis (1985b), following Selinker and Douglas (1985), advocates a 'multiple competence paradigm'. Tarone, in her influential 1983 paper referred to above, elaborates a continuum model. In discussing what seem to me the drawbacks of this kind of metaphor, I shall focus on Tarone's model as a convenient example; many of the criticisms I shall make, however, apply generally to models which account for variability in terms of multiple competence.

In Tarone's model, a learner's interlanguage competence is seen as encompassing a number of 'styles' or 'capabilities', distinguished from each other by the degree of attention paid to language forms, and capable of being located on a continuum from 'most careful' to 'most vernacular'. The term *vernacular*, as used by Tarone, does not carry its usual sociolinguistic connotations, but refers simply to spontaneous production in which there is minimum attention to formal accuracy. (It is important to make this point, since Tarone associates her model closely with that used by Labov (1969) in his studies of style-shifting. However, Tarone's 'styles' are by no means the same kind of thing as the sociolinguistic registers investigated by Labov.) Tarone's 'most careful style' is that used by the learner when making grammaticality judgements; performance in various elicitation tasks is what constitutes the operation of other relatively careful styles; 'attended speech data' represent a less careful style; unselfconscious spontaneous speech draws on the vernacular style. Language items may be differentially variable according to the style being used: Tarone cites studies which appear to show a systematic correlation between carefulness and correctness in certain cases – the more careful the style, the greater the mastery of the structure being investigated. (So for instance, in a study by Dickerson and Dickerson (1977), Japanese learners pronounced English /r/ correctly most often when they were reading a word list, less often when they were reading aloud, and least often when they were speaking freely.) Newly learnt structures, according to the model, can move along the continuum from the 'careful' end to the 'vernacular' end.

One thing that worries me about this model is the nature of the evidence for the so-called careful styles. This includes learners' intuitions of grammaticality, and their performance in tasks such as, for instance, elicited imitation or minimal pair production. I question whether such data can be taken as reliable evidence for the status of any aspect of a speaker's competence. If a language user only produces a given form in an imitation task, or judges it to be grammatical but does not use it, in what sense can we say that the form is really part of that person's idiolect? In one study cited by Tarone (Schmidt, 1980), some learners judged the structure, 'Mary is eating an apple and Sue a pear' to be grammatical, but were unable to produce it.

I would also judge this structure to be grammatical, but I doubt whether I use it myself. If I don't, then rather than saying that it is a feature only of 'my most careful style', it seems more sensible to say that the structure is not part of my productive idiolect at all. Again, I could probably manage certain imitation or minimal-pair production tasks in, say, Swahili or Vietnamese; but it would be misleading to take the resulting data as evidence for my 'careful style' in these languages, given that I don't speak a word of either of them. To put the criticism another way: can we really regard grammaticality judgements and performance on elicitation tasks as being on the same continuum as more and less careful styles of speech and writing?

In fact, I feel uneasy about the whole notion of 'style' and 'style-shifting' in this context. There are certainly times when people pay more attention to their language in order to get things right, but to what extent does it make sense to describe this as a process of 'drawing on a new style?' I find the French word *réimperméabilization* (= *reproofing*) difficult to say; if I need to say it, I slow down and make a special effort. And I often make the mistake in French of beginning a request 'Si tu pourrais . . .' instead of 'Si tu pouvais . . .' (= 'If you could . . .'); if I pay attention, I can avoid the mistake. But it seems to me odd and ponderous to describe what I am doing in these cases as 'shifting to a different style'. It would certainly not occur to me to use this kind of terminology to talk about variable behaviour in non-linguistic areas. I have recently changed cars, and (in accordance with Appendix 6b of Sod's Law) the wiper and indicator switches on the new car are the opposite way round from where they were on my old car. When I want to hit the indicator, I get the wipers about 40% of the time. If I concentrate, I can cut the percentage of errors to about 25%. And if – investigating my judgements of correctness – you asked me at this moment whether the wiper switch was on the right, I would have no difficulty in telling you – correctly – that that is the case. So – are we to say that in my 'non-careful driving style' I have an error-rate of 40%, in my 'more careful driving style' I have an error-rate of 20%, and in my 'most careful driving style' (when I am not even in the car) my performance is faultless? And when I stop getting it wrong, as I no doubt will one day, am I to account for this by saying that mastery of the rule has 'moved across the continuum' from my most careful (and most permeable) style to my least careful style?

If the notion of style seems inappropriate here and Tarone's model – a misleading metaphor rather than a useful conceptualization – this is because the data being discussed simply do not add up to anything that we can reasonably call a style. A style, if we are to use the word in something approaching its normal sense, is a bundle of features which are found together and which have a certain coherence. One variable feature alone doesn't make a style. Nor indeed do whole catalogues of variable features, as long as they are investigated independently and cannot be shown to co-vary systematically in groups. To justify the assertion that interlanguage variability involves style-shifting, it would be necessary at least to demonstrate that, in a particular interlanguage, a significant number of features all varied together purposefully according to the degree of attention paid to language form. But no such claim is made by Tarone.

Competence and performance

The real reason why this kind of model doesn't work well is that it describes features of performance in terms of competence. If an instance of variability is related to degrees of attention, this is presumably because there is an obstacle to successful spontaneous performance, and attention is needed to overcome the obstacle. For instance, a learner may find it difficult to decide in real time between two competing rules, or to recall an item from store, or to assemble a compound item, or to put his/her tongue in an unfamiliar position. And if variability changes over time (as new items 'move through the continuum' towards the vernacular style), this is presumably because difficult items become easier with practice. Notions like *difficulty* and *practice*, which involve considerations of performance, don't seem easy to handle with a model which essentially locates the sources of variability in differential competences. And perhaps for this reason, Tarone and the other writers mentioned have little to say about these notions. Yet they are surely fundamental to the type of variability under consideration here.

Bialystok and Sharwood-Smith, in their paper 'Interlanguage is not a state of mind' (Bialystok and Sharwood-Smith, 1985), argue for a view of interlanguage which pays attention to both *knowledge* and *the control of knowledge in real-time processing*. A dual model of this kind, in my view, makes it a good deal easier to talk coherently about variability. With such a dual model, the sources of variability can be seen as being located both in competing rules (competence) and in processing problems (performance), as appropriate. Mechanisms of change can be regarded as involving both analysis/reanalysis (changes in competence) and improvements in processing skill arising from practice (changes in performance). Similarly, fossilization of errors can be attributed both to failed analyses (defective competence) and to repeated difficulty in getting things right (defective performance).

For the 'man in the street' (and the average language teacher), it seems obvious that variability is related to performance factors as well as to competence. Knowing a language is one thing, but using it is another; it's harder to get things right when you're tired; you talk better after a couple of drinks; practice makes perfect; once you've made a mistake you're quite likely to make it again; your knowledge of a language can get rusty; the usage of the person you're talking to has an effect on the way you talk yourself; and so on. Such naive commonsense notions may not provide us with an adequate account of interlanguage behaviour, but it seems perverse to ignore them totally in favour of a model which explains all variation in terms of separately stored competences.

The input to interlanguage and the variety of variability

If we consider the input to interlanguage performance – the reasons why a particular learner's production is as it is, and not otherwise – we need to take into account the following factors, among others:

(1) Basic learning mechanisms such as perception, imitation and generalization, and the way in which these operate in the learner in question.

(2) The learner's aptitude for foreign language learning and use.

(3) The amount, type and content of the learner's previous exposure to the target language.

(4) The extent to which the learner has so far used the target language, and the ways in which he/she has used it.

(5) Whatever explicit information the learner has received about the target language.

(6) The nature of the learner's mother tongue, its similarities and differences with the target language.

(7) Other languages known to the learner.

(8) The learner's hypotheses about target language features: the generalization that he/she has made on the basis of the data so far attended to, and the equivalences that he/she has posited between target language features and features of the mother tongue or other languages.

(9) Habits of perception and production developed by the learner while using his/her mother tongue; while using other languages; while using the target language.

(10) Whatever universal language acquisition mechanisms or strategies can be shown to affect the learner's assimilation of the target language.

(11) The difficulty of specific target language features (determined both by their intrinsic complexity and by their similarity to or difference from mother-tongue features); the resultant problems the learner may have in understanding, learning, recalling, and accurately and fluently producing the features in question.

(12) Whatever universal language production mechanisms and strategies can be shown to affect the learner's performance.

(13) The learner's motivation, needs and attitudes.

(14) The degree of communicative success that the learner has so far attained with his/her interlanguage (and the resulting pressures towards improvement or fossilization).

(15) The load on the learner's processing capacity from moment to moment, and any resultant pressure on the learner to simplify, pidginize etc.

(16) The learner's morale, state of health and level of alertness or fatigue, and the implications of these factors for successful production at any point.

(17) Any input being received by the learner at a particular time, and the way in which this may affect production at that time.

(18) Any social pressures on the learner at a particular time which might encourage him/her to modify his/her performance.

Many of the factors listed above can obviously account for variable performance. In trying to produce a target language feature, a learner may have to decide between competing hypotheses drawn from different sources; he or she may be influenced by competing habits; habit may compete with hypothesis; explicit knowledge may compete with both habit and hypothesis; the difficulty of the feature may affect the learner's ability to produce it correctly; universal production strategies, or overloaded processing capacity, may encourage simplification and pidginization; the social need to sound 'correct' may encourage greater accuracy; the learner's perception of his/her moment-by-moment communicative success may also lead to a raising or lowering of standards; and so on.

It is not surprising, then, that learners are inconsistent in their production of some target language items. Given the number and complexity of the factors that affect interlanguage competence and performance, we obviously cannot expect to predict this variable behaviour in any very precise way. All we can hope to do is to gain a somewhat better understanding of the various mechanisms involved. Since these mechanisms are very varied, any models we use to help us conceptualize what is going on will need to be quite complex. Mutliple-competence models are clearly too simple and one-dimensional to be of very much use. Indeed, we may well find that the competence–performance distinction itself is too broad a metaphor for our purposes, and that more closely-defined concepts are needed if we are to organize our data efficiently.

The scope of variability: how large is the claim?

One's impression from reading articles such as those quoted is that their authors assign a great deal of importance to the type of variability under discussion. For Ellis, interlanguage 'is composed of a series of variable systems' (Ellis, 1985b). And he sees variability as the key to language development: 'The resolution of non-systematic variability underlies all language change' (ibid.). For Tarone, her data show that 'interlanguage behaviour varies systematically with elicitation task' (Tarone, 1983).

How variable is interlanguage, in reality? Let us suppose that a French learner of English, reporting the same incident at different times on the same day, produces three different variants of a particular tense rule. At one point she says, 'I have seen Lucy yesterday'; on another occasion she uses *saw* instead of *have seen*; on a third occasion she uses *see*. Despite the striking variability in the verb forms, it is unlikely that many of the other structural or lexical features in the utterance will be produced in different versions. It would be surprising, for example, if the learner substituted *you* for *I* on one of the three occasions; or if she said *I have seen . . .* but *Saw I . . .*; or if she alternated between saying *yesterday* and *today*; or said *ironed* instead of *seen* on one occasion. Her pronunciation will probably not be perfect, and no doubt one or two of the features will vary (she might for example sometimes pronounce an /r/ in the second syllable of *yesterday* and sometimes not). But experience tells us that most of the vowels and consonants are likely to be pronounced the same way (whether rightly or wrongly) each time. And in general, I think investigation will show that at any one time most features of any interlanguage are invariably right or wrong; that variable features are the exception rather than the rule; that synchronic variability is not in fact a characteristic feature of most learners' language; and that variability cannot plausibly be regarded as the major mechanism in language change. Many structures, surely, are learnt correctly from the beginning; some are learnt wrongly from the beginning and stay wrong (as often happens also with phonetic features). It is particularly difficult to see how the variability paradigms discussed can be applied wholesale to lexical knowledge – much of which develops by simple accretion – and yet lexis, after all, comprises the bulk of what anybody knows of a language.

The position of the authors quoted is perhaps open to the criticism that they are deriving a very general view of language use and development from limited data of a very particular kind – from those phonological and grammatical features which do exhibit variability. This sort of perspective might lead one, for instance, to say that a learner's interlanguage had entered a new stage of development because of alter-ations in the pattern of variability of a few phonemes and morphemes, but to treat his/her acquisition of 2,000 new words as developmentally unimportant. The data assembled by Tarone in her 1983 article comprise: one study of several learners' mastery of a subject-deletion rule; one study of the handling of 3rd-person -s by some Japanese learners; one study of Japanese production of English /r/; one study of Thai production of English /r/; one study of Arab learners' production of /θ/; one study of English negative patterns produced by Germans; and references to research by Krashen and LeCoco. While the findings quoted are interesting, they do not seem to me to go very far to justify the apparant generality of Tarone's claim that 'Interlanguage data from several studies have been presented, which show that IL behaviour varies systematically with elicitation task'. Clearly *some* interlanguage behaviour varies in this way. But how much?

This is not of course the first time that tricky grammatical features have been given a starring role in linguistic theory. We are all familiar with discussions of acquisition in which general and far-reaching hypotheses about language, language development, universals and the nature of the human mind have been supported by data derived from studies of the order of acquisition of a dozen or so morphemes. Variability research is typically concerned with that rather special category of problematic linguistic elements which tend not to be mastered successfully: those phonological and syntactic features which learners find especially difficult, and where competing interlanguage rules or habits lead to variability. While research can obviously contribute to our understanding of such matters, it is important not to overestimate their importance in language development. We cannot, without substantial further evidence, take variable behaviour as being characteristic of language acquisition as a whole.

Notes

1. I shall use the term *learner* to refer to anyone using a foreign language. This is imprecise but convenient; there is no single appropriate word that covers both those who are still learning the foreign language that they use, and those who have passed that stage.

Section Three:

VARIABILITY IN INTERLANGUAGE SYSTEMS

Interlanguage is the term coined by Selinker (1972) to describe the 'mental grammars' that learners construct in the process of acquiring a second language (L2). The 'rules' that make up the learner's mental grammars arc of different kinds (see p. 13 of the Introduction), but it is likely that at least some of them will be developmental, in the sense that they differ from the rules of either the learner's first language or of the target language. It is hypothesized – with considerable support from empirical studies of SLA – that learners pass along a continuum comprising a number of these mental grammars. That is, each grammar is a transitional one. The continuum is often referred to as the 'route' of development. The route involves the gradual complexification of each transitional grammar.

SLA research has been concerned with two related tasks; (1) to describe the transitional grammars of the interlanguage continuum and (2) to explain how the grammars are constructed. The two tasks are related because the *way* that the researcher chooses to describe an interlanguage grammar has implications for the kind of explanation that is provided. We can identify three basic descriptive (and, therefore, explanatory) approaches:

(1) **The linguistic approach**. This seeks to identify the linguistic properties of an interlanguage grammar and assumes that the primary causal factors in development have to do with the nature of language. That is, language is viewed as possessing certain universal properties which act as constraints on both the kind of rules the learner can construct and also the manner in which they are complexified as acquisition takes place.

(2) **The sociolinguistic approach**. This seeks to describe the relationship between interlanguage rules and context. The term 'context' can be defined in a number of ways, as explained in the Introduction. Implicit in this approach is the belief that the kinds of social meanings a learner wishes to express shape the rules that are constructed. That is, interlanguage reflects the learner's attempts to function as a social being.

(3) **The psycholinguistic approach**. This seeks to describe interlanguage rules and the way they develop as the product of internal processing strategies of a general, cognitive nature. That is, language learning is viewed as any other kind of learning in that it involves information processing. This processing is evident in both *learning* (i.e. deriving knowledge from data) and *using* (i.e. employing knowledge in production and reception).

Of these three approaches, only the sociolinguistic and the psycholinguistic consider the role of *context* in SLA. The linguistic approach views knowledge as decontextualized and discounts variability phenomena as 'performance'. In this section of the

67

book, therefore, there is no paper reporting a purely linguistic investigation of interlanguage. All four papers apply either a sociolinguistic or a psycholinguistic approach or both together.

Cutting across the distinction between a sociolinguistic and psycholinguistic approach is another important distinction – that between *knowledge* and *control* (Bialystok and Sharwood-Smith, 1985). Knowledge concerns the way language is represented in the mind of the learner – the actual 'rules' of the learner's mental grammar. Knowledge can be represented with differing degrees of analycity (e.g. can be more or less conscious to the learner) and is, therefore, variable. Control concerns the processing of knowledge in actual performance. This, too, is variable because the automaticity of retrieval of linguistic features differs; some features can be accessed more easily than others. Bialystok and Sharwood-Smith view the distinction between knowledge and control as a psycholinguistic one. The distinction is, however, equally applicable to a sociolinguistic model of interlanguage. It is possible to envisage contextual factors influencing both the way knowledge is organized and the way it is controlled. For example, knowledge may be internalized in relation to certain contexts of use (i.e. represented with regard to a particular topic, addressee or task) and also retrieval may be affected by the learner's perception of the social demands of a situation (i.e. how formal the language use needs to be).

These rather crude distinctions – between a sociolinguistic and psycholinguistic approach on the one hand and between knowledge and control on the other – will help us to interpret the research reported in the four papers of this section.

There are two papers which follow an essentially sociolinguistic approach and which investigate knowledge – those by Pavesi and Weinert. Both papers address the same question: to what extent is the interlanguage knowledge that arises in naturalistic and instructed contexts the same or different? The type of sociolinguistic approach involved is *macro* in nature. That is, it entails a comparison of learning in different domains (see Introduction, p. 7).

Pavesi examines lexical knowledge. This is particularly welcome as the acquisition of lexis has been relatively neglected in SLA research. She looks at the closed lexical sub-system of spatial prepositions (on, in, into, to, from, out of, across, through and at). Her study uses a non-equivalent control group design. The classroom learners were 48 Italian high school students, and the naturalistic learners 28 Italian workers in Edinburgh. Pavesi employs the techniques of implicational scaling (see Introduction, p. 16) to derive an acquisitional order for the spatial prepositions from cross-sectional data for each group of learners. She found that the acquisitional orders did differ for the two groups. They diverged in two principal ways. The instructed learners acquired 'into' much earlier than the informal learners (who, by and large, did not acquire this preposition at all). Also the instructed learners acquired 'to' before 'from', while the informal learners acquired these prepositions in the opposite order. Pavesi offers a detailed discussion of possible reasons for these divergences. In her conclusion she makes a number of points: (1) the learners' performance was variable but systematic; (2) the context of learning affects interlanguage development; (3) lexis may be more susceptible to the influence of instruction than grammar; and (4) the differences in acquisitional orders for the instructed and informal learners need not reflect differences in learning processes.

Weinert studies the acquisition of German negatives by Edinburgh school children over a four-year period. She relies on descriptions of the naturalistic acquisition of German negatives for her comparison. Data for the classroom learners were collected inside in the classroom and also from elicitation tests designed to tap spontaneous speech. The main difference between the classroom and naturalistic acquisition of negatives which she pinpoints is that the classroom learners appear to rely on formulas to a much greater extent. This is explained in terms of the extensive drilling of patterns such as 'Ich habe kein . . .' and 'Ich spiele nicht . . .' which took place. Apart from these formulas the same mechanisms appear to operate in both learning contexts. That is, there is evidence of learners creating their own systems, which 'linear' instruction is not able to subvert.

These two studies contribute to the growing body of research into classroom SLA. They provide further evidence for the complex effects of instruction. On the one hand, Pavesi finds that instruction can affect the order of acquisition; on the other, Weinert finds that instruction has no real effect. The studies need not be seen as contradictory on this issue, however. First, differences in order of acquisition need not reflect differences in learning processes (a point Pavesi makes strongly). Second, it is possible that some linguistic features are more susceptible to influence by instruction than others (a point borne out by other studies – see Pica (1985), for instance).

When differences do emerge – as in Pavesi's study – there is a real problem about how to explain them if there are no data on the actual language events that took place in the classroom and naturalistic contexts. The researcher is forced into speculation. It is for this reason that 'product' studies comparing tutored and untutored SLA need to be complemented with 'process' studies that document more narrowly the various contexts which arise in each domain. The 'macro' sociolinguistic approach is of value in enabling broad issues to be addressed, but it is the 'micro' approach which is the more likely to provide explanations.

The other two papers adopt a psycholinguistic approach. Kellerman *et al.* consider one aspect of control – the communication strategies which learners use to compensate for the lack of linguistic resources in expressing referential meaning. Towell examines the relationship between knowledge and control, arguing that the efforts which learners put into increasing their control over existing linguistic resources inhibits their ability to attend to new linguistic information. Although both of these papers provide descriptive information about interlanguage development and use, their primary aim is explanatory.

Communication strategies have aroused considerable interest in interlanguage research. It has long been recognized that one source of variability is the learner's attempts to communicate ideas when he lacks the linguistic means – in particular vocabulary – to do so. To describe this variability researchers have developed taxonomies of strategies consisting of categories such as 'paraphrase' (e.g. 'brother of my father' for 'uncle') or 'word-coinage' (e.g. 'airball' for 'balloon'). Kellerman *et al.* are critical of this approach. They note that such taxonomies have tended to proliferate. They code only surface phenomena and do not effectively describe the underlying mental activity which is involved. Also in such taxonomies the strategy type is dependent on the nature of the object being described, in particular whether it is concrete or abstract. Kellerman *et al.* argue that there is a need for a system which can be applied to all data and which affords prediction and explanation and not merely surface description. Kellerman *et al.* propose three 'archistrategies': (1) *approximation strategies*, which are holistic, involving the use of an alternative lexical item for a missing one (e.g. 'bird' for 'robin'), (2) *analytic strategies*, which are partitive, involving some form of decompositional analysis of the referent in terms of its conceptual, functional or perceptual attribute, and (3) *linguistic strategies*, which involve recourse to the learner's first language in some way (e.g. by 'borrowing' or 'foreignerizing'). These strategies can be employed cyclically and become embedded in each other as problems-within-problems develop. Learners at different stages of proficiency seem to prefer different strategies. Unremarkably beginners make frequent use of linguistic strategies; intermediate learners prefer analytic strategies; advanced learners make greater use of approximation strategies. Kellerman *et al.* emphasize that native speakers make use of the same strategies, with a general preference for approximation strategies. Thus the strategies constitute a universal solution to lexical problems. The account of communication strategies in Kellerman *et al.* provides an interesting – and convincing – way of systematizing an aspect of interlanguage control that previously appeared random.

Towell reports a longitudinal study of learner of L2 French. The study uses data collected over four years when the subject was at university in Britain. The focus of the study is non-systematic variability evident in two grammatical structures; 'c'est difficile + preposition' and 'pas de + article'. It is always difficult to determine whether variability in L2 data is random or systematic. However, Towell's careful documentation of the contextual conditions under which the data were collected together with ample illustration of the two structures suggests that the variability evident in the data is random. The question Towell poses is why non-systematic variability persists for so long despite the 'ideal' learning conditions this learner experienced. The answer, Towell argues, lies in the efforts the learner put into increasing *channel capacity*. He shows that although no development of *knowledge* took place (at least where these two structures were concerned), there were considerable advances in *control* of this knowledge. That is, the learner's capacity to perform in a more native-like manner with regard to processing variables such as speaking rate and length of runs between pauses developed considerably. Towell argues that non-systematic variability is the product of lack of knowledge and that this arises when the learner's efforts go into processing. In other words, the acquisition of control over existing linguistic resources occurs at the expense of the acquisition of new linguistic knowledge.

These four papers give some idea of why SLA researchers are interested in variability. They also illustrate some of the approaches which have been used to describe and explain variability. In particular, they show that variability is both the product of social and psychological factors and that an explanation requires a consideration of both. Furthermore, the study of variability in interlanguage needs to distinguish that variability which relates to knowledge from that which relates to control of knowledge. The true systematicity of interlanguage can only be identified by giving recognition to the interaction of social and psychological variables on these two dimensions.

Variability and Systematicity in the Acquisition of Spatial Prepositions

MARIA PAVESI
University of Edinburgh

Variability and systematicity in the acquisition of a second language have traditionally attracted much interest in interlanguage (IL) research. The study of these two aspects of learners' language has concentrated both on each one in isolation and on their interrelationship. Learners' language has been assumed systematic (Selinker, 1972), i.e. internally consistent and rule-governed. However, Labov (1970) for language systems in general, and Huebner (1985) for ILs in particular, have pointed out that the degree of systematicity of each separate part is an empirical question to be investigated individually. Learners' grammar has also been assumed inherently variable. Corder (1981), for example, defines IL as a 'dynamic, goal-oriented language system of increasing complexity (p. 90) where the emphasis is on the diachronic variability of the system.

The relationship between variability and systematicity was formerly seen as one of opposition: only categorical phenomena would be considered systematic. More recently, the adoption of sociolinguistic models and the associated statistical analyses have resulted in the recognition that variability in IL can be systematic (Andersen, 1978; Borland, 1983; Hyltenstam, 1977). The realization of a structure or a series of structures may vary according to linguistic and sociolinguistic contexts, yet such a variation may be regular and predictable. The recognition that variability can be systematic does not rule out the concept of variability which is not systematic and some authors (e.g. Ellis, 1985b; Labov, 1970; Huebner, 1985) distinguish between systematic variability and unsystematic variability: the first rule-governed, the second random and unpredictable.

At the moment we need to establish which factors are involved in these IL phenomena. Learning setting – classroom versus naturalistic, for instance – could be one of the variables affecting variability and systematicity in second language acquisition. IL could be more or less systematic depending on the type of language instruction. Classroom acquisition, for instance, could be (i) generally unsystematic, (ii) unsystematic in areas where naturalistic acquisition is systematic, (iii) systematic in areas where the latter is not. The degree to which and the domains in which IL under different types of exposure exhibits systematicity are, as pointed out earlier, empirical matters. Moreover, different learning settings with their correlates of presence versus absence of language instruction, and different linguistic inputs, may affect orders of acquisition, thus determining variability among learners. It has recently been suggested, however, that language environment does not affect the route of development, but simply the rate (e.g. Ellis, 1984a). Lightbown (1983), on the contrary, has reported a different order of acquisition for classroom learners as compared to learners with a richer language exposure. She suggested, though, that the difference between the order of her group of classroom learners and the 'natural' order is mainly due to an initial overproduction of the morpheme *-ing*, probably caused by the atypical frequency of the form in the teacher's talk as well as in the textbook. She supposes that the 'natural' order will emerge once the disrupting elements of the linguistic environment have faded away.

It must be noted, however, that research conducted on the influence of the language learning environment on the orders of acquisition (Pica, 1983b; Lightbown, 1983 and on transitional structures (Felix, 1981; Weinert, 1985) has been restricted to morphology and syntax. Little is known of the impact of learning setting on variability and systematicity in the acquisition of the IL lexicon. More specifically, the issue appears particularly complex as the target language lexicon generally lacks the systematicity inherent in target language phonology and syntax. We can, however, isolate closed lexical sets with a tight self-contained structure of meanings. Such sets lexicalize well-defined conceptual fields, i.e. classes of entities pre-existing or independent of the various systems of linguistic categorization, for example, the continuum of colour (Lyons, 1977).

Spatial prepositions are an example of such subsystems. The meaning of each spatial preposition is delimited and thus defined by those of all the others, so that a change in the meaning of one would affect the whole system. The number of features contained in the conceptual field of this subsystem is limited (e.g. movement versus location, positive versus negative direction, number of dimensions of the reference object), as is the number of possible combinations of such features (e.g. two-dimensional space + location, *on*; three-dimensional space + movement, + negative direction, *out of*). These limitations are presumably due to the way humans perceive space and should thus apply across languages.

Closed lexical subsystems such as spatial prepositions present us with a well-defined set of vocabulary items covering the same conceptual field in both target language and mother tongue. It is, then, worth investigating whether systematicity in the target language results in systematicity in learners' language.

In this paper we shall investigate the evidence for variability and systematicity in the production of some English prepositions by Italian speakers. The evidence will be discussed with the focus on the different kinds of linguistic exposure – classroom versus naturalistic – and their impact on the acquisition sequence of the features investigated. The prepositions investigated are: *on, in, into, to, from, out of, across, through, at+* (i.e., *at* and other zero-dimensional locationals). Idiomatic senses are not included in the studies.

Methodology

Subjects

Two groups of learners were chosen for this study. The first group comprised 48 Italian high school students whose ages ranged from 14 to 18. They had been studying English for between two and seven years, with an average of four years. All the subjects belonging to this group, except for three who had spent up to two months in Britain, had had only formal exposure to English. The method used by their teachers was a very traditional grammar-based one. All subjects in this group spoke standard Italian. Their school is a very academic type of high school. They were heavily exposed to formal English through the study of English literature and, more generally, through a substantial input of written language.

The second group comprised 28 Italian workers in Edinburgh – waiters for the most part. The subjects belonging to this second group had had only minimal instruction in English or none at all. Their ages ranged from 19 to 50. They had been in Britain for between three months and 25 years, six years on average. They had been exposed to the language naturally while at work, in their homes, or during recreation. I tried to find informants who spoke standard Italian or a regional variety close to the standard. Given that their level of education was generally quite low, and also on account of their semi-skilled occupation, it was assumed that their exposure to the formal registers of English was limited.

Elicitation procedure and scoring methods

The nine spatial prepositions were elicited orally by means of visual stimuli. The material included both pictorial clues and real objects: e.g. a map, boxes, and miniatures. The subject was asked questions involving the location or direction of one of the movable entities – for example a cat, a horse, Mary – in relation to one of the reference entities – a bank, a table, a house. For example, in the case of movement out of a three-dimensional space, the experimenter would ask 'what is John doing?' while showing the miniature going out of the post office.

The interviews were tape-recorded and lasted for an average of 20–25 minutes. Two examples were given at the beginning, then during the interview the learner was invited to reply speedily, supplying the first answer which came to mind. Each preposition was elicited eight times.

Two scoring procedures were employed for the data analysis. The first one included only performance in obligatory contexts – i.e. contexts where the preposition was required, e.g. when showing a horse jumping through a ring, the answer to the question 'what is the horse doing?' includes an obligatory context for the preposition *through*. The second analysis included performance in both obligatory and non-obligatory contexts. Learners' scores on each preposition were calculated on the basis of both how many times the preposition was supplied appropriately and how many inappropriately – i.e. when another preposition was required: for example *into* instead of *in*, in 'Peter is into the house'. The first analysis is called O-C performance analysis or scoring method, the second J-S performance analysis or scoring method. J and S are the initials of Johnston and Slobin (1979) who in their study on the acquisition of spatial prepositions by children learning their first language used a similar method of analysis to the one reported here.

The cut-off point for acquisition was set at the 80% level for both scoring methods. If the learner performed accurately at least 80% of the time the preposition was required, he received a score of 1 (+ in the tables) when using the O-C performance analysis. He received the equivalent score with the J-S scoring method when he performed accurately at least 80% of the time the preposition was required and did not supply it inappropriately more often than he had done appropriately.

We report the results calculated with both scoring procedures to better highlight the differences between the two groups. A fuller discussion of this issue is reported elsewhere (Pavesi, 1984).

Results

The two groups' production was analyzed using implicational scaling.[1] Both O-C and J-S scoring methods were employed for each group. In all four cases the scale was found significant – coefficient of reproducibility (c.r.) > 0.90 – (formal group, O-C analysis: c.r. = 0.91, J-S analysis: c.r. = 0.94; informal group, O-C analysis: c.r. = 0.92, J-S analysis: c.r. = 0.94). Tables 1a, 1b, 2a, 2b report individual performances for both groups and both methods.

It can be seen from tables 1a and 1b the implicational order for the formal group is the same for both scoring methods, and reads as follows:

ON > TO > FROM > AT+ > IN > INTO > OUT OF > ACROSS > THROUGH

Similarly, the implicational order found for the informal group is identical for both scoring procedures – see tables 2a and 2b.

ON > FROM > IN > TO > AT+ > OUT OF > ACROSS > THROUGH > INTO

Discussion

As expected our results show variability in both the formal and the informal group's performance on spatial prepositions. If it is the case that accuracy sequences reflect developmental ones, then the orders obtained may provide us with information about diachronic variability in the acquisition of spatial prepositions by Italian learners. Learners' performance on spatial prepositions is variable, going from no target-like use to a very close approximation to the English system for at least the spatial terms investigated. However, as shown by the validity of the various implicational scales learners' performance is not only variable, it is also systematic. The order in which prepositions appear in learners' language is predictable and implicational. That is, each learner's performance can be placed on a scale such as $A > B > C > D$, where the presence of the feature B in the learner's IL *implies* the presence of A but not that of C or D; the presence of C implies that of A and B but not that of D. Thus knowing that a learner possesses a given spatial preposition allows us to make valid predictions about which others he can use according to the target language. We know with a statistically significant level of probability that a learner who performs successfully on *out of*, will also perform successfully on other prepositions such as *on, to, from*, but not necessarily *across* and *through*.

Though variability in both groups' performance is systematic a comparison of the orders exhibited by the two groups shows points of divergence. The most striking difference is in the pair *in–into* with a smaller difference in the pair *to–from*. *In* appears earlier in the implicational sequence for the informal group than it does in

TABLE 1a

*Formal learners' performance on spatial prepositions: O-C scoring method**

	On	To	From	At+	In	Into	Out of	Across	Through
23	−	(+)	−	−	−	−	−	−	−
27	−	−	−	−	−	−	−	−	−
29	−	−	−	−	−	−	−	−	−
16	+	−	−	(+)	−	−	−	−	−
4	+	−	−	−	−	−	−	−	−
3	+	−	−	(+)	−	−	−	−	−
6	+	−	−	−	−	−	−	−	−
9	+	−	−	(+)	−	−	−	−	−
2	+	−	−	−	−	−	−	−	−
19	+	−	−	(+)	−	(+)	−	−	−
22	+	−	−	−	−	(+)	−	−	−
28	+	−	−	−	(+)	−	−	−	−
32	+	+	−	−	(+)	−	−	−	−
1	(−)	+	−	−	−	−	−	−	−
18	+	+	−	−	−	−	−	−	−
21	+	+	−	−	(+)	−	−	−	−
44	+	+	−	(+)	−	−	−	−	−
37	+	+	−	−	(+)	−	−	−	−
7	+	+	+	−	−	−	−	−	−
12	+	(−)	+	−	−	−	−	−	−
26	+	+	+	−	−	−	−	−	−
5	+	+	+	+	−	−	−	−	−
8	+	+	+	+	−	−	−	−	−
13	+	+	+	+	−	−	−	−	−
20	+	+	(−)	+	−	−	−	−	−
31	(−)	+	+	+	−	−	−	−	−
33	+	+	+	+	−	−	−	−	−
34	+	+	+	+	−	−	−	−	−
48	+	+	(−)	+	−	−	−	−	−
10	+	+	+	+	+	−	−	−	−
14	+	+	+	+	+	−	−	−	−
15	+	+	+	(−)	+	−	−	−	−
17	+	(−)	+	(−)	+	−	−	−	−
24	+	+	+	+	+	−	−	−	−
25	+	+	+	(−)	+	−	−	−	−
36	+	+	+	+	+	−	−	−	−
39	+	(−)	+	+	+	−	−	−	−
40	+	+	+	(−)	+	+	−	−	−
41	+	(−)	+	+	+	+	−	−	−
11	+	(−)	+	+	(−)	+	−	−	−
38	+	+	+	+	(−)	+	−	−	−
42	+	+	+	+	(−)	+	−	−	−
30	+	+	+	+	(−)	+	+	−	−
45	+	(−)	+	+	(−)	+	(−)	+	−
43	+	+	+	+	(−)	+	+	+	−
47	+	+	+	(−)	+	+	(−)	+	−
49	+	+	+	+	+	+	(−)	+	−
46	+	+	+	+·	(−)	+	+	(−)	+

* c.r. = 0.91

Deviations are in brackets

TABLE 1b
*Formal learners' performance on spatial prepositions: J-S scoring method**

	On	To	From	At+	In	Into	Out of	Across	Through
29	−	−	−	−	−	−	−	−	−
27	−	−	−	−	−	−	−	−	−
16	−	−	−	−	−	−	−	−	−
4	−	−	−	−	−	−	−	−	−
23	−	−	−	−	−	−	−	−	−
19	+	−	−	−	−	−	−	−	−
2	+	−	−	−	−	−	−	−	−
3	+	−	−	(+)	−	−	−	−	−
28	+	−	−	−	−	−	−	−	−
6	+	−	−	−	−	−	−	−	−
9	+	−	−	(+)	−	−	−	−	−
22	+	−	−	−	−	−	−	−	−
32	+	−	−	−	−	−	−	−	−
1	(−)	+	−	−	−	−	−	−	−
18	+	+	−	−	−	−	−	−	−
21	(−)	+	−	−	(+)	−	−	−	−
7	+	+	+	−	−	−	−	−	−
12	+	(−)	+	−	−	−	−	−	−
15	+	+	+	−	−	−	−	−	−
25	+	+	+	−	−	−	−	−	−
26	+	+	+	−	−	−	−	−	−
17	+	(−)	+	−	−	−	−	−	−
48	+	+	(−)	+	−	−	−	−	−
8	+	+	+	+	−	−	−	−	−
13	+	+	+	+	−	−	−	−	−
5	+	(−)	+	+	−	−	−	−	−
20	+	+	(−)	+	−	−	−	−	−
30	+	+	+	+	−	−	(+)	−	−
31	(−)	+	+	+	−	−	−	−	−
33	+	+	+	+	−	−	−	−	−
34	+	+	+	+	−	−	−	−	−
38	+	+	+	+	−	−	−	−	−
44	+	+	(−)	+	−	−	−	−	−
45	+	(−)	+	+	−	−	−	(+)	−
41	+	+	+	+	−	−	−	−	−
42	+	+	+	+	−	−	−	−	−
10	+	+	+	+	+	−	−	−	−
14	+	+	+	+	+	−	−	−	−
24	+	+	(−)	+	+	−	−	−	−
36	+	+	+	+	+	−	−	−	−
39	+	(−)	+	+	+	−	−	−	−
11	+	(−)	+	+	(−)	+	−	−	−
40	+	+	+	(−)	+	+	−	−	−
41	+	(−)	+	+	+	+	−	−	−
47	+	+	+	(−)	+	+	−	−	−
49	+	+	+	+	+	+	(−)	+	−
43	+	+	+	(−)	+	+	+	+	−
46	+	+	+	+	(−)	+	+	(−)	+

* c.r. = 0.94
Deviations are in brackets

TABLE 2a

*Informal learners' performance on spatial prepositions: O-C scoring method**

	On	From	In	To	At+	Out of	Across	Through	Into
51	−	−	(+)	−	−	−	−	−	−
52	−	−	−	−	−	−	−	−	−
71	−	−	−	−	−	−	−	−	−
77	−	−	−	−	−	−	−	−	−
75	−	−	−	−	−	−	−	−	−
58	−	−	−	(+)	−	−	−	−	−
85	+	−	−	−	−	−	−	−	−
74	+	−	(+)	−	−	−	−	−	−
63	+	+	+	−	−	−	−	−	−
69	+	+	+	−	−	−	−	−	−
73	+	+	+	−	−	−	(+)	−	−
57	+	+	+	−	−	−	−	−	−
72	+	+	+	−	(+)	−	−	−	−
50	+	(−)	+	+	−	−	−	−	−
55	+	+	+	+	−	−	−	−	−
53	+	+	(−)	+	−	−	−	−	−
56	+	+	+	+	−	−	(+)	−	−
76	+	+	+	+	−	−	−	−	−
61	+	+	(−)	+	−	−	−	−	−
62	+	+	(−)	+	−	−	−	−	−
67	(−)	+	(−)	−	−	−	−	−	
70	+	+	(−)	+	−	−	−	−	−
54	+	+	+	+	−	−	−	−	−
60	+	+	+	+	+	−	−	(+)	−
64	+	+	+	+	+	−	−	−	−
65	(−)	+	+	(−)	+	−	−	(+)	−
68	(−)	+	+	+	+	−	−	−	−
59	+	+	+	+	+	−	−	−	−
66	+	+	(−)	(−)	+	+	−	+	+

* c.r. = 0.92
  Deviations are in brackets

that for the formal one. Simultaneously, *into* does not occur at all in the informal group while it comes immediately after *in* for the formal group. As for *to* and *from*, formal learners favour the former over the latter, while the reverse is true for informal learners.

Context of learning appears here to have a direct influence on the sequence of acquisition. *Into* is characteristic of formal registers and does not always occur in informal speech. In informal registers, *in* is often favoured over *into* with the meaning of movement into a three-dimensional space (e.g., 'put the milk in the fridge' instead of 'into the fridge'). Thus formal learners, who are almost exclusively exposed to formal English and have very little contact with informal speech, will exhibit a higher performance on *into*. They will often produce utterances such as 'the horse is jumping into the box' or 'the duck is going into the cupboard'. Informal learners, on the other hand, presumably receive input with a high proportion of *in* being used with both meanings of location and movement. (Compare the 217 occurrences of *into* as opposed to 3,123 of *in* in the London-Lund corpus of 192,000 words of educated speech (Brown, 1985).) It is possible, then, that the type of input could account, at least partially, for informal learners' low performance on the more specific prep-

TABLE 2b
*Informal learners' performance on spatial prepositions: J-S scoring method**

	On	From	In	To	At+	Out of	Across	Through	Into
51	−	−	−	−	−	−	−	−	−
52	−	−	−	−	−	−	−	−	−
53	−	−	−	−	−	−	−	−	−
58	−	−	−	−	−	−	−	−	−
67	−	−	−	(+)	−	−	−	−	−
71	−	−	−	−	−	−	−	−	−
75	−	−	−	−	−	−	−	−	−
77	−	−	−	−	−	−	−	−	−
85	−	−	−	−	−	−	−	−	−
50	+	−	−	−	−	−	−	−	−
70	+	−	−	(+)	−	−	−	−	−
57	+	+	−	−	−	−	−	−	−
63	+	+	−	−	−	−	−	−	−
69	+	+	−	−	−	−	−	−	−
73	(−)	+	+	−	−	−	−	−	−
72	+	+	+	−	−	−	−	−	−
74	+	(−)	+	−	−	−	−	−	−
55	+	+	+	+	−	−	−	−	−
61	+	+	(−)	+	−	−	−	−	−
62	+	+	(−)	+	−	−	−	−	−
76	+	+	+	+	−	−	−	−	−
56	+	+	+	+	−	−	(+)	−	−
54	+	(−)	(−)	+	+	−	−	−	−
65	(−)	+	+	(−)	+	−	−	−	−
59	+	+	+	+	+	−	−	−	−
60	+	+	+	+	+	−	−	(+)	−
64	+	+	+	+	+	−	−	−	−
68	(−)	(−)	+	+	+	−	−	−	−
66	+	+	(−)	(−)	+	+	−	−	−

* c.r. = 0.94
Deviations are in brackets

osition. It should also be noted that the use of *in* for both location and movement corresponds to that of the Italian *in* 'in' and *dentro(a)* 'inside' in the mother tongue.

It is possible moreover that correction by the teacher may influence formal learners' high performance on *into*. It is difficult in fact to believe that our informal learners, some of whom had been in Britain for several years, hardly ever heard *into* being used. It seems unlikely that the amount of exposure could be the only reason for the difference between the two groups and in particular for the absence of the preposition in informal learners' IL. An utterance like 'she came in the restaurant' would be accepted or at least understood by native speakers and therefore not questioned but the same utterance might provoke correction from an Italian teacher of English. Non-native-speaking foreign language teachers have often been reported to be stricter than their native-speaking colleagues. Ferguson (1983) reports non-native-speaking English teachers marking as serious errors register-bound choices: that is, forms which typically occur in spoken, informal language.

Our findings on the acquisition of *into* by informal learners agree with those of Mougeon *et al*. (1979) who also found the preposition to be very late in the speech of Canadian-French children learning English. The delay was attributed by the authors to the lack of distinction in the mother tongue between *in* and *into* as well as the infrequency of the latter preposition in casual speech (notice that in the same study *into* was also late-acquired by English monolingual children). Input, however, seems unlikely as an explanation for the late occurrence of *in* on the implicational scale for the formal group, when compared to that for the informal group. The point will not be fully discussed here, since its explanation relies on data which are not presented in this paper. It should be noted, however, that formal learners' low performance on *in* may be related to their high performance on *into*, presumably because they generalized the latter to contexts where the former was required (e.g. 'Peter is into the house'). When using an O-C performance analysis only four learners appear to have acquired both *in* and *into*. While the implicational pattern leads us to expect that learners will exhibit *in* only, or neither preposition, a high number of learners (nine) reach the 80% level of accuracy with *into* and, unexpectedly, not with *in*. The number of deviations in this particular section of the implicational scale decreases when performance in non-obligatory contexts is included (J-S method): only three learners exhibit target-like performance on *into* and not on *in*. Such a performance pattern indicates that formal learners tend to operate with only one preposition, *in* or *into*. At lower levels of general performance *in* is used, but as soon as *into* appears in learners' IL their performance on the former preposition drops, to pick up, presumably, later and coexist with target-like performance on *into*. If this picture is corroborated by data on substitutions (that is, by an error analysis), formal learners' behaviour is shown to mirror that of informal learners. Informal learners exhibit only *in*, formal learners both *in* and *into* but, for the most part, not both together. The tendency not to distinguish in the preposition between location and movement characteristic of Italian and other languages as well as of Pidgins and Creoles (Traugott, 1974) would thus be extended to these learners' IL. Type of exposure would then mainly determine which preposition, *in* or *into*, is chosen for the expression of both spatial concepts.

Turning now to the pair *to–from* we hypothesize that formal learners rely more on routine learning derived from classroom drilling. Formal learners may initially learn verbs of movement holophrastically in combination with the preposition to – e.g. 'the children are going to the park', or when *into* was required, 'John was going to the kitchen'. Informal learners who are not given explicit language practice would, on the other hand, fall back on the system of the mother tongue which does not distinguish in the preposition between location and movement (the distinction between the two meanings being usually lexicalized by the verb). They produced utterances such as 'Peter is going from the house in the bank' or 'the children are going in the park' (instead of 'to the park') much more often than formal learners did.

The influence of the Italian system of spatial relational terms may also account for the relatively early mastery of *from* by informal learners. The Italian *da* is a spatial preposition which with inanimate objects expresses only movement away from a zero- or one-dimensional point. Moreover, in English the distinction between movement and location is always coded in zero-dimensional positive locatives (e.g. 'I went to the cinema', 'she was at the cinema'), but it is not always so in zero-dimensional negative locatives (e.g. 'we came straight from the department', 'she is from Milan'). As in Italian the distinction is never coded, Italian learners may be facilitated in performing on a preposition which has both directional and locational meaning. If this is true, formal learners' better performance on to – a preposition which has only the meaning of movement and does not stand in a one-to-one relationship with any Italian preposition – is unexpected, and may really be the outcome of explicit teaching which emphasizes the collocation of the preposition with verbs of movement. In support of this interpretation it should be noted that Mougeon *et al.* (1979) also found *from* to precede *to* in the speech of their Canadian children. French, like Italian, does not have an equivalent for 'to' and does not distinguish in the preposition between location and movement. No language instruction was reported for the children who took part in the Canadian study.

Conclusion

The results of the present investigation into the acquisition of English spatial prepositions by Italian learners indicate that, although variable, learners' performance is systematic, i.e. predictable on the basis of an implicational order.

Context of learning – classroom versus naturalistic – seems to affect some of the stages of learners' developmental continua. The acquisition of lexis may thus be more susceptible than parts of the grammar to external factors such as input frequency and presence or absence of language instruction. Yet, as noticed by Lightbown (1983), differences in orders do not necessarily reflect differences in acquisitional processes. Learners' total production must be taken into account and the pattern of acquisition must be carefully examined before any claims concerning underlying processes can be made.

Note

1. Implicational scaling is a statistical technique which in IL studies is used to establish whether within a group of features each one occurs in learner's speech or is acquired according to a predictable and systematic pattern. When the scale is valid (coefficient of reproducibility ≥ 0.90) we will be able to predict individual learners' linguistic behaviour on the basis of the point reached on the scale. Given the pattern $A > B > C > D$, we will know, for example, that a learner's IL exhibits feature C it will also exhibit features B and A but not necessarily D. The scales employed in this study are bimodal. The value for each feature is either + or −, where + means 'acquired' and − means 'non-acquired'.

Processes in Classroom Second Language Development: the acquisition of negation in German

REGINA WEINERT

University of Edinburgh

The question of whether, to what extent and how second language development is affected by the learning environment has attracted considerable interest among SLA researchers and language teachers in recent years. This interest is at least partly due to the fact that the results of SLA research, in particular of the morpheme order studies, with informal or mixed subjects have led some researchers to formulate implications for language teaching. Thus attempts have been made to apply knowledge gained about language acquisition[1] in one setting to practical problems of language development in another. Many researchers therefore feel the need for a closer look at the language development of learners who have been exposed to the target language (TL) in the classroom only, and to compare this with the development of naturalistic learners.

Inherent in the view that language development in classroom-only settings ought to be investigated separately from SLA in naturalistic settings, is of course the assumption that the former differs markedly from the latter and that this may have an effect on the processes of language development. The problems of dividing learning settings into 'formal' and 'informal' without further analysis of the exact nature of each environment have been demonstrated repeatedly in the literature (Krashen, 1976; Allwright, 1984; Ellis, 1984a), often with particular reference to studies attempting to measure the effect of instruction on proficiency. It has also been argued that classroom settings may share crucial characteristics with naturalistic settings[2] (Allwright, 1984; Ellis, 1984a). The present author does not deny the possibility that classroom and naturalistic settings share common properties. However, it is her contention that there are considerable differences between the two settings in terms of organization of input and interaction. With the exception of immersion programmes, some comprehension approaches and task-based teaching, the following represent essential characteristics of most language classrooms, irrespective of particular syllabus, methods and techniques employed. These features are not typically found in naturalistic settings and furthermore constitute a deliberate and principled attempt, recognized by most teachers, at guiding target language development.

(1) Skill-getting precedes skill-using, i.e. aspects of the language[3] have to be mastered before they can be used in natural language.
(2) Following the principle of (1), teaching proceeds essentially through presentation of TL items or aspects in one form or other; followed by practice of these items to achieve mastery of the TL aspects in the form of imitation, drill,

meaning

83

substitution exercises etc., which may be structured to allow learners to express their own meaning to a very limited degree; followed by 'activity' designed to capture some aspects of natural language use, during which learners are expected to apply what they have learnt previously.

(3) In most cases description or explanation of the TL is provided to varying degrees of explicitness. Usually this forms part of presentation, or of error correction and explanation.

(4) Aspects of the TL are selected for teaching in a linear order and selection is based on notions of what it is the learner needs to know (either because of what is considered 'essential' or 'basic' knowledge of the TL or because of more specific communicative needs of particular learners), and on notions of grammatical and/or functional complexity, derived from a variety of TL descriptions. Recycling of items is done for remedial purposes. It is only during 'activity' that the opportunity arises for a coming together of the various items and aspects taught.

(5) Errors are frequently corrected, particularly during practice. Remedial teaching in terms of 2 and/or 3 is frequently carried out, and learners are required to produce the corrected versions.

It is because of these differences that it makes sense to compare classroom second language development with naturalistic SLA at all. Briefly, classroom teaching attempts to develop language through presentation and practice for use in 'activity',[4] whereas naturalistic learners develop language essentially through 'activity'. The deliberate and principled attempts at structuring the learning environment in terms of 1–5 imply, at least implicitly, that guidance in TL development activates learning processes which are, presumably, more efficient than those found in naturalistic SLA. The model of second language learning implied regards language learning largely as a matter of memorization, be it of chunks of language or of an analyzed system of rules, and as a transfer from stored language knowledge to automatic language use reflecting that knowledge, through practice. Therefore comparison between the actual performance and learning processes of classroom language learners with those of naturalistic learners potentially yields important insights into the kind of processes which operate when human beings acquire second languages.

In keeping with the above perspective, i.e. maintaining that classroom and naturalistic settings differ in essential characteristics, two main aims in recent approaches to the study of classroom second language development can be identified:

(i) To investigate to what extent classroom language development involves the same or different processes from those apparently involved in naturalistic SLA.

(ii) To determine to what extent various aspects of the classroom which constitute a deliberate and principled attempt on the part of the teacher to guide language development affect or do not affect the language and language development of learners.

Considering the popularity and enormous impact of the morpheme studies, it is not surprising that researchers of classroom language development should have attempted to establish whether morpheme rank orders obtained in naturalistic or mixed settings would also be found in the classroom. If this was the case, it would indicate the existence of similar acquisition processes in both types of setting. The majority of classroom studies focus on this area of language development. However, results of these studies are contradictory and difficult to interpret, presenting a largely inconclusive picture. The difficulties inherent in performance analysis *per se*[5] are confounded by uncertainties as to the exact nature of the learning environment and the use of different elicitation tasks. Furthermore, studies which do report disturbed orders may not necessarily be taken as evidence against the hypothesis that processes in classroom second language development are the same as those in naturalistic SLA, since classroom learners may have received very different input from naturalistic learners. Lightbown (1983) suggests the possibility of different surface phenomena stemming from differential input, rather than indicating different underlying processes. Detailed analysis of teaching materials, teachers speech etc. in her study supports this view for her data. It is also the view of the present author that performance studies of seemingly unrelated grammatical morphemes present only a partial and potentially misleading picture of SLA due to their focus on linear orders of acquisition in TL terms. They do not reveal a great deal about *processes* underlying the construction and development of interlanguages.[6]

To date there are only a handful of studies which have investigated processes in classroom second language development, giving consideration not only to target-like structures and functions in the learners' language but also to non-target-like structures and functions and to target-like structures with non-target-like functions. Although the paucity of these studies and the limitations of some of them do not at present justify the conclusion that classroom second language development follows exactly the same principles as naturalistic SLA, they do provide some evidence that very similar processes are involved, and support the view that classroom learners act upon the language input available to them in whatever form to create and develop their own systems of communication, rather than react directly and immediately to the guidance of teachers to develop the target language (Ellis, 1984; Felix, 1981, 1982; Lightbown, 1983; Pavesi, 1984; Pica, 1983b, 1985; Pienemann, 1984; Schumann, 1978b.) Furthermore some classroom practices may in fact be detrimental to learners' progress by blocking their own mechanisms for dealing with language input (Lightbown, 1983).

The purpose of the present study is to further investigate differences and similarities between classroom and naturalistic second language development. The study is concerned with the *course* of development only.

Language subsystem

The area to be investigated is negation. There are two reasons for this choice:

(1) A problem with the study of ILs is that they may operate with units other than those used for the analysis of full languages and the TL in particular. The structure–function relationship of negation was assumed to be readily identifi-

able even within IL systems. Thus it was considered unlikely that learners would express negation using items which were completely unrelated to negation in the TL, and, more importantly, would use items related to negation in the TL to express completely different functions.

(2) Negation has been widely researched in the naturalistic SLA of German and of other languages, offering data for comparison.

The investigation will be restricted to:

(a) Learners' *placement* of the negator in relation to the sentence and the verb in main clauses. Of the different verb types, the copula, possessive 'haben', main verbs, modals and auxiliaries will be considered.

(b) Learners' *choice* of the negative particle (excluding holophrastic usage). Reference will be made to different (object) NPs.

Negation in German

Placement of the negator in relation to the verb

In main clauses where the subject is in initial position the negator is placed after the finite verb.

Examples:

Main verb	ich koche nicht
	'I cook not', i.e. I don't cook
Copula	ich bin nicht gross
	'I am not tall'
Modal	ich kann nicht kochen
	'I can not cook'
Auxiliary	ich habe nicht gekocht
	'I have not cooked'

In subordinate clauses the negator precedes the verb:

Use of negative particles 'nein', 'nicht' and 'kein'

'Nein' is used holophrastically in answer to yes/no questions, to negate part or whole propositions at sentence or text level, as a response to commands etc. It is not used sentence internally. 'Nicht' and 'kein' are used for sentence internal negation. 'Kein' is used to mark indefiniteness of NPs or objects, otherwise 'nicht' is used. 'Kein' is also marked for gender and case; however this aspect will not be discussed in this paper.

Examples:

| Copula | das ist kein Buch |
| | 'that is not a book' |

| As opposed to | das ist nicht das gute Buch |
| | 'that is not the good book' |

| Possessive | ich habe kein Buch |
| 'haben' | 'I have not a book' |

| As opposed to | ich habe das gute Buch nicht |
| | 'I have the good book not' |

The use of 'kein' in types of the above structures containing the copula and possessive 'haben' and indefinite NPs is obligatory. The choice of negative particle with main verbs (excluding possessive 'haben'), modals and auxiliaries is more complex. Indefiniteness can be marked optionally, 'nicht' can be used for emphasis etc. Thus the following are acceptable sentences:

| Main verb | ich fahre kein Auto |
| | 'I drive not a car' i.e. I don't drive |

| | ich fahre *nicht* Auto |
| | 'I drive not car', i.e. I don't drive |

The same sentences are possible with modals and auxiliaries. The rules governing optional and obligatory marking of indefiniteness with regard to structures containing main verbs, modals and auxiliaries are too complex to be discussed in this paper. They will only be referred to marginally in the data analysis.

Naturalistic SLA

Placement of the negator and sentence structure

L1 and naturalistic learners of German typically proceed from external negation to sentence internal negation and within the latter from preverbal to postverbal negation. External negation typically precedes the item(s) or sentence to be negated. Learners initially negate single words followed by one or more constituent negation and sentence negation. Within sentence internal negation learners distinguish finite main verbs from other verb-types such as the copula, modals and auxiliaries. Finite main verbs are negated preverbally at the same time as other verb types are negated postverbally.

Choice of negative particle

Naturalistic learners select 'nein' as a negative particle before they use 'nicht'. This applies to both sentence external and sentence internal negation. Data on the development of 'kein' is very sparse. This is partly due to the fact that it does not seem to appear in early L2 acquisition to any great extent. Lange (1979) reports sporadic occurrences of 'kein' during the early stages which are similar to those found in early L1 acquisition. Instead of 'kein' learners use 'nicht ein'. Felix (1978) reports that first regular occurrences of 'kein' always appear with 'nicht'. Later, while 'nicht ein' is still used, 'kein' appears target-like. Unfortunately (Lange, 1979) only reports on the use of 'kein' for 'nichts' and does not give examples of other uses (e.g. for 'nicht'), which he considers 'not productive' in terms of the TL.

TABLE 1
Naturalistic SLA examples: placement of the negator and sentence structure

sentence external negation, (NEGX/S)	sentence internal negation
nein kaputt	no verb (Subject NEG X)
('no broken')	das nein aua
nein helfen	('that no sore')
('no help')	Milch nicht da
nein spielen Katze	('milk not there')
('no play cat')	
preverbal negation	*postverbal negation*
nein du nicht kommt	ich kann nicht
('no you not come')	('I can not')
du nicht spielen Keller	das ist nicht so
('you not play cellar')	('that is not so')
Julie nicht spielt mit	Ich fällst nicht runter
('Julie not plays with us')	('I fall not down')
	(Felix 1982)

TABLE 2
Naturalistic SLA examples: Choice of negative particle

use of 'nein'	use of 'nicht ein'	use of 'nicht'
nein kaputt	das ist nicht eine Schaf	nicht fahren (Lange 1979)
('no broken')	('that is not a sheep')	('not drive')
ich nein essen	das ist nicht ein Hund	du nicht spielen Keller
('I no eat')	('that is not a dog')	('you not play cellar')
		(Felix 1982)

double negative with 'nicht' and 'kein'	use of 'kein' target-like
Ich hab nicht keine	Ich hab keine Auto
('I have ____')	('I have no car')
Ich seh die kein nicht	nein, da ist keine (Puppe)
	(Felix 1978)
('I see it ____')	(no, there is no (doll))

Subjects

The study is part of a cross-sectional and longitudinal investigation into the acquisition of German in the classroom by English-speaking children and adults. Subjects of the present study were 42 English-speaking children aged 11–16 at a secondary school in Edinburgh representing each of the first four years of instruction in German. German was their only second language. With the exception of the first year subjects, who were picked at the very beginning of the school year, subjects considered by their teachers to be fairly typical for their year were chosen.

Subjects had been exposed to teaching based on a communicative syllabus. However, within the structure of the syllabus there was room for the isolation of grammatical points (implicitly or explicitly). Teaching was based partially on the textbook *Deutsch heute* (especially in the first year), which includes summaries of grammatical points, explanations of grammatical structures and grammar-based exercises. In addition, typical 'communicative' activities were engaged in. In general the teaching approach can be described in terms of the five characteristics listed in the introduction in this paper. More detailed information will be provided at the relevant points in the discussion of the data.

Data elicitation

An approximation to spontaneous oral production was considered the only valid source of data for the purposes of this study since:

(a) it is spontaneous spoken language use which classroom teaching seeks primarily to develop;
(b) it is spontaneous spoken language data which is available from naturalistic SLA studies for comparison.

Data for the longitudinal study consist of utterances produced during classroom observations and of elicited responses outside the classroom with pairs of subjects giving and requesting information about personal data, collected during the first four months of German instruction of the first year only.

Cross-sectional data for the 1st–4th year were obtained at approximately month 8 of the school year. Data were elicited by means of individual oral interviews lasting between ten and fifteen minutes. Subjects were asked questions concerning their own personal circumstances, e.g. family background, hobbies, school subjects etc. The majority of questions were information questions to avoid simple yes/no answers. Questions were designed to potentially elicit a large proportion of negative constructions based on the interviewer's assessment of the likelihood of certain facts to be true of the subject. Examples included: 'Wo lernst du Karate?' with most but not all subjects not learning karate. The entire questionnaire potentially yielded a reliable number of negative responses without the questions seeming absurd to the subjects. Contexts were created to allow for the use of different verb and object types. A proportion of the questions were designed to elicit affirmative, descriptive answers. Thus a reasonable mixture of negative, affirmative, short and elaborate answers were allowed for in order to divert subjects' attention from the purpose of the elicitation. In addition a small listening task was administered, designed to elicit some further structures containing the copula, difficult to elicit by means of questions. Learners were asked to spot false statements.

Learners' exposure to negative structures

The learners were introduced to and extensively drilled in the following structures during the first year of instruction in the listed order:

(a) das ist *Kein N*
('that is not a *N*')

(b) ich habe *Kein N*
('I have not a *N*')

(c) Subject copula nicht adjective
(e.g. ich bin nicht gross)
('I am not tall')

(d) ich main verb nicht gern X
(e.g. ich spiele nicht gern Fussball)
('I don't like playing football')
'gern' is an adverb expressing 'liking' or 'enjoyment'.

(e) ich kann nicht infinitive
(e.g. ich kann nicht schwimmen)
('I can not swim')

From the 2nd year the learners were also given general word order rules, including the placement of the negator after the verb. Whenever possible, comparison with English was made.

Description of data

Some preliminary comments concerning the subjects' reaction to the interviewer's questions seem appropriate at this stage, as they shed some light on some of the effects of the nature of the classroom. Given the conditions of the elicitation task within the school context, it is not surprising that subjects felt their ability to speak German correctly was being assessed. However, the interviewer noted some striking examples of subjects seemingly unable to treat her questions at face value, i.e. as real questions. This was particularly true of the lower two years. Subjects would 'invent' cats, hobbies, etc., as though it seemed inappropriate to them to negate the assumptions of the questions. Furthermore they appeared to be guessing the purpose of the interview, frequently asking for confirmation as to the appropriateness of their answers, not only in terms of TL norms, but also in terms of the kind of responses which might be expected of them. In other words they treated the interview as a game or exercise of some sort, to which they had not been given the rules, or detailed instructions. More advanced learners tended to respond more directly to the questions but also in much more detail than was required, which suggests an emphasis in the teaching on complete sentences and practice in responding to oral examination questions, requiring learners to display as much of their TL knowledge as possible. Subjects in lower years also, not infrequently, refused to respond to certain questions or instructions, on the grounds that they 'hadn't done it yet' in class, rather than attempt to negotiate meaning.

Thus the learners were constrained by classroom practices to such an extent that they found it difficult to treat the second language outside the classroom, in (admittedly formal) conditions of natural language use, as a means of communication, and had at times to be asked specifically to do so.

Formulaic speech

It was observed during the longitudinal study of the first four months of instruction and during data collection as part of the cross-sectional study, that 1st year learners relied heavily on routines and patterns in speech production. To a small extent they were used for routine classroom activities, i.e. learners would respond to instructions such as:

'Hebt die Hand'
('lift your hand')
'Zieh die Jacke aus'
('take off your jacket')
'Frag . . . .'
('ask . . . .')

and would produce formulas on appropriate occasions, e.g.

'Lisa fehlt heute'
('Lisa is absent today')
'Trevor fehlt auch heute'
('Trevor is also absent today')
'Ich habe mein Heft vergessen'
('I have forgotten my exercise book')

However, the use of routines and patterns extended beyond these routine activities. Evidence for the largely formulaic status of learners' utterances is manifest in a number of ways. Learners produce and respond to questions with the meaning of other questions. Most common are confusions of 'Wie heisst . . .?' with 'Wie alt . . .?' patterns. Examples include:

S1: Wie heisst du? (What is your name?)
S2: Ich bin zwölf Jahre alt. (I am 12 years old)

and during a card game:

1: Hast du ein Heft? (Do you have an exercise book?)
S: Nein, das ist keine Heft. (No, that is not an exercise book)
1: Hast du einen Pullover? (Do you have a pullover?)
S: Nein, das ist kein Pullover. (No, that is not a pullover)

Learners also combine parts of questions with parts of other questions:

S: Wie alt dein Geburtstag?
    ('How old your birthday')
S: Hast du Geburtstag?
    ('Have you a birthday')

and they respond to questions using part of it:

1: *Lernst du* Karate?
S: Nein, *learnst du* gern nicht Karate.
1: Bist du gross?
S: Nein *bist du gross*
1: Hast du eine Katze?
S: Nein *hast du eine Katze*

Explanation for the extensive use of routines and patterns can be found in the teaching. During the first four months, which were observed regularly between once and twice a week, subjects received very little input. They were drilled extensively in the use of a limited set of questions and answers concerning personal data such as name, age, brothers and sisters, pets etc. The use of routines and patterns also accounts for a large proportion of 1st year learners' negative structures.

Considering the beginners' status of our learners, the high proportion (90%) of postverbally negated sentences containing finite main verbs[7] is surprising. Naturalistic learners distinguish finite main verbs from other verbs, placing the negator in front of finite main verbs, at the beginning stage of sentence internal negation. Postverbal finite main verb negation is evidence of a later acquisitional stage. However, there is evidence that these structures when produced by our learners are formulaic, rather than being generated by a learnt system of TL negative rules. In almost 75% of cases of postverbally negated finite main verbs, subjects insert the adverb 'gern' into the sentence where it is inappropriate or not required. In a number of cases 'gern' is also inserted into sentences containing 'sein'.

Structures of the kind 'Ich *main verb* nicht gern *X*' (corresponding to the English 'I don't like __ing *X*') were the first negative main verb structures to be introduced (at about 3½ months) and were drilled extensively over a long period, with a limited set of verbs, 'spielen' being the most common. This also accounts for the fact that subjects always choose 'nicht' appropriately as negative particle in sentences containing main verbs.

Approximately 85% of all structures containing possessive 'haben', all of which contain indefinite objects, are negated appropriately with 'kein'. Again this can be explained in terms of formulas. Learners had been drilled extensively in the use of formulas, using them at times randomly and at times combining parts of different formulas in ways which are to my knowledge not the case in naturalistic SLA. This may be explained in terms of constraints on memorization and as a result of the emphasis in the teaching on memorization of language chunks. Furthermore the learner is required to produce utterances in the TL from the very beginning and is under constant pressure to respond to the teacher. He is therefore not given the chance of a silent period, nor of selecting from the input those items which will serve him as formulas, unlike naturalistic learners. Because of this, and due to the close interrelatedness of the forms and functions of the structures involved, learners do not always maintain clearly defined contexts for their use.

Placement of the negator and sentence structure in classroom data

First year data include a considerable amount of non-TL-like negative structures, indicating some processing of the input and IL creation by learners. Learners produce one-word-negation and sentence external negation; sentence internal negation in structures without verbs; preverbal negation with main verbs at the same time as postverbal negation with other verb types.

Thus despite the emphasis on memorization of TL-like structures in the teaching, 1st year classroom learners produce very similar structures to those found in naturalistic acquisition, indicating similar input processing and IL construction.

While the use of formulas decreases between 1st and 2nd year, there is a considerable increase in the use of the above non-TL structures by 2nd year learners. The proportion of postverbally negated finite main verbs drops from 90% for the 1st year to 60% for the 2nd year. Instead preverbal negation is used by 70% of subjects. There are now also cases of possessive 'haben' being negated preverbally. At the same time all structures containing the copula 'sein' and the small number containing modals, are negated postverbally. Thus 2nd year data resemble early naturalistic data more closely than do 1st year data.

Third year learners do not produce sentence external negation. There are a number of negative structures which do not contain a verb. Preverbal negation is restricted to finite main verbs, excluding possessive 'haben'. At the same time finite main verbs are also negated postverbally, except by one subject. The data now also include a greater number of modals and a few auxiliaries, all of which are negated postverbally.

Choice of negative particle in classroom data

First year learners show evidence of their own particle system. The use of 'nein' is generally restricted to sentence external negation. Only one example of sentence internal negation with 'nein' was found. Although learners use both 'nicht' and 'kein' in their respective obligatory contexts, they also use both inappropriately, i.e. using 'kein' instead of 'nicht' and vice versa.

A closer look at the data reveals that, despite some target-like performance, learners do not distinguish the functions of 'nicht' and 'kein', but rather use both to mark negation only.

Earlier I argued for the formulaic status of structures containing main verbs and possessive 'haben' negated appropriately with 'nicht' and 'kein' respectively. All responses elicited were either of the type 'Ich spiele nicht (gern) X', or 'Ich habe *Kein*', with either brothers, sisters or pets as indefinite objects. With regard to sentences containing the copula, a larger variety was elicited. Structures were of the following type (excluding negation):

(a) Subject copula adjective
    (with a large variety of adjectives used)
(b) Das ist indef N
    (with a large variety of nouns)
(c) Subject copula indef N

Subjects supplied 'kein' in half of all obligatory contexts, supplying 'nicht' inappropriately in the other half. 'Nicht' was supplied appropriately approximately 75% of the time, in the remaining 25% of cases 'kein' was used instead. Thus despite the early use of 'kein' by classroom learners in comparison with naturalistic learners, learners do not distinguish the respective functions of 'nicht' and 'kein', but rather select one or the other, or both, to mark negation, with a slight tendency to favour 'nicht' as a negative particle. The lack of TL indefiniteness of 'kein' in learners' ILs is further indicated by occasional structures such as 'das ist keine ein Sessel'. The relatively early use of 'kein' can be explained in terms of the teaching. After 'nein' 'kein' was introduced, approximately two months before 'nicht' and structures containing it were drilled extensively.

First year learners also use the occasional double negative e.g. 'Ich habe nicht keinen Bruder'. Thus again, once learners move away from the use of formulas in their production of the TL, they process the input and produce output in ways very similar to naturalistic learners. This includes the use of 'nicht ein' instead of 'kein', indicating lack of marking for indefiniteness even when 'kein' *is* used; the tendency to favour 'nicht' over 'kein' as a negative particle; the occasional double negative.

As with 1st year learners, the use of 'nein' by 2nd year learners is restricted almost entirely to sentence external negation, although it occasionally appears within the sentence. Similarly to 1st year learners, 2nd year learners use 'nicht' and 'kein' both appropriately and inappropriately, i.e. using 'nicht' instead of 'kein' and vice versa. However there are differences in the use of these two negative particles. The inappropriate use of 'kein' instead of 'nicht' is restricted almost entirely to sentences containing main verbs. Many of these structures do in fact contain indefinite objects. However, since all of them are negated preverbally it is highly unlikely that subjects were operating according to the target rule. 'Kein' was almost never supplied where required. The proportion of the use of 'kein' with main verbs is relatively small (20%). (Comparable naturalistic data were not available.)

Fourth year learners categorically negate structures containing finite main verbs, modals, auxiliaries and the copula, postverbally. Thus once learners cease to rely entirely on memorization of formulas in their L2 production, their development towards postverbal negation is essentially the same as that of naturalistic learners, i.e. from sentence external to sentence internal, and preverbal to postverbal, with finite main verbs being distinguished from other verb types.

At the same time the use of 'kein' and 'nicht' in structures containing the copula is distributed in the following way: 'kein' is supplied when required only 4% of the time, in 96% of cases 'nicht' is used instead. 'Nicht' is supplied almost 98% of times required, 'kein' is used in approximately 2% of cases instead.

Thus the tendency to favour 'nicht' over 'kein' as a negative particle, becomes very strong with 2nd year learners indicating that the influence of the teaching during the first year with its early emphasis on 'kein', has diminished substantially.

Third year learners do not use 'nein' sentence-internally: 'nicht' and 'kein' are both used. Learners no longer use 'kein' inappropriately instead of 'nicht' and in structures containing 'sein' they never use 'kein' where required, but instead always use 'nicht'. Thus 3rd year learners' tendency to favour 'nicht' as a negative particle is even stronger than that of 2nd year learners. The difference may again be explained in terms of the use of formulas. Second year learners' utterances included a number of 'das ist *Kein*' structures which had been drilled extensively in the first year of instruction. Such data were not found for 3rd year learners.

Like 3rd year learners, 4th year learners do not use 'nein' as a negative particle and 'kein' is not used appropriately. Learners supply 'kein' when required in 'sein' constructions only 5% of the time, using 'nicht' instead in all other cases. However, subjects sometimes use 'kein' appropriately in constructions containing main verbs and indefinite objects where either 'kein' or 'nicht' would be appropriate (20% of the time).

Examples include:

ich fahre kein Auto
ich koche kein Mittagessen
ich lerne kein Französisch

This may indicate that subjects are beginning to distinguish the functions of 'nicht' and 'kein'.

As was the case with the placement of the negative particle, the use of negative particles with formulas by our classroom learners has also been reported for naturalistic learners.

'Nein' is used only in the 1st and 2nd year, i.e. in the very early stages. Differences are mainly surface differences. Thus the early use of 'kein' by classroom learners is a result of its early introduction in the input and extensive drilling of structures containing it, and the absence of 'nicht' in the early input. However, over the years, 'nicht' establishes itself clearly as the favourite negative particle.

Unfortunately, data on the development of marking indefiniteness are virtually non-existent, both for our classroom learners and for naturalistic learners. However, the lack of marking for indefiniteness is a feature of both types of early learners' language.

Summary and discussion

Despite some early TL-like performance, which can be explained in terms of the limited input and the use of routines and patterns, learners are found to process and analyse the TL input to construct their own IL system of communication. This is apparent in the use of non-target-like negative structures which are not found in the input. Moreover, the change from sentence external negation to sentence internal preverbal negation to postverbal negation, with finite main verbs being the last to be categorically negated postverbally, observed from the 2nd to the 4th year, resembles very closely the development of negation in naturalistic SLA. Thus we are justified in assuming that these changes are developmental. With regard to choice of negative particles, learners also create their own system. Although comparable data are sparse and some differences in surface phenomena can be observed, classroom learners' performance evidences at least some similar processes in the acquisition of negative particles compared with naturalistic learners. This includes the use of unbound 'nein' in the early stages of acquisition, i.e. in sentence external negation; marking for negation only before marking for indefiniteness; a preference for 'nicht' over 'kein' as a marker for negation.

Since the kind of structures produced by naturalistic and by our classroom learners are not found in the input, language development, in the area of negation at least, cannot be explained in terms of input and interaction only, but rather has to be seen as evidence of internal acquisition mechanisms (not necessarily language specific).

Considering the formal nature of the elicitation procedure and the difficulties encountered in attempting to obtain spontaneous natural language data from classroom learners, these results take on all the more importance in our attempt to determine what kinds of process operate in second language development. It appears that to a large extent the same mechanisms operate irrespective of the learning environment. However, the structure of the classroom and classroom activities designed to develop TL performance and requiring immediate production from learners can result in heavy reliance on routines and patterns, blocking for a time learners' processes of IL construction and development, including the ability to treat language as a means of communication for negotiating meaning. More specifically, one might ask at least two questions about the nature of the effect of the classroom on L2 development in this study:

(1) Since 2nd year learners' language closely resembles very early naturalistic learner language, what happened in the 1st year? Can it be regarded as a necessary step towards L2 acquisition, in the same way as the 'silent period' may be regarded as preparation for later IL production, or would learners actually have proceeded to IL construction and production sooner if they had not been required to produce immediately and 'correctly'?
(2) In terms of choice of negative particle 3rd year learners resemble early naturalistic learners more closely than do 1st and 2nd year learners. Is it possible that the acquisition of marking for indefiniteness would have started sooner if learners had not received early input which focused on 'kein' exclusively before introducing 'nicht'?

Conclusion

The results of this and other studies suggest that naturalistic and classroom second language learners process language data in similar ways to construct and develop their own systems of communication. In the light of the results of the present study we may ask ourselves whether organization of input and interaction in terms of the Presentation–Practice–Activity principle always results in a temporary 'blockage' of IL construction, at any point in the development. We may also ask to what extent and how this may be a necessary or at least helpful preliminary to acquisition, and to what extent and how it may impede it. Ultimately these questions relate to the issues of what triggers acquisition and what constitutes the optimal environment for what we now know to be a highly complex, systematic and organic process of development.

Notes

1. The use of the terms 'acquisition' and 'learning' is neutral with regard to Krashen's distinction and is intended to signify 'development'.
2. The observation that classroom and naturalistic settings may share crucial characteristics was in fact made retrospectively, in view of the similarities of development in the two types of setting.
3. 'Language' or 'language system' is used to refer to all aspects underlying a speaker's use of it, i.e. including grammatical, semantic, lexical, pragmatic etc. features.
4. This is not to deny, however, that there may be considerable differences between classrooms with regard to individual teachers' interpretation of the PPA-Principle.
5. For a detailed review and criticism of morpheme order studies see Long and Sato (1984).
6. For a detailed review and criticism of classroom morpheme order studies see Pica (1983b).
7. Because of its special status in the data, possessive 'haben' is treated separately from the other main verbs.

Appendix

TABLE 1
Classroom data* examples: placement of the negator and sentence structure

Formulas

I: Wo lernst du Karate?
    ('Where do you learn Karate?')
S: Ich lerne nicht gern Karate
    ('I don't like learning Karate')
I: (statement) Zola Budd spielt Fussball
    ('Zola Budd plays football')
S: (corrected statement) Zola Budd spielt nicht gern Fussball
    ('Zola Budd doesn't like playing football')
I: Wo spielst du Gitarre?
    ('Where do you play the guitar?')
S: Ich spiele nicht gern Gitarre
    ('I don't like playing the guitar')
I: Bist du müde?
    ('Are you tired?')
S: Ich bin nicht gern müde
    ('I don't like being tired')
I: Bist du faul?
    ('Are you lazy?')
S: Ich spiele nicht gern faul
    ('I don't like playing lazy')

Sentence external negation (NEGX/S)

L   nein hässlich
    ('no ugly')
L   nein das ist ein Haus
    ('no that is a house')
L   nein das ist ein Sessel
    ('no that is an armchair')
L   nein mein Vater ist schön
    ('no my father is good-looking')
L   nein Zigaretten
    ('no cigarettes')
L   nein ich lerne Karate
    ('no I learn Karate')

Sentence internal negation

no verb (subject NEG X)

ich kein gross
('I not tall')   ·
ich nicht gern faul
('I not _____ lazy')
ich keine Rugby
('I not Rugby')
nein ich keine Katze
('no, I no cat')

Preverbal negation

Zola Budd nicht spiele Fussball
('Zola Budd not plays football')
Zola Budd nicht spielen Fussball
('Zola Budd not play football')
Gordon Strachen nicht spielt Eishockey
('Gordon Strachen not plays ice-hockey')
Gordon Strachen nicht spiel Eishockey
('Gorden Strachen not play ice-hockey')
ich keine arbeitet
('I no/not work')
ich keine lerne Karate
('I no/not learn Karate')
ich keine hast ein Hund
('I no/not have a dog')
ich keine habe Haustiere
('I no/not have pets')

Postverbal negation

ich kann nicht spiele Gitarre
('I can not play the guitar')
ich bin nicht gross
('I am not tall')
Hamburg ist nicht in England
('Hamburg is not in England')

---

*Unless otherwise stated, data are taken from the cross-sectional part of the study. Examples marked 'L' are taken from the longitudinal study.

TABLE 2
Classroom data examples: choice of negative particle

Use of 'nein'

L   nein hässlich
    ('no ugly')
L   nein das ist ein Haus
    ('no that is a house')

Ich habe nein Katze
('I have no cat')

ich nein (koche)
('I no (cook)')
ich habe nein Freundin in Deutschland
('I have no friend in Germany')

Use of 'nicht' and 'kein'

'nicht' in obligatory contexts:
sie ist nicht gross
('she is not tall')
ich bin nicht faul
('I am not lazy')
Zola Budd spielt nicht Fussball
('Zola Budd plays not football')
ich spiele nicht gern Rugby
('I play not Rugby')

'kein' in obligatory contexts:
ich habe keine Schwester
('I have not a sister')
ich habe keinen Bruder
('I have not a brother')
das ist keine Tür
('that is not a door')
das ist keine Tafel
('that is not a blackboard')

'kein' used inappropriately:
Hamburg ist kein in England
('Hamburg is not in England')
mein Hund ist keine gross
('my dog is not tall')
Ich bist keine müde
('I am not tired')
ich keine spiele Fussball
('I no/not play football')
ich keine Klavier spiele
('I no/not piano play')

'nicht' used inappropriately:
das ist nicht eine Tafel
('that is not a blackboard')
das ist nicht eine Tür
('that is not a door')
Ich habe nicht Katze
('I have not a cat')
die Usher Hall ist nicht ein Museum
('the Usher Hall is not a museum')
ich habe nicht Bruder
('I have not a brother')

double negative
Ich habe nicht keinen Bruder
('I have _____ brother')

Strategy and System in L2 Referential Communication

ERIC KELLERMAN
THEO BONGAERTS
NANDA POULISSE

Introduction

This paper deals with the ways in which second language learners compensate for vocabulary deficiencies while performing referential communication tasks. Referential communication has been defined by Glucksberg, Krauss and Higgins (1975: 305) as taking place in 'situations in which the participant's task is to construct a message that enables someone else to know what that message refers to'. It will be argued here that previous research on the strategies used by second language learners to overcome lexical gaps in referential communication ('communication strategies') has failed to come to grips with the systematic principles underlying the use of such strategies. Because of a tendency to concentrate on the construction of descriptive taxonomies of *ad hoc* learner behaviour, such research has (a) failed to distinguish clearly the psychological process from the linguistic product, and (b) failed to consider the linguistic and non-linguistic constraints that influence the particular choice of strategy in ongoing discourse. As a result, an unnecessarily diverse number of types of strategy have been isolated and reported in the literature, at least some of which are confounds of strategies, their linguistic realizations and the specific attributes of the referents themselves.

Only one major category of communication strategy will be considered here, namely what Faerch and Kasper (1983b) call *compensatory strategies*. In our framework, compensatory strategies are used in referential communication typically when the speaker has to resort to *ad hoc* solutions to bridge linguistic (e.g. lexical) gaps without sacrificing the integrity of his intended message. Because such strategies are ultimately designed to refer, they will also be called referential strategies in this chapter. Those strategies by which the learner reduces the communicative goal in order to avoid linguistic problems ('reduction strategies', Faerch and Kasper 1983b) will not be considered.[1]

It is contended here that despite the apparent diversity of strategy types suggested by descriptive taxonomies to be found in the literature, the number is actually very small. In fact we propose that there are only three, which we call analytic, approximative and linguistic. Furthermore, we think it likely that the linguistic realizations of strategies are constrained. Some of these constraints are imposed by the properties of the referent whose L2 lexical label is unknown. Others have to do with the need to distinguish the referent from an array of competing referents. All in all, the limited number of strategies we propose coupled with these constraints make it likely that linguistic variation in L2 referential communication will be systematic and to some extent predictable.

This paper begins by underlining the similarities between a learner's compensatory strategies in L2 and other forms of compensatory behaviour available to all native speakers. Then a number of problems that beset the traditional view of compensatory strategies are examined. As an alternative to this view, a process-oriented treatment of such strategies will be proposed. The sections that follow consider the importance of collecting both L1 and L2 data from the same subjects performing the same tasks, and the cyclic and hierarchical fashion in which strategies are applied. Finally there is a brief account of two recent experiments in L2 referential communication.

The non-uniqueness of compensatory strategies

Although research on second language learners' *ad hoc* solutions to linguistic problems arising during speech production (i.e. their *communication strategies*) now stretches back to Varadi (1973), there seems to have been little attempt to place such research in a more general context of language behaviour (Bialystok, 1984, is an honourable exception; see also Poulisse, Bongaerts and Kellerman, 1984). This appearance of insularity is strengthened by the common use of strategy labels like Borrowing, Foreignization and Transliteration, all of which indicate that the learner solves his communicative problem by resorting to other (non-target) languages. While such strategies are also available to native speakers with referential problems (obviously provided they have some knowledge of another language and they anticipate linguistic common ground with their interlocutors), such strategies will, it is true, be used much more frequently by learners. However, this difference between native and non-native speakers is one of degree and not of kind. Even allowing for strategies based on other languages, it is doubtful whether there are any forms of L2 strategic behaviour which do not have their analogue in communication typically involving only native speakers. Take the following situations:

(1) teachers explaining words and expressions to children (or non-native learners);
(2) experts explaining technical terms to laymen;
(3) native speakers temporarily unable to retrieve a word[2];
(4) native speakers having to describe some referent for which they do not have a name (perhaps because there isn't one);
(5) native speakers taking part in TV quizzes where the object is to enable their partners to guess the word on a card without using the word under severe time constraints;
(6) Aphasics suffering from anomia.

These activities have features in common. A name for a particular referent cannot be retrieved, or must be withheld, or is not understood by the listener so that the referent must be labelled, relabelled or described in such a way that it can be recognized by the listener. It matters little whether it is the speaker or the listener who causes the compensatory behaviour to take place, or whether it is an activity stretching over several conversational turns or a single one. The motivation for the compensatory behaviour may differ from communicative situation to situation, as the above list suggests, but the processes underlying the choice of strategy are essentially drawn from the same small reservoir of options. One might argue that in the case of the second language learner, however, there is the added problem of a reduced *linguistic* competence in the L2 to contend with. But since in all the above situations it is a missing word that triggers the need for a compensatory strategy in the first place, to introduce the notion of reduced L2 competence is only to delay dealing with the issue of how the lexical gap is bridged. The learner's problem is indeed more acute if it means that he is unable to encode the preferred strategy as efficiently as he might were he a native speaker (which may lead to the use of strategies-within-strategies, Bialystok and Fröhlich, 1980; Ammerlaan, 1984; Kellerman, Ammerlaan, Bongaerts and Poulisse, 1986) but it is not qualitatively different. Consequently, we would argue that learners have the same 'compensatory capability' as native speakers by virtue of the fact that they *are* native speakers themselves.

Problems with the traditional view of communication strategies [3]

Problems of classification

Practical experience[4] shows that it is difficult to analyse any learner text satisfactorily using existing, product-orientated, taxonomies. It is almost inevitable that the analysis will contain a number of arbitrary decisions as to what is or is not a communication strategy, and what sort of communication strategy has been located. In this respect, a perusal of the literature on communication strategies reveals a tendency to illustrate strategy types with isolated examples rather than to demonstrate practically how such classificatory schemes can be applied to cohesive speech or writing, a reflection, we feel, of the general discomfort felt in analysing texts with current taxonomies.

Before classification can start, a reasonably foolproof means must be found of *locating* strategies in a text. While researchers in the past have been aware of the danger of confusing an *ad hoc* strategy with a systematic IL rule (since the two could be indistinguishable as far as linguistic form is concerned), it is only recently that systematic attempts have been made to expedite the location procedure. One way of doing this is to make use of such textual indicators of problematicity as hesitation phenomena, false starts, marked intonation, gesture, crossings-out, or metacommunicative activity. Another way is to make careful use of retrospective comments elicited from the learner about problems encountered. The two methods can be used in tandem, of course. (For a discussion of the value of the latter approach, see Poulisse Bongaerts and Kellerman, 1986.)

Even if the problem of which stretch of speech or writing represents an underlying strategy is solved to the researcher's satisfaction there still remains the problem of classification. This will prove a complex task if one resorts to the multiplicity of taxonomies and strategy types recorded in the literature (Poulisse *et al.*, 1984 list about 50 strategies, a number of these being more or less terminological variants). Most taxonomies to date suffer from two major deficits: (a) the definitions of strategies they contain are imprecise and difficult to apply in a cohesive text; (b) taxonomies are merely descriptive. No attempt is made to investigate what interplay of psycholinguistic mechanisms determine the particular choice of strategy in a given situation. In other words, descriptive taxonomies are product-oriented, not process-orientated.

To illustrate point (a) briefly, let us look at a number of what are known as Intralingual Strategies (Poulisse, Bongaerts and Kellerman, 1984), i.e. those which typically do not appeal to the learner's L1, but which are realized exclusively using the resources of the L2. The difference between Approximation (Tarone, 1977), Generalization (Faerch and Kasper, 1980), Exemplification (Faerch and Kasper, 1980) and Semantic Contiguity (Bialystok and Fröhlich, 1980), and likewise between Circumlocution (Tarone, 1977; Faerch and Kasper, 1980), Description (Bialystok and Fröhlich, 1980: Faerch and Kasper, 1980), Paraphrase (Tarone, 1977: Faerch and Kasper, 1980) and Word Coinage (various authors) is hard to discern.

Approximation and Semantic Contiguity, for instance, refer to the substitution by the learner of a known lexical item for a potentially more valued (but unknown or irretrievable) L2 target with which it shares enough attributes to satisfy the learner (say *chicken* for *duck*). Often the relationship between target and substitute is one of class membership, ducks and chickens both being part of the superordinate class *edible (domesticated) birds*. Generalization is similar: the use of a more general word than is strictly necessary in the discourse (*bird* for *robin*). Exemplification entails the use of a hyponym for a superordinate term (e.g. *tables*, *beds*, *chairs* for *furniture*).[5]

Circumlocution and Description mean the use of descriptions of the properties of the referent (e.g. function, location, shape, colour), though how the strategies differ, if they differ at all, is not clear. Finally, Paraphrase has been used variously as a blanket term for Circumlocution, Description and Exemplification (Faerch and Kasper, 1980), and Circumlocution, Description and Word Coinage (Tarone, 1977). (See further Poulisse *et al.*, 1984.)

Another problem with the product-orientated approach concerns the existence of 'mixed' strategies. Take the following two examples from Tarone and Yule (1983). The first is labelled Circumlocution, defined by them as '[the description of] properties of the target object or action (i.e. the colour, size, shape, function etc.)'; the second is labelled Approximation, 'in which the speaker uses (a single target language vocabulary item or structure) which shares a number of semantic features with the target lexical item of structure':

> The colour is, uh, dark, and uh . . . the size is just, uh, uh, as a hand . . . it is made of uh, la, leather.

> It's a kind of the mitten.

It is not clear whether the two examples refer to the same item (presumably some kind of glove), but the problem is how a traditional taxonomy would classify a possible utterance such as 'It's a kind of mitten made of leather', where one has both Circumlocution and Approximation present.

Compensatory strategies and their linguistic realizations

The case of Word Coinage is one which most clearly points to the uncertainty in many classification schemes as to what types of data a taxonomy is supposed to capture. A Word Coinage is usually identified by virtue of its form as a novel compound noun, thus showing evidence of having been created by productive morphological rules in the L2 (*airball, flowerist*). One of its most obvious properties (at least as far as can be seen from examples in the literature) is its high degree of semantic motivation. As such, Word Coinages are really descriptions which are realized grammatically as compound or derived nouns. (Compare such sanctioned nouns as (E.) *hairdryer*, (Fr.) *sèche-cheveux* etc.)

The tendency of most taxonomies to concentrate on the grammatical properties of Word Coinage rather than on its referential ones may lead to absurdities. For instance, if Learner *A* describes a balloon as *a ball with air/a ball in the air*, and Learner *B* says *an airball*, then a traditional product-oriented taxonomy would call the first utterances Description or Paraphrase, and the second word coinage. Similarly, if Learner *A* describes a triangle as *a figure with three corners*, this would be a Paraphrase. Learner *B*'s *three corner* is Word Coinage. Thus, a product-orientated classification scheme would list *a ball with air* and *a figure with three corners* under one heading, and *airball* and *three-corner* under another, ignoring the fact that both *a figure with three corners* and *three-corner*, and *a ball with air* and *airball* refer to the identical sets of criterial attributes of a triangle and a balloon respectively. A Word Coinage is thus a grammatical phenomenon (whose exact nature and extent in the learner's utterances may well be dependent on his perceptions of the L2), and like other forms of syntactic structure (e.g. NP + postmodification in the case of *ball with air/figure with three corners*) does not belong in the company of strategies designed to refer at all.[6]

Compensatory strategies and properties of the referent

One further problem with the product-orientated approach is its failure to show clearly the relationship between the act of referring and the properties of the referent itself. Suppose the learner does not know the appropriate L2 words for the referents *moon* and *knife*[7], and comes up with, 'it's in the sky' for the former and 'you use it for cutting' in the latter. A conscientious descriptive taxonomy (e.g. Bialystok, 1983) would classify both as Descriptions, but would then further divide them into (a) description of location for *moon* and (b) description of function for *knife*, as if the choice of description strategy were at the discretion of the learner. Taken to its logical conclusion, a product-orientated taxonomy would have to go on subdividing strategies indefinitely (e.g. description of cutting function). What is lost in this sort of detailed classification is the fact that the contents of both Descriptions of *moon* and *knife*, suggestive of different (sub)strategies, simply reflect the differences between the referents themselves. The criterial attribute of most knives is their ability to cut; moons are not normally perceived to have functions (cf. Miller and Johnson-Laird, 1976: 229, 232). Hence once the compensatory referential strategy has been chosen by the learner (i.e. Description), the attributes of the referent itself will have a crucial part to play in its realization. There is therefore no point in reporting the frequency of, say, descriptions of function if this frequency only reflects the frequency of the criterial attributes of the referents themselves. The predominance of functional descriptions reported in some studies (e.g. Bialystok, 1983) thus merely reflects the large number of concrete objects that had to be communicated in the L2. Most concrete objects have functions, and it is function which usually differentiates one concrete object from another. If the task consists of communicating abstract concepts such as 'faith', 'hope' and 'charity', descriptions of function are unlikely to surface in large numbers.

Towards a process-orientated taxonomy of compensatory strategies

All in all, we believe that there are three kinds of compensatory 'archistrategy' in referential communication. So far we have obliquely referred to two of them. These are cognitive in nature; the third, which we have not yet mentioned, is linguistic.

Approximative strategies

The first 'archistrategy' makes use of substitute lexical items for missing targets which, the learner realizes, may not quite fill the bill linguistically, but which are drawn from the same semantic field. The linguistic target, as projected by the learner, is actually unknown, uncertain or forgotten, but the word or words chosen in compensation label a referent potentially sharing enough attributes with the target referent for sufficient sense to get through to the interlocutor. Such strategies are holistic, requiring the listener to determine what referent X is like – by inferring the attributes of a conceptually related referent Y, if Y clearly is not the speaker's intended target. Those strategies known as Approximation, Generalization and Exemplification are of this type. We shall call them *approximate strategies*, and their outcomes *approximations*.

Thus if a learner substitutes *bird* where he would have preferred the L2 word for *robin* (generalization), the listener will no doubt refer in his mind's eye to some such bird as robin, sparrow, etc., but not ostrich. In other words, it is the listener who has to extract the criterial properties of the referent from the word presented. In the case of *bird* for *robin*, we may assume that the speaker relies on shared assumptions of prototypical category members (Rosch, 1977). We may also assume that if the intended referent is not a 'good' member of the category *bird* (e.g. *ostrich*), or if it is of importance to specify robins rather than sparrows, then the learner will endeavour to constrain the generalization via hedges of various kinds ('a sort of . . ., not a . . . but rather more a . . ., with a red breast', etc.). The same sort of strategy is apparent in the use of category member substitution, where one category member replaces another (e.g. *chicken* for *goose*). Here too, there may be qualification on the *part* of the speaker (e.g. 'a big chicken for Thanksgiving' for *turkey*).

Analytic strategies

The second 'archistrategy' takes the form of a sort of decompositional analysis of the referent in which one or more of the conceptual/functional/perceptual attributes of the desired target are made explicit. Here there is no attempt by the speaker to make do by substituting another referent for the preferred one (approximation). The intention is for the listener to build up a picture of the target referent itself from the speaker's description. The traditional category of description (or Circumlocution or Paraphrase) is of this analytic type, which we shall refer to from now on as an *analytic strategy*, and its outcome as an *analytic description*.

Analytic strategies select attributes of the target referent so that the interlocutor will be able to reconstruct the referent from what are effectively a series of clues. Analytic descriptions may have elements of other strategies embedded in them, or they may themselves be embedded. Thus *robin* may be referred to by generalization (an approximative strategy) as 'a bird', with a subsequent description such as 'it has a red breast'.

What attributes of the target referent will be selected by an analytic strategy will depend, amongst other things, on a range of task-related factors. We have already suggested that the particular attributes of the referent will determine in some degree what form the compensatory strategy will take. If the referent is a knife, we may expect a strategy to capitalize on the knife's function as a cutting instrument since this is its most distinctive attribute. Thus the linguistic form of the strategy is initially constrained by the choice of archistrategy, linguistic or cognitive.

A further constraining factor on the form of strategies is the context in which strategies are to be used. If we return to the example of knife, then learners may be expected to select its cutting function as the attribute to refer to in the absence of the target lexical item *knife*. However, such a claim will only be valid if *knife* is represented in a context free of other *knives* or cutting instruments. If there is an array of such instruments, reference to the function of knives is not going to lead to successful communication, since function no longer remains a distinctive attribute. When reference is made to the concept of knife, function is indeed a criterial attribute; this is what gives knife its 'knifeyness'. But when it is a question of selecting one amongst many knives, then we need to distinguish amongst competing referents. Thus the learner may refer to a particular knife as *the large sharp thing* as distinct from *the small blunt one*. The context effectively neutralizes this normally criterial attribute of 'knifeyness' (Olson, 1970).

Linguistic strategies

There is a third class of strategy which we have termed *linguistic*. These have also been called *interlingual* in Poulisse *et al.* (1984), in that they resort to solutions afforded by other languages (usually the speaker's L1). Such strategies typically (but not exclusively) define the population of non-native speakers. Linguistic strategies rely on presupposed (or hoped-for) shared linguistic knowledge on the part of the listener (cf. Tarone and Yule 1983). They have been referred to in the literature as

Borrowing, Foreignization and Transliteration. Borrowing occurs when a word or two of a non-target language is inserted in the speech stream without adaptation. It is in effect a code-switch; foreignization is the creation of L2 words by the application of supposedly L2-based morphophonemic conversion rules to an L1 (or other L) word (Du.) *alimentatie* 'alimony' → (E.) **alimentation*; (Du.) *pincet*, /pIn' set/, 'tweezers' → (E.) /'pInset/). Transliteration has been used to describe the translation of L1 (or other) idioms and other collocations as well as to morphophonemic conversion of single words. All these strategies are thus lexical. Many studies of communication strategies have mentioned the fact that less proficient learners resort to their L1s more readily than more proficient ones, but there has been very little work to date on what conditions have to be met for a speaker to resort to strategies like transliteration and foreignization. Some of the ideas on transferability developed in e.g. Kellerman (1977) might be relevant here.

The cyclic nature of strategy application

Let us assume that a learner, wishing to refer to a given object in the L2, realizes that he does not know the appropriate word for the object. He now has a number of choices. If he chooses to compensate for the missing lexical item by means of an analytic strategy requiring verbalization of some distinguishing attribute of the object but linguistic means again do not permit this, the learner is faced with a further choice. He may decide to select other, less favoured, attributes, or he may attempt to analyse the preferred attribute itself into its component attributes. Similarly, if he chooses to use an approximation, but his lexical knowledge does not permit him to select the one he would find most satisfactory in his L1, he may be forced to resort to one of the other strategies. In other words, we must allow for the possibility of strategies being embedded within other strategies (cf. Bialystok and Fröhlich, 1980) or being hierarchically related to each other.

Suppose we use the example of robin again. If an analytic strategy is to be used, then the learner may say something like, 'it has feathers and a red . . . *borst*' (Dutch, = E. breast). The overall strategy is analytic, but while that strategy is being executed a new problem crops up, that is, how to name the concept labelled 'borst' in Dutch. In this case the problem is solved by an embedded linguistic strategy. It might, for example, have been solved by an approximative strategy ('chest') or by an analytic one ('the part between throat and legs'). In other words, problem-solving procedures may apply cyclically to increasingly small linguistic domains within the overall strategy. It is thus quite possible that a single utterance may represent two strategies simultaneously.[8]

The need for comparative data

In certain tasks the difficulties experienced by the speaker may not only be due to a reduced linguistic proficiency but also to the inherent difficulty of the task. The description of complex abstract shapes, for instance, creates problems for native speakers as well as for learners, though the problems are more involved in the latter case. In order to determine what the effect of a reduced linguistic proficiency is on the form of referential strategies and their linguistic realizations in such a task, it will be necessary to have protocols for each shape by each subject performing both as native speaker of his L1 and learner of his L2. Otherwise it is impossible to determine what is an attempt to solve the referential problem, and what is a strategy compensating for a lexical gap.

To illustrate this point, if we present a series of complex unconventional shapes to a group of learners and ask them to describe them, we would not be able to tell whether the descriptions of labels afforded the shapes were representative of what this group would do were they performing in their own language. This may be because these shapes are unlikely to have commonly accepted names in any language or because the task is perceived not to require simple labelling of shapes. Thus the fact that Dutch learners of English may describe a rhombus standing on one of its points as a series of lines or as two triangles joined base to base cannot be taken as *prima facie* evidence of lack of knowledge of the word 'diamond' without the necessary comparative data to show that the same task would have been performed differently in the L1. Yet relatively few studies have used comparative data (see Poulisse *et al.*, 1984).

Two experiments on L2 referential communication

In the following paragraphs, two recent experiments on referring in a second language are briefly described. The first (Ammerlaan, 1984) shows how comparative data can reveal systematic differences between L1 and L2 behaviour within the same subject; these differences can probably only be attributable to a reduced lexical store in the L2. Ammerlaan's data reveal a clear tendency towards analytic descriptions in the L2, most probably a result of the nature of the task, as is the considerable detail to be found in most protocols. The second experiment (Bentlage, 1985a) is in some senses similar in that sets of learners were required to describe abstract shapes. Unlike Ammerlaan (1984), it permitted interaction. Here, a clear preference for approximations is revealed (with the exception of one group of subjects). Again this tendency may be attributed to the particular requirements of the task.

1. Ammerlaan (1984)

Kellerman, Ammerlaan, Bongaerts and Poulisse (1986) reanalysed data from an earlier investigation (Ammerlaan, 1984) into the way that 17 university-level Dutch learners of English named or described 11 abstract shapes both in Dutch and English. The task was carried out with the goal of enabling a (hypothetical) native speaker of the language of description to accurately draw the shape from a recorded transcript. There was no feedback during the task. (For a similar approach, see Simons and Murphy, 1986.) Results showed that while learners used exactly the same approach in L1 and L2 to the description and naming of a particular shape in the great majority of cases (c. 88%)[9], there were nevertheless a number of cases where the L1 and L2 protocols of a particular learner for a particular shape diverged (c. 10%).

In this 10%, all but one case represent clear evidence for revised referential strategies motivated by the absence of the appropriate L2 lexis. The L2 protocols tended to be longer in terms of words and revealed evidence of attempts to break shapes up into less complex (and more easily nameable) components. Thus there was a clear difference at the *global* level of description, where the L1 protocol was more likely to consist of a holistic (thus approximative) strategy, i.e. one that named the entire figure (*ruit*, 'diamond'). In the L2, the absence of a known translation equivalent for *ruit* led learners to select what we have called a partitive strategy, whereby the shape was described via its component figures. This strategy is *analytic*. Thus Dutch *ruit* might become in L2 English *two triangles* or *two roofs of a house*. A third strategy noted in the data, also analytic, described the shape as if it were a map and reduced it to its ultimate components of lines and angles. This approach we call *linear*, viz.

> Two lines starting in one point . . . er one goes to the left side and the other goes to the . . . right side erm . . . and erm . . . they're about er 3 cm. long and er . . . then on top of each of these lines on the left one there's a line which starts at the end of er the first line and erm . . . goes to the right ending in er one point and on the . . . right line, on the top of that there's starting another line . . . er going to the left and er it ends in the same point as the line I described just er before.

Learners report that these linear descriptions are difficult to do – they are also difficult to reconstruct.

There are 18 pairs of protocols where L1 and L2 do not match. In 16 cases, the Dutch strategy is holistic (approximation). Of the 16 equivalent English protocols, 6 are partitive and 10 are linear. One Dutch case is partitive (analytic); here the English equivalent is linear. The one exception, the eighteenth pair, is the case where the Dutch description is linear and the English one holistic.

The three strategies thus seem to be ordered, with holistic strategies being preferred to analytical ones. Impressionistic support for this ordering can also be found from a perusal of the protocols within a given language. That is, subjects prefer to use holistic strategies to accomplish the description of ever smaller levels of detail in the figures. The L2 protocols suggest that these levels of detail require greater use of analytic strategies than in the L1.

If the language in which the task had been carried out was irrelevant to the descriptive approach used, and changes in description from protocol to protocol reflected unforced changes of mind as to the best way to describe a shape, then we would expect to find an even distribution of holistic, partitive and linear strategies across both languages in the 10% of cases where L1 and L2 do not match. But we do not. The holistic strategies are with one exception in the L1.

The linguistic strategies of Borrowing, Foreignization and Transliteration are scarcely in evidence at this level of proficiency. Other research has tended to suggest that these strategies characterize less advanced learners (see Bentlage, 1985a for recent discussion). In this respect, the small number of L1–L2 differences must also be attributed to the high proficiency level of the subjects.

2. Bentlage (1985a, b)

Bentlage (1985a, b; Bentlage, Bongaerts and Kellerman, forthcoming) conducted a replication of Krauss' experiments (see the listing in e.g. Glucksberg *et al.*, 1975) with Dutch learners of English at four levels of proficiency, P1 (schoolchildren in their second year of English, 13–14 years old), P2 (fourth year of English, 15–16 years old), P3 (sixth year of English, 17–18 years old) and P4 (second year university students, eighth year of English, 19–20 years old).

The task, performed by dyads, required one subject (the Director) to describe a series of abstract unconventional shapes such that they could be identified and placed in the right order by a second subject of the same sex and nominal proficiency (the Matcher) divided from the Director by an opaque screen. The procedure was repeated six times per dyad, the order of presentation being different on each occasion, and note was taken of the time it took for the dyad to complete each trial.

Bentlage found that by some measures P1, P2 and P4 all performed the task more efficiently than P3. Whereas all groups took less time and needed fewer words as the trials progressed, P3 needed the most words to successfully complete the six trials. However, the efficiency of the P1 group at least partly derives from the fact that they were also the most willing to resort to their native language and even their local dialect. This is consonant with other findings reported in the literature showing that there is a negative correlation between use of the L1 and level of proficiency. In fact more than 50% of P1's final references were based on Dutch. P2, P3 and P4 made decreasing use of their L1 (perhaps because they are more institutionalized and certainly in the case of P4, more proficient).

However, P3 performed strikingly differently from all the other groups in terms of the distribution of compensatory strategies chosen. While P1, P2 and P4 used about three *approximative strategies* (e.g. 'it looks like a UFO') for every two literal *analytic strategies* in Trial 1, P3 used about five times as many analytic strategies as approximative ones. Analysis of the references made to every figure in each group in Trial 1 showed that *initial* analytic strategies (i.e. those referring to a new figure *before* the Matcher had a chance to intervene) were less likely to lead to successful interpretation (and the establishment of the final reference) by the Matcher than approximations. Thus it seems that in this task approximations were the preferred strategy, presumably because they required less effort to execute than long analytic descriptions, and, given the nature of the task, should usually prove sufficient for recognition purposes. This would at least partly explain why P3 seemed less efficient in establishing final references.

At this stage we do not know whether the preference for initial analytic descriptions is a quirk of this particular group, or an age-related factor, true of most 17–18 year olds. Perhaps we have here a genuine L2-related phenomenon which can be related to critical proficiency, in that these learners, not having the lexical means available for successful approximations, are nevertheless able to 'overcompensate' via the considerable means they do have. Unfortunately we do not have the P3 group performing the same task in their native language for comparison (though we note that Yule and Tarone, 1986, have recorded a tendency for non-natives to over-elaborate in their descriptions). Further research is needed here.

As expected, P4 were able to perform the task more efficiently using fewer compensatory strategies. Thus efficiency, as measured by time and number of utter-ances needed to complete the six trials appears to be a matter of linguistic competence. P1 and P4 were the most native-like in their performance, though for P1 the relevant native language was Dutch rather than English.

Conclusion

In this chapter, it has been suggested that the study of communication strategies, and in particular compensatory strategies, should be located within existing research in referential communication. Furthermore we think it is important to free such research from a product-orientated approach to these phenomena (i.e. one that is merely descriptive) in favour of one that looks at the processes underlying the utterances of second language learners. This shift in emphasis leads to a simplification of terminology as well as a gain in psychological validity. In other words it is important to investigate not only what sorts of strategies are used by speakers, but what it is that motivates their selection. This will necessitate an abstract characterization of strategies that does not depend on situational factors such as task requirements or item-specificity.

We have proposed three 'archistrategies' which we believe will subsume all the strategies identified in previous research. The first two, approximation and analytic strategies, are cognitively based. The former is holistic, substituting a label from the semantic field for the lexical item; the listener is required to infer what the relevant shared attributes of the substitute are. The latter utilizes attributes of the referent explicitly, inviting the listener to form a conceptual picture of the referent. The third strategy is linguistic; learners make use of the lexical resources of their L1s and possibly the morphophonemic rules of the L2 to 'invent' labels for referents. Stra-tegies may be employed cyclically, embedded within each other as solutions to problems-within-problems. Bentlage's study shows that learners at different profici-ency levels seem to prefer different types of strategy, at least in their initial references to shapes.

The study by Ammerlaan (1984) demonstrates the importance of having compara-tive data available in L1 and L2. In order to understand how a reduced linguistic proficiency affects a task, we must be able to say how a native speaker would have performed the same task under the same conditions. Ammerlaan's data show evidence of an ordered range of approaches to description moving from holistic to partitive which operates across L1 and L2. It is the systematic differences in choice of strategy in pairs of protocols which demonstrates the existence of compensatory strategies.

Notes

1. The discussion will be restricted to verbal strategies, though the potential importance of gesture, mime and pointing in the study of language behaviour is acknowledged.
2. Here is a recent example:

   Shrieking in a most unmanly fashion, I retreated through the door where stood a Dowayo waif of about six who looked at me quizzically. Stress had somewhat disrupted my lexicon and I could not find the word for 'scorpion'. 'There are hot beasts within!' I cried in an old testament voice. The child peered inside and with an expression of profound disdain stamped the scorpion to death with his bare feet. [Nigel Barley, *The Innocent Anthropologist*. Penguin, 1986.]

3. This section will not provide a survey of the research to date on communication strategies. Readers interested in such surveys are referred to Faerch and Kasper (1983b) and Poulisse, Bongaerts and Kellerman (1984).
4. This practical experience is derived, *inter alia*, from the Nijmegen Project on Compensatory Strategies.
5. It may well be that there *is* no label for the superordinate category in the L2, in which case the learner may unwittingly be doing exactly what native speakers of the L2 have to do. For instance, there is no generic term for 'nut' in French; a Francophone will have to specify what sort of nuts were included in his 'assortment panache'; an Anglophone can simply say 'a bag of mixed nuts'. Similarly, in American Sign Language, there appears to be no generic sign for 'fruit'. Instead, signers use a composite sign consisting of reduced signs for prototypical fruits, such as 'orange, apple, pear', plus the sign for 'etc.' (Bellugi and Klima, 1979). As in the French example above, the superordinate category is represented by a list.
6. Some word coinages may be more strictly referential strategies in our sense if they are *ad hoc* translations from the L1 or some other language. As such, they could be classified as linguistic strategies, under the heading of transliteration.
7. Referents will be indicated by capitals. The word in capitals should be seen to represent the object independent of the name it has in any given language.
8. Thus if an English learner were to refer to a wristwatch in French as 'une cloche', we would have both an approximation and a foreignization at the same time. It could be argued that the latter is embedded in the former on the grounds that the learner would first have to have associated *watch* to *clock* and then converted it morphophonemically.
9. That is, the same descriptive elements were mentioned, usually in the same order.

Variability and Progress in the Language Development of Advanced Learners of a Foreign Language

R. TOWELL
University of Salford

Introduction

In this paper I will discuss the vertical or diachronic dimension of interlanguage development on the basis of data derived from a longitudinal study of advanced[1] learners of French. My aim will be to further the discussion of the possible causes of variability along this dimension by examining data which have been collected within the narrow set of criteria proposed by Ellis (1985b:124) for the existence of non-systematic variability. I shall attempt to show that non-systematic variability exists in the data (alongside systematic variability) and shall then search for explanations to account for this phenomenon, giving particular consideration to the explanatory power of concepts such as 'knowledge and control' (Bialystok and Sharwood Smith, 1985), 'channel capacity' (Cook, 1985), 'strategies' (Faerch and Kasper, 1983) 'formulas' (Fillmore, 1979) (Raupach, 1984) and 'temporal variables' (Grosjean and Deschamps, 1975).

I shall argue in particular that more attention should be paid to the development of channel capacity as measured by temporal variables and that these factors should be taken into account in any discussion of interlanguage development.

Ellis (1985b: 124) puts forward five criteria which, he suggests, must be met if a discussion of non-systematic variability is to be made possible. He states non-systematic variability can be held to exist when:

(1) the two forms occur in the same situational context;
(2) the two forms perform the same illocutionary meaning;
(2) the two forms occur in the same linguistic context;
(4) they occur in the same discourse context;
(5) there is, in the manner of their production, no evidence of any difference in the amount of attention paid to the form of the utterances.

The data discussed in this article meet these criteria as they are taken from a series of recordings[2] made with the same British undergraduate student at different times throughout her four-year long undergraduate course. This particular student came from Northern Ireland where she had been studying French from the age of 11, i.e. for at least seven years before coming to university. She had only visited France on one occasion before coming to Lancaster. During the recording period she spent a year as an assistant in France and then returned to Lancaster for the fourth year of her course. One recording was made each term and the same types of question and the same tasks were reintroduced each year. In each case the recording was made on a one-to-one basis in an informal setting with a native speaker of a similar age already known to the learner. The style of speech used by the learner consistently corresponds to that of a 'vernacular' (Tarone, 1982). The 'discourse domain' (Selinker and Douglas, 1985) relates to the home of this student, i.e. Northern Ireland, and the presentation of the subject takes the form of responses to the same (or very similar) questions and sometimes gives rise to a re-telling[3] of an anecdote recounted earlier (akin in some ways to the use of 'episodes' by Selinker and Douglas).

The way this particular set of data has been collected should therefore exclude explanations of variability on the grounds of sociolinguistic differences along a 'capability continuum' (Tarone, 1979; 1982; 1983), on the grounds of differences in 'monitoring' (Krashen, 1981) or attention (Tarone, 1982), on the grounds of different 'discourse domains' (Selinker and Douglas, 1985) on the grounds of 'backsliding' because of 'new and difficult' intellectual subject matter or . . . a state of anxiety or . . . a state of extreme relaxation' (Selinker, 1972: 214), on the grounds of differences in the situational or linguistic context or indeed on the grounds of differences of personality between learners. In so far as it is possible over a four-year study these factors have been held constant and therefore cannot provide an explanation for variability in the use of language.

This is, of course, not to say that such factors do not provide an explanation for variability elsewhere in the data. The research design here corresponds to Tarone's 1983: 159) request for 'longitudinal studies which use a variety of elicitation tasks and keep the data from these tasks separate from one another'. It is therefore equally possible using data from the same corpus to exploit the 'synchronic' dimension, within the limitations imposed by the variety of tasks, to show that the factors mentioned above do cause variation, but for the purposes of this paper I have decided to examine a small part of these data where these factors have least influence.

Characteristics of the developing interlanguage

I will therefore present aspects of the data with special emphasis on non-systematic variability and then examine concepts from various psycholinguistic approaches in an attempt to find an explanation for this phenomenon.

Systematic and non-systematic variability

Two examples will suffice to demonstrate the kind of variability which occurs and which apparently fails to systematize even over a lengthy period of time.

I. 'c'est difficile de/à'

In Term Five (Year Two) of the data collection, the following utterances occurred within the limited context outlined above:

(1) * c'est difficile à sortir pendant les soirs
(2) * c'est difficile aller au cinéma (said without pause and a unified intonation pattern)

(3) * il y a toujours des taxis mai c'est difficile à trouver
(4) * c'est difficile à commencer à vivre . . .
(5) c'est difficile d'être garçon et catholique

Clearly 1, 2, 4, 5 provide a very similar linguistic context in so far as the basic structure used is the same, viz. 'c'est difficile + *Infinitive*' and the illocutionary force is the same as each statement is part of a description of the problems associated with living in Northern Ireland in the late seventies. Yet the utterances do not use the same linking preposition:

(1) c'est difficile *à* + Infinitive
(2) c'est difficile *ø* + Infinitive
(4) c'est difficile *à* + Infinitive
(5) c'est difficile *de* + Infinitive

In so far as it is possible to identify a norm for spoken French the most common form would be 'c'est difficile *de* + Infinitive.' The 'c'est difficile à' form exists, as does 'il est difficile de' but they are consistently differentiated by native speakers.

Il est facile + de + (Pron) + Inf + (Noun) = Formal language
    difficile
C'est facile + de + (Pron) + Inf + (Noun) = Informal Language
    difficile
C'est facile + à + Transitive Infinitive = where 'ce' is a neutral pronoun with an identifiable referent resulting from an NP movement

The relationship between these structures can be shown by the similarity in meaning between

Il } est { facilie *de* faire quelque chose = Quelque chose } est difficile *à* faire
C' }   { difficile   C'   }

This last point relates to example (3) above where 'c'est difficile à trouver' would be possible if it is acceptable (and in some varieties it would be) for 'des taxis' to be the referent for 'ce'. In most cases, however, one of three alternatives would be more acceptable:

(1) Il est difficile d'en trouver;
(2) C'est difficile d'en trouver;
(3) Ils sont difficiles à trouver;

where it is clear that the infinitive 'trouver' has an object.
The examples (1) to (5) demonstrate that in Term Five

á)
de }   are variably used where 'de' would be more appropriate
ø)   in either formal or informal language

The variability in the use of 'à' and 'de' persists throughout the data, although the use of ø does not appear after Term Five.

In order to understand more clearly this phenomenon and even if it takes us beyond the narrow context of the initial data set it is worth listing the examples in the data for the occasions in other terms where the speakers uses:

c'est +   { facile }   + (*Prep*) + *Infinitive*
           { difficile }

because it seems to demonstrate a pattern of learning which exemplifies the failure (in the four years available) to systematize a pattern which native speakers, in the main, do not confuse.

In Terms One and Two the only form to occur is

c'est   { facile }   de + *Infinitive* + *Object*
         { difficile }

Term One:

(6) je trouve que c'est très facile uh de faire des amis parce que . . .
(7) et c'est très facile aussi de faire des amies spéciales . . .
(8) sur le campus c'est plus facile d'être une étudiant que . . .
(9) c'est peut-être difficile de distinguer entre la vie dans la maison et dans l'université
(10) j'aime j'aime le cours mais c'est difficile de maintenir le niveau de travail.

Term Two:

(11) mais dans les choses comme uh le travail manuel c'est très difficile pour une femme de dire que elle est égale . . .
(12) mais c'est difficile de d'avoir des opinions comme ça . . .

In Term Four, however, the pattern changes and 'c'est difficile *à*' is the only form which occurs:

(13) * uh c'est difficile à connaître les professeurs
(14) * uh c'est difficile à les connaître
(15) * c'est plus facile à ouvrir une boîte
(16) je je trouve l'accent de du Midi très (laughs) c'est mais la le vrai accent du Midi c'est très difficile à comprendre
(17) * j'ai une amie qui habite à Voreppe elle est de Montpellier et c'est très difficile à comprendre.

In Term Five the state of confusion cited in examples (1)–(5) is reached where both structures co-exist but with an unacceptable degree of variability, producing a number of erroneous utterances as in Term Four.

In Term Seven we find:

(18) c'est une ville que c'est facile de d'aimer de s'eloigner de (!)
(19) * c'est peut-être très facile à s'habituer plus facile à s'habituer à quelque chose qu'on reconnait un peu.

In Term Eight we find

(20) ça c'est plus facile à comprendre des quelqu'un riche (= de (la part de) quelqu'un de riche).

In Term Ten we find:

(21) c'est facile d'aller d'Irlande du Nord à Belfast d'Irlande du Nord à Lancaster
(22) * et souvent c'est plus facile à faire quelque chose
(23) * c'est difficile à trouver les peut-être quelque chose pour le mettre dedans
(24) * (le russe) c'était difficile à parler
(25) à cause de ça c'était difficile uh par exemple de reconnaître des choses comme adverbaux (= adverbiaux)
(26) mais s'il faut habiter à Morecambe c'est Morecambe c'est très difficile à . . . (unfinished sentence).

In Term Eleven we find:

(27) c'est difficile à expliquer parce qu'il faut vivre dans. . . .

In Term Twelve we find:

(28) donc c'est plus facile de de s'accoutumer à le (= au) sens d'humeur
(29) * les différences entre les deux styles je crois que c'est c'est difficile d'expliquer
(30) bon familier c'est um difficile á expliquer hum un peu comme. . . .
(31) un peu non c'est difficile à expliquer mais c'est pas très intellectuel.

where (29), (30) and (31) were produced in rapid sequence in response to a question about differences in the style of American and French films.

Examples (22) and (23) in Term Ten show the infinitive followed by an object in the 'c'est difficile à' structure (just as in Term Four), and example (29) in Term Twelve shows the transitive 'expliquer' with 'de' where 'ce' refers back to 'les différences': the same 'error' in different guises.

Although this is only a single example and the data relatively sparse, the pattern of learning suggests that in Year One only one form is available: 'c'est difficile de' and this is used correctly. Once, however, the 'alternative' 'c'est difficile à' is introduced in Term Four this at first replaces 'c'est difficile de' and then in Term Five the two structures are seen to compete, along with other possibilities. They then continue to compete in examples in the rest of the data covering a further two years.

Another noticeable feature of the data is the very high density of 'c'est'. The consistent overuse of 'c'est' has been commented on by Raupach (1984:124): 'It is true that "sentence schemata" (Lyons, 1969:178) such as "c'est" and "il y a" belong to the standard repertoire of native speakers of French, an accumulation to the effect that nearly all sentences in a performance follow this schemata must, however, be regarded as non-idiomatic and typical of second language production.' Thus both my data and Raupach's data from a German student at a similar level shows a systematic overuse of 'c'est' (and 'il y a') and my data appear to indicate continuing non-systematic variability in the use of:

c'est $\left\{ \begin{array}{l} \text{facile} \\ \text{difficile} \end{array} \right\}$ + *Prep* + *Infinitive*

The learner is not able, it seems, to learn to keep these competing structures apart as native speakers in the main, do.

2. 'pas de'

A second example concerns the use of 'de' after 'pas'. The target language rule, as stated by Ferrar (1967:123) requires that 'de + ø' should be used after 'pas': when 'the noun is negative in quantity, i.e. when "no", "not a", "not any" means "no amount of", "no number of" but that "un", "une", "du", "de l'", "de la", "des" remain unchanged in a negative sentence when the noun is negatived as to its identity (i.e. when the meaning is that it is not that kind of thing).' It is also true that 'un, une' can be used after 'pas' in a statement of contrast and to mean 'a single one'. One of the consequences of this rule is that the form 'pas un' is not infrequent: it will occur, for example, in sentences with 'être'. The learner who has simplified the rule (as, indeed, it is expressed in some grammar books) to read 'after "pas" use "de" without an article' is confronted with a reality which the over-simplified rule does not capture. All the following examples are of the 'negative in quantity' type, but the rule is not consistently applied.

As in the example for 'c'est facile/difficile à/de' above the pattern of learning here seemingly goes from 'correct' language use to 'incorrect' language use. In Term Five (Year two) this particular student produced the following utterances, which are all correct in terms of the target language norm:

(32) il n'y a pas de liberté en Irelande du Nord
(33) il n'y a pas d'autobus
(34) il n'y a pas de taxis
(35) il n'y a pas d'autobus.

In Terms Eight (Year Three), however, when she was actually living in France, again in the same circumstances for recording, she produced the following erroneous utterances.

(36) * il n'y avait pas un trève
(37) * ils ne portent pas des mitraillettes

This was repeated in Term Eleven (Year Four) by:

(38) * il n'y a pas de des écarts.

This variability called for further investigation beyond the very narrow confines of our data base and other examples confirm an impression that this variability is non-systematic:

(39) Term 2   (Year 1):   * il n'y a pas le différence entre
(40) Term 6   (Year 2):   il n'y a pas de choses pour . . .
(41) Term 6   (Year 2):   * je ne peux pas trouver des questions
(42) Term 6   (Year 2):   vous n'avez pas d'expérience des choses comme ça
(43) Term 7   (Year 3):   * j'achète pas de la viande pas souvent.

(44) Term 7   (Year 3):   il n'y a pas de théâtre
(45) Term 7   (Year 3):   il n'y pas de théâtre
(45) Term 7   (Year 3):   il n'y a pas de grands grands montagnes
(46) Term 9   (Year 3): * je n'avais pas un but particulier
(47) Term 10 (Year 4):   il n'y avait pas d'autres occasions de la faire
(48) Term 10 (Year 4):   je n'avais pas assez d'expérience
(49) Term 10 (Year 4): * je n'avais pas des idées
(50) Term 10 (Year 4):   il n'y a pas de contact
(51) Term 10 (Year 4): * il n'y a pas des séminaires tous les semaines
(52) Term 10 (Year 4):   si on n'a pas de technique.

Even within this extremely narrow range of linguistic contexts, we find a pattern of accurate and inaccurate use of the forms which is very difficult to explain. Most of the verb forms here involve 'avoir', particular 'il y a' but there is no consistent pattern. The presence of a following vowel does not suffice to create a pattern. A transfer of an L1 usage fails to explain the distribution. I, at least, cannot find a linguistic explanation for the non-systematic variability which appears to persist over a four-year period.

Whilst Ellis's footnote (1985b:130): 'Presumably the learner eliminates such forms (erroneous forms RT) (rather than trying to exploit them functionally), because subsequent input demonstrates that they are not present in the target language . . .' does not put a time limit on the exposure needed to eliminate such forms, it seems to me that if they have not systematized in the spontaneous speech of a learner after eleven years, including a year in the relevant country, then some kind of explanation is called for.[5]

These data suggest to me, therefore, that non-systematic variability persists over time to a considerable degree alongside those other areas where systematicity finds a ready explanation. The data here cover a four-year period during which the exposure to the language has been enormous including positive and negative, inductive and deductive information about the language and yet it would seem that any move towards systematicity, even if it eventually takes place (perhaps along a form–function separation as suggested by Ellis, 1985b), it is nonetheless extremely slow, suggesting that some explanation is needed to account for the failure of an intelligent adult to make better use of the implicit and explicit information available in an attempt to approximate to native speaker behaviour. Given the limitations imposed by the selection of the data this explanation can only really come from a psycholinguistic framework dealing with mental processing.

Mental processing

While the learner is apparently not learning to differentiate and/or control the structures we have just examined, she is nonetheless making considerable progress elsewhere and this can be best described under the general heading of 'mental processing', which has been dealt with in the literature in a variety of ways.

In an attempt to 'reconceptualize' some of the essential issues in this area Bialystok and Sharwood Smith (1985:104) propose a 'theoretical framework which is based on the assumption that explanations of learner performance should be related to two separate components, namely the way in which the language system is represented in the mind of the learner (the categories and relationships in the long-term memory), and the processing system for controlling that knowledge during actual performance'. The two components 'knowledge' and 'control' are then related respectively to the 'vertical' and 'synchronic' dimensions of interlanguage growth. The vertical/knowledge dimension contains variability and 'the primary cause of this variability is changes in knowledge including the amount, nativeness and analysis of that knowledge' (1985b:109). The synchronic/control dimension includes within it those 'control procedures' which relate to the efficiency with which the retrieval of linguistic forms is executed. 'This efficiency, also referred to as automaticity, is the basis of fluency' (1985b:109).

Cook (1985) taking stock of recent Chomskyan thinking, takes a slightly different stance. He reminds us first of a distinction to be made between *development* – the real-time learning of language by children – and *acquisition* – language learning unaffected by maturation sometimes called the instantaneous acquisition model (1985: 4–5).[6] In L1 acquisition universal grammar may be present in the brain from the start: the fact that it takes years to 'unfold' is not part of the grammar. The process of 'unfolding' depends on many factors, an important one of which may be that part of cognition which includes 'the systems of information processing involved in handling language, which can be called *channel capacity*' (1985:7). Applying this distinction to second language learning Cook suggests that 'some aspects of channel capacity are not transferred to a second language' (1985:11) and 'development is not necessarily reliable evidence for acquisition in a second langage: the L2 sequence of development may reflect the re-establishing of channel capacity for using the language, rather than language acquisition per se' (1985:11). Cook adds that 'errors may be the result of channel capacity rather than of acquisition per se' (1985:13). It is not entirely clear what the relationship might be between Cook's *channel capacity* and Bialystok and Sharwood Smith's *control*. Both refer to processing mechanisms but place the emphasis on different aspects of those mechanisms. *Control* stresses the sensitivity of those mechanisms to different situations, *channel capacity* stresses the cognitive skills which may or may not have developed in the L2.

Fillmore (1979) and Raupach (1984) in dealing with this same area refer to 'formulaic expressions' which are seen to play an important role in the development of fluency and these also seem to blur the Chomskyan distinction between 'competence' and 'performance'. Raupach (1984:116) in particular has suggested that formulae may be indicators of processing units and in defining these (1983; 1984) has made use of the measurement of temporal variables such as speaking rate, pause/ time ratio, articulation rate, length of runs between unfilled pauses and the proportion of runs of differing lengths.

To some extent also mental processing has been dealt with via the concept of 'strategies': learning strategies and communicative strategies (Faerch and Kasper, 1983b). Is it possible to examine the data in question using these concepts in order to gain an insight which might also illuminate the non-systematic variability, and the continued use of non-target-like forms outlined above?

Changes in mental processing as shown by the use of increased knowledge, formulas, and communicative strategies

As is immediately obvious from the examples cited above the use of 'c'est' and 'il y a' as sentence schemata is extremely frequent in the data. In part it could be assigned to the category of a communicative strategy known as 'formal reduction' (Faerch and Kasper, 1983b:52–3) which is employed when an area of 'problematicity' is encountered. This 'strategy' is obvious in the next example, where also the strategy of 'restructuring' is used.

In Term Two (Year One) the student recounted an anecdote of what happens when there is a bomb in her street. She wanted to say that the bomb explodes, or possibly is exploded by the army, but for reasons of syntactic, morphological or lexical uncertainty had difficulty in expressing this idea:

(53) et quand le la bombe uh doit quand la bombe et quand il y a l'explosion

The initial attempt has 'la bombe' as subject of a verb, perhaps 'devoir' but despite two attempts she cannot continue with this structure and changes it to the frequently used 'il y a + Noun' giving rise to so-called 'formal reduction' and increased frequency of the formula 'il y a + noun'.

The same story is told in Term Eleven (Year Four) but the element of 'problematicity' is no longer there because the amount of knowledge has increased:

(54) et puis on fait exploser l'armée euh le fait exploser

Faire + Infinitive is now an available, easily accessed structure so formal reduction is not necessary. It is also true that the 'restructuring' of (54) is different to that of (53) in so far as the restructuring of (54) merely replaces 'on' as subject by the more precise 'l'armée' (as a native might do) whilst in (53) the restructuring involved 'resorting to' an 'easier' structure.

In this sense the use of formulas, of particular strategies and changes resulting from increased amounts of knowledge are several sides of the same coin, but the increase in the amount of knowledge is probably the most significant factor.

Another example proving the same point is available from a comparison of a Term Two (Year One) utterance with a Term Eleven (Year Four) utterance of a similar kind.

Term 2:
(55) 'c'est très uh maintenant c'est très habituel on doit sans penser je crois on
    doit le faire sans penser'

Term 11:
(56) 'mais on s'habitue très facilement et uh puisqu'il faut s'habituer il faut vivre
    donc il faut s'habituer et parce qu'on s'habitue euh on ne le reconnait pas
    comme une situation très triste.

Knowledge of the appropriate verb 's'habituer', 'puisque' and of 'parce que' allows a much more sophisticated, planned response to be offered where the reduced form 'c'est' of (55) is no longer needed.

Knowledge is not, however, to be measured only by its amount. As suggested above the nativeness of the knowledge is also important. As Raupach's (1983:205) data also indicate the early stages of the advanced learner's interlanguage contain many instances of generalizations expressed by 'quelque chose comme ça', but as progress is made these vague approximations take on a more authentic form and the methods of hesitating or changing direction become akin to those used by native-speakers. It is doubtful whether these should be considered part of the linguistic system as such, but they certainly add to the impression of native-like language.

Term Two (Year One):
(57) oui il y a toujours des choses comme ça.

Compare this with Term Eight (Year Three):

> (58) . . . parce que *bon* la fête c'est quelque chose très fa euh familial donc euh il y a encore *tous les trucs* de Noël *tous les* grands repas *tout ça* le sapin de Noël *tout ça*.

Which is perhaps not a great deal more precise but much more authentic with the use of 'bon' to change direction, of 'donc' to add a logical structure, and the repetition of 'tous les . . . tout ça'.

This evidence certainly supports the idea from Bialystok and Sharwood Smith that vertical dimension variability responds to the growth in 'knowledge' and also demonstrates the important role of those 'schemata' and/or 'formulas' which are necessary at a certain stage but which can be replaced as knowledge of the appropriate term becomes available.

The importance of knowledge offers the possible explanation that the non-systematic variability outlined above is caused by lack of knowledge. In one sense this is self-evidently true: there are systematic target language rules which the native speakers use (these have been roughly sketched in above) and the non-native speaker does not use these rules consistently in her language production, despite the fact that she has been exposed to various kinds of inductive and deductive sources of information about the language. Yet, on the other hand, there are numerous examples in the data of 'correct' uses: how could these be produced without 'knowledge' of the rule? And, at the same time, this, admittedly small, sample of data has been collected in such a way that other situational causes of variability cannot be said to have produced the variability in this case.

One possibility to which I shall return later is that these examples are particularly lengthy examples of U-shaped learning. But if this is so, why does the curve take so long to evolve a 're-structuring' of the language system?

Using, at least initially, the division suggested by Bialystok and Sharwood Smith, I would like to propose that the answer may lie in the area of 'control', although my proposal may conflict with the total separation of knowledge from control. In their article Bialystok and Sharwood Smith show that the variability of control is related to the synchronic dimension and its explanation 'requires qualitative models which reflect not the amount of knowledge that the learner has but the psycholinguistic conditions under which that knowledge may be demonstrated' (1985:110): control variability is separated from cognitive variability 'which reflects a change in the learner's knowledge over time' (1985:110) and systematicity belongs in the cognitive dimension: 'it is our claim that systematicity reflects the cognitive underpinnings of language acquisition (1985:116).

My evidence here is of non-systematicity which persists over time in a stable data collection environment: my problem is why that non-systematicity persists for so long. The explanation may lie in 'the psycholinguistic conditions under which that knowledge may be demonstrated' but 'conditions' here has nothing to do with external differences in the situation but a lot to do with the internal consequences of the constant pressure on the learner to process language as fast as possible. I wish to suggest that part of the learners' 'psycholinguistic conditions' is a constant demand to process language at a near-native speed. The actual manifestation of that pressure is the habit of native speakers of 'switching off' or of interrupting or of finishing sentences for the learner. In terms of cognitive effort the learner may be required to pay attention to that part of the mental processing of language, which is associated with ensuring a reasonable speed of utterance and the cost may be an inability to internalize all those possible patterns which are evidenced in the language to which the learner is exposed, or at least to economize on overall cognitive effort and internalize just those elements which will provide the greatest return.

In order to assess the evolution of 'control' within the confines of the data outlined above, it is possible to compare various measurements of 'temporal variables' as outlined by Grosjean and Deschamps (1975) for comparative data in French and English with native speakers and used for non-native speakers of French by Raupach (1983, 1984). These provide a way of comparing various aspects of the mental processing of language with relatively objective data.

The variables used are:

(1) Speaking rate: normally expressed in syllables per minute and calculated by dividing the total number of syllables produced by the total time taken to produce the utterance (including pause time) and multiplying the result by sixty. It allows comparisons of how much time it takes to formulate and produce the speech.

(2) Articulation rate: normally expressed in syllables per second and calculated by dividing the total number of syllables produced by the amount of time taken to produce them (not including pause time). This measure gives an indication of the speed at which speech is being produced.

(3) Pause/time ratio: gives the percentage of the time spent speaking as a proportion of the whole.

(4) Length of runs between unfilled pauses: this is the mean (or median) number of syllables between unfilled pauses of no less than 0.2 seconds (or in some cases 0.25 seconds). The figures here, especially with small amounts of data, must be interpreted with great caution as a small number of fillers such as

'bon' with pauses on either side can considerably reduce the average. This figure can be supplemented as in Table 2 by an indicator of the percentages of runs of different lengths.

The following two tables indicate comparative data for the particular learner studied in this paper. The data have been severely limited in order to ensure comparability. The figures are based on approximately four minutes of speech in which in Year One and in Year Three virtually the same anecdote was retold on the subject of what happens in the street when a bomb is discovered. The object of the comparison is to provide a comparative statement about the learner's ability to perform virtually the same act with an interval of two years. These figures should not be taken as suggesting a norm of any kind: the analysis of similar exercises by other speakers, or of the same speaker performing another exercise, suggest that these variables are extremely sensitive to individual and contextual variation.

TABLE 1
Comparative data for a single subject in the same situation talking on the same topic in different years

	Year 1	Year 3	Native speaker norms in interviews (Grosjean and Deschamps)
Speaking rate	118.20 syll./min.	195.20	264.00
Articulation rate	3.07 syll./sec.	3.69	5.21
Pause/time ratio	64.03	88.02	84.45
Length of runs between unfilled pauses	4.30 (mean)	8.40 (mean)	12.00 (median)

TABLE 2
Comparative data between the subject cited in Raupach (1984) and data from my subject. Raupach's subject (R) was measured before and after a period in France of a term. My subject (RT) was measured in Year 1 and then in the second term of the year abroad

Data	R before	R T Year 1	R after	R T Year 3
Length of runs between unfilled pauses	5.55	4.30	8.70	8.40
Utterances with 1–4 syllables	54.26	65.30	27.74	34.40
5–10 syllables	34.57	30.61	36.13	34.40
11+ syllables	11.17	4.08	36.13	31.08

The tables also include, for reference, figures obtained by Raupach for a similar subject answering questions on subjects such as student life in France and Germany before and after a period of residence in France. The data analysed represent about ten minutes' recording. Equally for reference are the figures obtained by Grosjean and Deschamps for native speakers in radio interviews.

From these figures it is clear that between Year 1 and Year 3 the student increased her speaking rate by 65%, her pause/time ratio by 37%, her articulation rate by 20%, and the length of runs between pauses by 95%. At the same time the number of utterances between 1–4 syllables fell by 30.4%, the number of utterances between 5–10 syllables increased by 3.79% and the number of utterances of 11 syllables and above increased by 19.91%. The same degree of variation is also seen in the data provided by Raupach on the effect of a term abroad.

These changes are certainly large enough to indicate that the student has progressed to a stage where the language can be processed much more quickly and in much larger units. It is probable that such a change makes greater demands on the overall channel capacity and in consequence the learner may be obliged to assign a greater amount of the channel capacity to processing at the expense of other aspects of linguistic cognition. The learner is in fact constantly rquired to perform a balancing act and this probably lasts throughout the learning process until some kind of threshold is reached. It may even be that learners have to attain native speaker processing norms if fossilization is not to take place. Non-systematicity will continue to be present as long as the attempted processing speed continues to be more than the channel capacity can take and the learner, especially in interaction with a native, is always under pressure to process language more quickly.

It is not, however, obvious why certain items of linguistic structure should be more vulnerable to changes in the balance between processing and other aspects of cognition. It might not be unreasonable to suggest, however, that some parts of the linguistic system might be more 'peripheral' than others and that the learning of these peripheral items might be sacrificed in favour of other less peripheral items until such time as the 'balancing act' allows the luxury of dealing with these non-central elements. This in turn might help explain the U shape learning pattern: it may be that the system will tolerate ambiguity for considerable lengths of time if that part of the system is not central to its functioning so the learning of some items might have a larger U-shape than others. Only carefully controlled experiments could hope to discover whether the items thrown up by naturalistic data collection can be seen to vary in experimental conditions. There is certainly room for a great deal of research to discover the sub-elements of cognitive variability. Lightbown (1984:244) points out that 'work . . . where the emphasis is on memory and information processing . . . is not generally seen as being part of the mainstream in SLA research'. This may in fact be a rather dangerous omission and lead researchers into failing to compare like with like. If, as may be the case, the non-systematic variability referred to above, is caused by an insufficient channel capacity for the learner to process the knowledge, it would indicate that the learner's performance, if studied cross-sectionally at a given moment in time might reveal a large number of errors (or a particular score of right answers in obligatory contexts, as in the morpheme studies) because the learner has overstretched her channel capacity. Another learner might have fewer errors, because that learner is not attempting to process language at the same speed and might therefore seem to have 'acquired' more. But comparisons between the two would be misleading unless figures were available for the temporal variables for each learner. The temporal variables, like Brown's (1973) mean length of utterance, can act as a comparative base on which performances can be compared.[7]

Conclusion

I have argued that evidence provided by data from the language learning of advanced learners indicates that despite large amounts of exposure, despite implicit and explicit instruction in the language, non-systematic variability persists over a long period of time. I have further argued that whilst 'knowledge' is undoubtedly a major factor in explaining cognitive variability along this diachronic axis, it will not suffice to explain the persistence of non-systematic variability. I would wish to propose that the explanation may lie in the concept of 'control' if the 'psycholinguistic conditions' and the 'processing constraints' mentioned by Bialystok and Sharwood-Smith include not only those created by the external conditions but also those internal psycholinguistic constraints associated with the development of channel capacity. Knowledge and control are presented as a dichotomy: it seems to me that there must be at least some interaction between these two aspects. There is a point at which that which is controlled becomes automatized or internalized which implies some kind of interface between the two systems, within a cognitive developmental framework in a similar way to that outlined by McLaughlin (1978:319). If this is the explanation of the persistence of non-systematic variability, then research in second language acquisition in general would benefit from measuring control or channel capacity via temporal variables in order to ensure an adequate basis for comparison between subjects.

Notes

1. Cook (1985:13) has rightly remarked with reference to interlanguage study that 'one conceptual problem, however, is that L2 learning is seldom complete in that few learners ever approximate to native competence; all their grammars are interlanguages. Hence the instantaneous acquisition model is difficult to apply, because there is no settled final competence, no "steady state" grammar.' This remark explains the use of 'development' in the title of the article and also stresses the value of using evidence from advanced learners as this is likely to be as near as one can get (after 11 years and a year abroad) to native speaker competence.
2. The data used as a primary source for this article represent part of a larger corpus of data collected from five undergraduate students at the University of Lancaster over a four-year period. The total corpus represents approximately fifty thousand words.
3. This is, however, a genuine re-telling and not a repeat in the sense that the interviewer has never heard these answers before and in some cases there is a three-year interval between the use of the same anecdote in an answer.
4. *Indicates an utterance where the choice of 'à' or 'de' is different from that which would be made by a native speaker. Where other kinds of mistake are made by the learners an interpretation of what was meant is added in brackets.
5. Limitations on space prevent extensive exemplification from other students, but similar analysis of the performance of other students suggests a similar pattern of non-systematic variability in the data examined to date.
6. S. W. Felix (1984) refers to the same distinction as the logical problem of language acquisition and

the developmental problem of language acquisition and argues (p. 142) that the possible separation between these two aspects can be resolved by the proposal that 'the principles of universal grammar are themselves subject to an innately specified developmental process'. It is not clear how this would affect the L2 learner whose maturational processes have been completed.

7. Rosansky (1976:410) has commented on the lack of a comparative basis for the morpheme studies.

Section Four:

VARIABILITY AND SOCIAL CONTEXT

The two articles in this section examine how language and social context are inter-related. The first article, by Roberts and Simonot, is concerned with how communicative competence in a second language (L2) is developed. This is investigated by examining the way the L2 learner interacts with native speaker interlocutors in different social contexts. The second article by Edwards is concerned with linguistic competence (defined simply as 'language ability') and the situational factors that help to determine the level achieved by different language users. Roberts and Simonot report on a study of L2 users, who are members of an ethnic minority community in Britain. Edwards' subjects are West Indian Patois speakers resident in Britain. However, Edwards states that these speakers' competence appears to operate in the same way as L2 learners'. It seems appropriate, therefore, to include such a study in a book about SLA. Indeed, we need to recognize that there is no inherent difference in the acquisition and use of a second language and a second dialect.

These articles raise a number of important questions, of which we will consider two here. The first is a matter of definition – precisely what do we mean when we talk about 'social context'? The second concerns the relationship between language use and language learning – does the way a second language/dialect is used in particular contexts affect the development of competence in that language/dialect?

Roberts and Simonot help us to understand what is meant by the term 'social context'. They isolate three meanings of 'context'. First we can talk about the context that is created as a particular interaction unfolds. Second, we can use context as a generic term to refer to the type of interactive situation of which a particular interaction is an exemplar (e.g. the context of 'gatekeeping interactions'). Third, context can refer to the wider social setting in which the learner/user operates. It is this third meaning which the term 'social context' refers to. Turning to Edwards' article, we can see what kinds of variable may be important in determining how the social context influences language use and language development:

(1) the educational background of the subjects;
(2) the sex of the subjects;
(3) the subjects' attitudes to different social groups comprising the society in which they live, in particular their attitudes to members of their own 'ingroup' and members of the 'outgroup';
(4) the network of the subjects' social relationships (e.g. whether they mix mainly with other second language/dialect speakers or with native speakers/standard dialect speakers).

From the Roberts and Simonot article, we can add a fifth variable:

(5) the type of interaction habitually engaged in (in particular whether this is instrumental or 'personal' in nature).

Let us now consider the relationship between social context and language *use*. You will recall from the Introduction and the articles in Section One that the basis of a sociolinguistic approach to SLA research is that L2 use, like any other language use, is influenced by social factors. You will also recall that this influence can be investigated in terms of style-shifting and/or in terms of interactional sociolinguistics. Roberts and Simonot choose the latter. They compare the ways in which their L2 learner subjects interact in two different social contexts. The first consists of 'gate-keeping situations', where there is a power imbalance between the L2 speaker and the native speaker. The particular type of gatekeeping situation they examine consists of estate agent encounters. The second consists of learner–researcher 'conversations', where the interactions are more relaxed and personal. Roberts and Simonot concentrate on the *strategies* used by both the language learners and the native speakers rather than the *linguistic* properties of the learners' speech in the two settings. This makes a refreshing change, as SLA research has been over-occupied with morphosyntactic features. Through careful qualitative analysis, Roberts and Simonot show that the learners' interactional strategies vary both according to context and also according to their individual personalities. Of the variables of social context considered above the ones seen as paramount are the learners' social network and the type of interaction they engage in.

Edwards considers the relationship between social context and linguistic *ability*. She points out that whereas the use of Patois by British West Indians is related to such factors as level of education and attitudes towards white society, actual ability (measured in terms of the number of dialectal features which are defining characteristics of Patois) is not. The key factor determining competence to use Patois is social network. Edwards found that her subjects exhibited highly variable abilities; those with the highest levels were those who mixed mostly with other West Indians, while those with the lowest levels were those whose social networks included members of the white community. Edwards suggests that Patois competence may be related to the extent to which her West Indian subjects choose to display group solidarity. Thus different social factors seem to predict when Patois is used and the degree of competence in Patois achieved by individual speakers. We can envisage highly competent speakers who actually use Patois very little and, conversely, speakers who are not very competent, but nevertheless use Patois frequently.

What then is the relationship between use and acquisition of a second language/dialect? First, we should be warned by Edwards' research that use and acquisition are not necessarily the same thing. What determines use may not be the same as what determines acquisition. Who you mix with and how often you mix with them may be the crucial factors governing acquisition. How educated you are and what you think about the 'outgroup' may govern how and how much you use the second dialect. Such a view is also implicit in the position adopted by Roberts and Simonot. Their L2 learners developed limited competence in English because they had limited opportunities to engage in informal conversations with native speakers. Their perceptions of themselves and the perceptions which native speakers have of them as minority ethnic workers determine to a large extent both when they use English and how they use it (i.e. what kinds of strategy they employ). Thus, restricted networks of use lead to restricted interactional opportunities, which affect how successful acquisition is.

Thus, although competence and use may not be related to the same social variables, the two must be seen as closely interlocked. Frequency of opportunity to use a second language/dialect must surely govern the level of competence achieved. But, more important, perhaps, is the type of opportunity that is experienced, or, to put it another way, the quality of the interaction engaged in. Roberts and Simonot provide illustrative evidence to suggest that the acquisitional opportunities afforded by instrumental interactions of the kind that take place between an L2 learner and an estate agent may not be ideal for language learning, not least because they do not obtain the kind of simplified input which promotes acquisition. Yet for many learners – in particular, ethnic minority workers – these are the only interactions which they habitually experience. Thus, lack of competence in English is, in part at least, due to the failure to accomplish acquisition interactionally. Conversely, the West Indian speakers with the highest levels of Patois competence are those whose social network is predominantly West Indian and who, therefore, are likely to experience the right interactive and affective environment for learning Patois.

In considering the relationship between use and acquisition we also need to make clear what we mean by 'acquisition'. Edwards defines competence in terms of a set of grammatical features. Roberts and Simonot are more concerned with the development of strategic competence. Now, it is perfectly possible for a learner to develop a high level of *strategic competence* without developing a corresponding high level of *linguistic competence*. Indeed, this is exactly what Roberts and Simonot suggest occurs in the case of one of their learners. This learner is adroit at managing conversations, even when he is in a disadvantaged position, as in the estate agent encounter, but his control of English grammar and lexis is very limited. It is interesting to speculate that the type of social context that frames an L2 learner's development may help determine what *type* of competence is developed. Meisel (1980) has distinguished two types of learner – (1) the functionally orientated learner, who is primarily concerned with getting his message across, and (2) the structurally orientated learner, who is predisposed to discover the linguistic system of the L2. Which orientation a learner favours may in part be the result of his psycholinguistic disposition (Meisel's interpretation), but it may also be determined by the interactional requirements of the typical social contexts the learner is required to use the L2 in.

Finally, we would like to draw your attention to the fact that what is learnt from the social context of second language/dialect use is not just the second language/ dialect. Learners also learn about their own social identity. As Roberts and Simonot emphasize, it is not just language acquisition that is interactionally accomplished, but one's actual social position. Social context shapes through interaction what Rampton calls 'the socio-cultural world of the learner'.

'This is my Life': how language acquisition is interactionally accomplished

CELIA ROBERTS
MARGARET SIMONOT
Ealing College of Higher Education

Introduction

We are interested in how contexts created by interlocutors reveal learner and native speaker strategies and either encourage or discourage language acquisition. In order to do this, we have to examine factors which we assume have a bearing on motivation to acquire. One of the most crucial factors for minority ethnic workers, in a society where structural racism exists, is the degree of inequality in an interaction. Language alone will not alter power structures which either give or deny access to equal opportunity, but language can create a local interactional context in which the power imbalance is adjusted to give more equal treatment. So, we are also interested in whether these strategies help learners towards a more equal partnership in this interaction, and in future interactions. We are not simply concerned with whether the encounter was smooth, whether information was adequately exchanged, although these are significant indices of a successful transaction. We are particularly concerned with whether the encounter provides an experience for the learners which will help them to interact more equally in the types of activity where they are most likely to use the target language.

In order to examine the contexts in which adult minority ethnic workers[1] can acquire English as a second language through interaction, it is necessary to ask what these contexts are. So, we begin the paper by arguing for the need to deepen our understanding of the context in which most inter-ethnic communication takes place. We first give a brief outline of the research project on which this paper is based.

Data: The European Science Foundation project on adult second language acquisition

The data examined in this paper were collected as part of the project, *Second Language Acquisition by Adult Immigrants*, which has been funded by the European Science Foundation since May 1982. It is a cross-linguistic longitudinal study of untutored acquisition of a language by adults from a total of six source language backgrounds and five target languages.

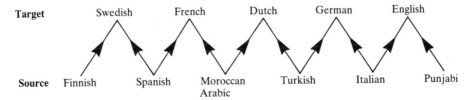

133

The British team has been working with two ethnic groups: Italian and Punjabi.

Each Italian and Punjabi informant has been interviewed at approximately six-week intervals by the project researchers. The interviews have consisted of free conversation, specific tasks agreed across all teams and external recordings, some of which have been role plays, and some naturally occurring situations.

Data have been collected in this way for each informant over 2½ years. The data used here were collected during the end of the study when the informants had been working with the project for at least eighteen months at the time of recording and had been in the country for a maximum of 2½ years.[2] The data used in this paper come from two Italian informants in two different contexts: in a non-studio recording – in an estate agent's – and in conversation with project researchers.

Context

Before analysing the data in detail, it is worth trying to tease out what we mean by the different contexts and why we should bother.

Until quite recently, with some notable exceptions, SLA has focused on quantification and on the acquisition of interlanguage forms at a relatively low level. There is now increasing interest in examining communication strategies across a range of activity types which entails the integration of context. As Selinker and Douglas (1985) point out, examining communication strategies in context is likely to be 'intractable to quantification'.

The exceptions to quantification work such as that by Hatch and her associates (1980) and the phenomenon of 'convergence' by native speakers (Long, 1983a) still raise many questions about the notion of context. Levinson (1983) in an extensive tour around the notion of context concludes that we still have no clear idea of what it is except that it is 'whatever (excluding semantics) produces inferences'. It is quite possible to produce lists of features (Hymes, 1964; Lyons, 1977) but, as Levinson points out, how are we to decide what is relevant at any time?

In addition to the work of linguists and sociolinguists, social psychologists have argued for the need to include in our understanding of interactional context, the motives, values and perceptions of the interactants (Giles and St Clair, 1979; Giles and Saint-Jacques, 1979). We need, as Beebe and Zuengler argue (1983) to 'build a more expansive, integrated model'. But what should we invest in and at what point do we stop integrating?

Linguists and psychologists have been battling with the question of the perimeter fence of context ever since Bartlett (1932) suggested that in order to make sense of interaction we do not construct a context any larger than we need for interpretation (see Brown and Yule 1983 for a useful discussion). But this poses great problems for the analyst in trying to work out what is the context constructed by interlocutors in order for them to make sense of the interaction. We cannot assume that we can reconstruct that context because that presupposes a normative world. But we know how difficult it is to establish international communicative norms because of a lack of shared cultural presuppositions. Consider, for example, the so-called international visual symbols used on roads or lavatory doors. They can be misunderstood with disastrous consequences. As linguists analysing inter-ethnic communication in a society of structured inequality, like Britain, we know we cannot make any normative assumptions.

So, we are faced with the urgent need to relate SLA to the actual contexts of situation in which adult learners have an opportunity to acquire, but with the difficult problem of deciding what that context is. Selinker and Douglas (1985) put the case for finding a way to limit the context in order to understand how learners use context to create an interlanguage. What, in fact, they seem to be proposing and what we are concerned with in this paper, is to find ways of deepening the context.

A good example of the difficulty of deciding how deep to go in excavating context before an adequate interpretation can be made is given in a recent overview of work on understanding and misunderstanding in the ESF project (Perdue, 1986). Perdue discusses how highly co-operative researchers adjust the input to the informant. He then refers to the work on convergence in SLA (see Long, 1983a) and remarks that this work assumes that native speakers will be highly co-operative and willing to adjust.

However, in the type of highly instrumental interactions that are often the only contacts with TL speakers that adult second language acquirers have, no such co-operative attitude can be assumed. In the ecology of second language acquisition by ethnic minority workers, the context of any interaction must go deep enough to account for the fact that native speakers, more likely than not, are not providing the support that in Long's words 'cocoons' the learner.

In the type of interpretative or qualitative research in which we are engaged, we need to take account of three contexts:

(1) The context created as the interaction unfolds.
(2) The contexts of previous similar interactions.
(3) The wider social context of living as a member of a minority ethnic group.

We use the term context to encompass both what are frequently defined as 'linguistic' and 'social' contexts. With Fowler and Hodge (1979) we feel that to separate the terms out would be to imply that some language has no social import. Rather, we see language and society as parts of a dialectic process in which language both expresses but simultaneously constructs social systems and structures. As Halliday (1978) has said, language learning is:

> also a social process, the construal of reality is inseparable from the construal of the semantic system in which the reality is encoded.

These contexts, which are becoming increasingly refined through the work of ethnomethodologists and linguistic and social anthropologists, are continually working on each other in an interaction to produce a 'triangulation' (Cicourel, 1974) of interpretations which should help us to understand how interactions are successfully accomplished and to what extent their success or lack of it determines the overall tempo and order of the acquisition process.

The way in which context is mutually constructed in interaction (context one) has been explored in depth by a number of sociologists and sociolinguists – notably

Goffman (1974), Cicourel (1974), Gumperz (1982a) and Garfinkel (1967). The anthropologist, Frederick Erickson has provided a detailed analysis of the context of counselling interviews (1982). He explains how encounters 'have a life of their own':

> Encounters occur within a general social system, and social and cultural influences affect to some extent what happens within the encounters. But encounters also seem to have a life of their own. Persons in encounters are able to make choices among optional specific ways of acting from moment to moment to accomplish those courses of action. Choice is possible among various attributes of status to be attended to or ignored. One person's communicative choices from moment to moment constrain the choice of others, and in this sense single individuals are not the sole cause of what happens; social interaction both constitutes and is constituted by the circumstances of enactment. Individuals are part of an ecosystem when they engage one another in interaction. [p. 181]

Relating this to second language learners in an instrumental encounter raises such questions as:

> What strategies do you need to get the maximum useful information?
> How do learners negotiate comprehensible input?
> How is topic choice and topic control negotiated?
> How can learners be adversely affected by an 'ecosystem' dominated by the native speaker?

The second context, that of previous similar interactions, argues for a wide data base of interactions between minority ethnic workers and white staff in institutional settings. It is only by building up such a wide data base that we can see what is typical and systematic in interactions in which the minority ethnic worker seeks access to information and resources where there is a linguistic imbalance and different cultural assumptions. Many such interactions have been termed 'gatekeeping' encounters (Erickson, 1982). Although such encounters are highly differentiated, it seems from analysis, ethnographic observation and informant comments that they are perceived by minority ethnic workers as being very similar experiences. There is clear evidence from informants and from data in Britain that any encounter with a native speaker in a position of authority or identified as an official is perceived as an interrogation. Evidence from the French ESF team suggests that this may also be true of minority ethnic workers in France (Deulofeu and Taranger, 1984). The experience of each individual encounter feeds into the structured experiences that minority ethnic groups and the white majority group build up of each other. The white 'gatekeeper' brings to the encounter the ideology of the institution they represent. The minority ethnic client brings his or her experience of discrimination. The stereotypical notions brought to the encounter will be triggered or reinforced by the experience of each particular interaction. These experiences will be unique to the individual but they will also tend to form part of the structured experiences of the group to which the individual belongs. It is this combination of ethnography and analysis of naturally occurring data which extends the analyst's 'interpretative repertoire'.

The third context area, the wider social context, relates to these structured experiences. The socially disadvantaged position of minority ethnic workers has been widely described and the facts of discrimination against these groups documented.

We have argued, therefore, for a deepening of our understanding of how interactants create contexts by examining the notion of contexts at different levels. We have, further, suggested that an appropriate methodology must not only include the collection and analysis of data of naturally occurring situations but must also include an ethnography of the learner in which informants comment on their own interactions (self-confrontation) and are encouraged to talk about their experience of and attitudes towards language and interaction in British society.

The informants

The two informants studied here are from an Italian speaking background. Neither had had any exposure to English before arrival in this country. Over the previous two and a half years in the case of A and the last two in the case of S, the ESF project has provided an excellent opportunity to study the amount of contact each has had with the host society and target language.

Given that their reasons for coming to England were quite different – one came in order to maintain a longstanding relationship with his bilingual girlfriend, the other to break a drug addiction problem, the extent of their contact has been highly comparable.

S is by trade a cook, and found himself a job as cook's assistant in an Italian restaurant, where he worked for the duration of his time in the UK. The other workers in the restaurant were also non-native speakers of English and some of them were Italian so at work S had little chance to acquire English. He lived in a rented bed-sit in a house where there were some English people but one did not get the impression that S got to know them well. With his girlfriend he spoke mainly Italian, though he was able to ask her for help with the language when he needed it.

S has had, then, almost no social contact with English speaking people; his learning environment consisted mainly of bureaucratic encounters to do with the purchase and sale of cars and motorbikes, their registration here and a number of related issues. At one point he was considering setting up as an entrepreneur in order to export cars to Italy, but this plan foundered.

The monthly encounters in English with members of the project research team were from S's point of view an important part of the acquisition process. He referred to them as 'school' and although he never received any formal instruction from them, he seemed to think they were of considerable benefit to his English.

A, who trained in Italy as a radio technician and industrial electrician, also spent the first year working in an Italian restaurant as a washer-up and then as a barman. He shared a flat with an Italian friend in a house in which, again, there were no native speakers of English. Initially he attended English language classes for about six hours a week but his attendance was sporadic and he jettisoned the idea after about three months. After being interviewed for a year, A got a job in a small Swiss-owned bakery as an electrician. This work is closer to his own background but again provides him with little opportunity to speak English.

His contacts, then, like S's, have been mainly with institutions: companies where he has applied for jobs, the administration concerned with being a car owner, flat and estate agents, travel agents for holidays in Italy, and since the arrival of his wife and son a year ago, with schools, doctors, dentists etc. In one interview he said explicitly that he had no opportunity for social conversation outside the project.

The above reflects the reality of the statement that adult workers have to learn to communicate by communicating in order to learn. This process takes place in an indifferent and sometimes hostile social environment in which the learner has strong instrumental goals to achieve. In this sense the Italian workers we study here are typical of ethnic minorities in European society.

They are, from the outset, disenfranchised by their lack of the language which in turn leads to a loss of rights at work and in their private lives. We see here language performing the function of perpetuating the power structure and in turn being a product of these structures.[3]

Analysis

In this section we study the two encounters with the estate agent and the two conversations with researchers. We shall examine them from the point of view of the three contexts suggested above and what the learners may have learnt. In order to begin to answer the question 'How is language acquisition interactionally accomplished?' we shall look at:

(1) Presuppositions – which includes the wider social context and expectations of previous similar encounters.
(2) The context created by the interlocutors and the strategies used for conversational involvement.
(3) What the learners may have learnt.

Estate agent encounters

The informants were accompanied by a source language researcher and had been asked to make enquiries about available houses for sale in an estate agent's office. Neither S nor A were attempting to buy a house at the time of the data collection. However, both had considered it as a possibility for the future. A already had considerable experience in looking for rented accommodation through agencies and was likely to be familiar with much of the terminology of house descriptions.

Presuppositions

The estate agent's aim is to sell property and they earn a commission on each house sold. It is therefore in their interests to match house and client as accurately as possible from the outset of negotiations, since if a customer makes an offer for a property they have to estimate the reliability of the customer and assess the likelihood of their being able to get a mortgage by the right date, etc. In the first encounter, though, which is what is examined here, their aim is to ascertain the client's wishes and to provide him with details of suitable properties.

It is in the estate agent's interest to sell houses to customers but they do not want their time wasted with unrealistic demands. We may expect, therefore, a degree of co-operation from the native speaker but it is a provisional co-operation which is likely to need to be constantly negotiated or maintained. The estate agent clerk is there to provide a service but as in many gatekeeping encounters, assumptions about the client and lack of smoothness in the interaction may mean that 'the customer is not always right' (Perdue, 1986). For the SL speaker, experiences of dealing with officialdom may give rise to expectations about being interrogated. Similarly, any experience of workplace negotiating or information exchange with officials may have caused second language speakers to develop ways of stating their case which are in Brown and Levinson's term 'bald on record'. In other words, speaker perspective is more directly and explicitly conveyed than in most native speaker interactions. For example, 'This is very important to me.'[4]

Both S and A give very brief opening statements and then wait for the clerk to question them:

(1) *S* I want to buy a house
     A Yes er + I'd like to buy an house

In inter-ethnic advice interviews a similar strategy is also frequently used (Gumperz, personal communication): state very little and wait for the official to ask questions. Later in the encounter *S* uses a very personal negotiating style, making his point very explicitly:

(2) *S*   it's important for me two bedroom because have the + the brother and
           the sister (?uh?)
     EA (yeah I see) yeah
     S   is very important for me and er work in central London I work in the city
           + in Holborn

Such strategies in other 'gatekeeping' encounters have frequently either led to a deterioration in the overall emotional tone of the encounter or, in the case of the first strategy, the interaction remains dominated by the native speaker with little evidence of conversational co-operation. *S*'s and *A*'s interactions contrast in this respect. Although *S* brings some of the presuppositions to the encounter which can lead to imbalanced or unsatisfactory contact, he has a series of strategies to maintain conversational involvement which allow him to progress the conversation in the way he wants. *A*, by contrast, experiences a lop-sided encounter. We could sum up the differences by characterizing *S* as using initiating strategies and *A* reactive strategies.

It is important to state here that we are not necessarily characterizing these strategies as those used only by non-native speakers. Many of them may be used by native speakers. What is interesting here is the way in which *A*'s and *S*'s strategies create a particular type of encounter and so a particular type of learning environment for themselves.

Created context: strategies for conversational involvement

S uses three main strategies for both taking control of the topic and for collaborating topically. The interaction could have foreclosed around the eleventh turn when the clerk simply states that they have no houses at that price in the area. However, *S*, the optimist conversationalist, uses the first of several strategies to maintain conversational involvement. In doing so, he also creates an 'ecosystem' in which the clerk becomes customer-orientated, sensitive to his objections even before they are explicitly raised, as in examples (3), (4) and (5).

(3) *EA* you want a house though do you

(4) *EA* . . . I think you'd get a house there for about thirty five, forty thousand . . . but that's
   S   too long

(5) *EA* three bedrooms but erm + +
   S   ?but?
   EA but I don't/think you'd find it difficult
   S   ?for this price?
   EA yeah yeah especially three bedrooms + + you can take the list and have a look (but)
   S   (yeah yeah)
   EA I can't think of anything really

In all three examples the clerk explicitly acknowledges that *S* will not be happy with what she is offering. His strategy is to ask questions which will elicit expert information. He does this five times in the interaction and on each occasion it is when the interaction has reached a relative impasse and looks like closing. For example:

(6) *EA* I haven't got any houses around forty thousand for sale I dont think erm I'll give you our list
   S   ?yeah what you think?

(7) *EA* yeah but I think you'll find it very difficult to get at you/to get a three bedroomed house for forty thousand we just haven't got anything like that
   S   ?how much you think it cost for three bedroom?

His second strategy to maintain conversational involvement is to make general and impersonal comments which induce further comments and suggestions from the clerk. He does this on three occasions:

(8) *EA* then you might get one for about fifty or sixty + or say forty eight sixty something like that
   S   very expensive area anyway
   EA well this/this is expensive this is less expensive

(9) *EA* take you twenty five minutes I suppose twenty minutes twenty five minutes
   S   anyway for er forty thousand very complication

> *EA* (yeah you've got a) very difficult + erm even two bedroomed flats is not
> too easy now.
> (10) *EA* I can't think of anything really
> *S*   yeah
> *EA* that would be suitable
> *S*   yeah I know is not easy for found
> *EA* no no
> *S*   okay
> *EA* might be agents in Haringey they might have something

His third strategy is to give a personal view or explanation. For example 'Too long', 'I no like this area for me', 'for me plenty difficult'. But in each case his remark is either highly collaborative or mitigated for example with a laugh. The only occasion when this strategy fails him is when he talks about how important it is to have a large house because of his brother and sister. And at the end of the encounter when again he tries to justify his need by explaining that he will soon be joined by three people from Italy. Here *S* presents personal information as if it could be integrated into the clerk's advice-giving schema. However, on neither occasion does the clerk interpret the explanations as turn-offering opportunities when she can provide more information.

The estate agent's interview with *A* is an encounter dominated by the native speaker. The agent has the power to grant or withhold a service and he exercises this right by assuming the role of the one who initiates topics (75% of the topic movement originates from the agent) and who has the right to ask questions. The predominance of questions from the agent (14 out of a total of 19 are asked by him, excluding clarifictory questions) lend an almost interrogation-like quality to the interaction. It is the agent who raises all the important questions of price, area, site of house and facilities. *A*, however, collaborates with this lop-sidedness and in so doing, lends the encounter a superficial appearance of smoothness, despite the fact that this perpetuates the inequality in which he is the subordinate party.

This behaviour on his part has the advantage of allowing *A* to achieve short-term goals, i.e. to be given details of houses on the market but its long-term effects serve to reinforce his position as a disadvantaged ethnic minority worker.

The strategies he uses are essentially of a reactive nature and include:

(a) Waiting for the other to demand information rather than offering information oneself.
(b) Developing only those themes which the estate agent has already implicitly sanctioned by having introduced them, i.e. essentially an elaborative rather than innovative approach.
(c) Omitting any affective response to information which has a negative bearing on *A*'s wishes.

One might initially assume that this could be defined as avoidance behaviour (cf. Faerch and Kasper, 1983) but this would imply that *A* has in fact changed goals. In none of these examples do we find evidence of this, nor of a 'change of plan' which would imply that *A*'s strategies were evidence of 'achievement behaviour' (*ibid*). Instead, *A* seems from the outset to have set himself a responsive rather than initiatory agenda, and this certainly leads to his short-term goals being successfully achieved.

We examine each of the above in turn.

(a) The receptive strategy or 'only speak when spoken to'

A's opening statement (see (1) above) does no more than give a minimal response to the estate agent's query about what *A* wants.

In this extract, one might well have expected *A* to expand upon his wishes in line 006 but he does not until explicitly called upon to do so:

(11) 003   *EA*   ?can I help you?
     004   *A*   yes er + I'd like to buy an house
     005   *EA*   yes
     006   *A*   yes
     007   *EA*   ?up to what price?
     008   *A*   about er + thirty thousand pounds

Similarly, later, he has expressed a wish to find a two-bedroomed flat, but does not object to the information that an apartment under discussion only has one. He leaves it to the estate agent to imply this:

(12) 033   *EA*   Blackstock Road er er that's a one bedroomed flat
     034   *A*   yeah
     035   *EA*   its not two bedrooms
     036   *A*   mhm

(b) The elaborative approach

Perhaps one of the reasons for the apparent harmony of this encounter is to be found in the way in which *A* develops conversational involvement by using the agent's information to move the encounter forward. For example, when, near the start of the encounter, the estate agent says there are no houses available, *A* counters with:

012   *A*   ?what about the flat?

a question which produces a lot of information about flats in the right price bracket.

Later, too, *A* responds and invites further contribution on the topic the agent has initiated:

(13) 027   *EA*   there's a very nice one we've got
                  + twenty-six nine-fifty + in Whiteman Road + +
     028   *A*   ?its a ground floor?
     029   *EA*   ground floor flat yes

One notes, though that *A*'s response in line 028 only comes at the third of the possible turn transition points and then only after a longer pause as if to make absolutely sure that he has the right to speak.

Both these examples are evidence of familiarity of the conventions of such an encounter, based presumably on previous experience. The clearest example of such co-operation occurs when the agent asks for *A*'s address:

(14) 060   *EA*   ?and your address?
     061   *A*   is ninety eight
     062   *EA*   ninety eight
     063   *A*   Maple Grove
     064   *EA*   + + Maple Grove ?and that's?
     065   *A*   NW 12
     066   *EA*   ?is there a phone number?
     067   *A*   yeah <gives number>

(c) Omission of affective response

We mention this particular feature of the interaction mainly by way of contrasting it with *S*'s strategies. *A*'s real needs to have two bedrooms, for example, are just as pressing as *S*'s, but he does not bring his own perspective explicitly into the encounter in the same way. This certainly contributes to smoothness of the interaction but does not necessarily gain the sympathy of the agent.

What the learners may have learnt

S has negotiated:

   (i) the information he needs;
   (ii) considerable recycling of the same information.

He has also been exposed to a language teacher's dream lesson on modals and politeness markers, 'You might perhaps', 'I think' etc.

Interestingly, during the course of the interaction *S* uses 'I think' twice and complex utterances such as 'I know is not easy' and 'how much you think it cost for three bedroom?' This may be an example of the acquisition process in which second-language speakers 'take up the other's words' (Mittner, 1984) and start appropriating these words themselves.

More significantly, this interaction is characterized by none of the features of misunderstanding and stress in unequal encounters which so frequently cause minority ethnic workers to seek to avoid such encounters and so limit further the opportunities for contact with native speakers. Although *S* opens the conversation in a way which is likely to lead to an unequal encounter, with the clerk questioning him, he rapidly establishes topic control and strategies for maintaining conversational involvement. In this respect, his performance contrasts quite dramatically with all the other informants in the project.

When we come to look at *A*'s encounter with the estate agent, quite a different pattern emerges. *A*'s strategies for negotiation are characterized by keeping a low profile. Unlike *S*, he does nothing to put himself on a more equal footing with the agent and is content to leave initiatives with him. As a result, *A* comes away with the service he required – in minimal terms – but he has achieved this by allowing the dominance described above to continue.

From this interview, then, *A* may well draw the conclusion that the native speaker can be relied upon to carry an interaction forward. This reliance naturally puts the L1 speaker in the position of being the person who provides the lexis and who will pick up on any lack of clarity in the informant's production.

It would seem from what *A* has said elsewhere that this kind of behaviour is consistent for him and so, given that his learning takes place mainly in interactions, what he learns is to a great extent dependent on what is offered, not what he himself demands.

Conversations

Presuppositions

Conversation is, by its very nature, not usually propelled forward in the same way that a strongly goal-orientated interaction such as the interview in the estate agent's office is. The participants' expectations of topics to be covered, and their goals in a more instrumentally guided interaction as in the latter case are more clearly defined and carry the interaction forward on a more clearly defined course.

Neither *S* nor *A* have had much opportunity for social conversation outside the project. *A* even stated at one point that he hardly had to talk English at all apart from in the project interviews. By the time these data were collected regular sessions with the researchers had established a basis of confidence and trust and the informants looked to the conversation sessions as an opportunity to get advice on practical issues and obviously considered that they had some pedagogic value. *S*, for example, actually referred to data collection sessions as 'school'. But he also used these meetings as a relaxed occasion at which to talk about himself in English.

Created context: strategies for conversational involvement

The conversation between *A* and the researcher is characterized by the unpatterned and unhurried nature of the interaction which should create an environment in which relaxed learning is possible.

This environment is created by the native speaker still remaining in control of the interaction by means of topic initiation. Each of the five main subject areas of the conversation are raised by her. In contrast, though, to the estate agent encounter, *A* is actively encouraged to contribute in this supportive encounter. This happens in the following way:

Once the topic has been introduced, the researcher on several occasions explicitly invites *A* to collaborate and expand an item as in the following extract where *A* is responding to a question:

(15) *A*   the job is about the maintenance of the + whole electrical parts of er +
the houses
　　M   uhuh so its within houses it's + it's not er + ?It'll be wiring and things
like that will it?
　　A   yes
　　M   right
　　A   to to check <the> wiring − <drawn out>

A further strategy the native speaker employs to encourage contributions from *A*
is to forego turns in a way that almost amounts to a flout of conversational rules as
in this example:

(16) *A*   to to check <the> wiring – <drawn out>
　　M   yes
　　A   and er to repair + and er + * <ma>* – <= but>
well now I don't remember very well
　　M   mm mm

Here the interviewer allows two pauses within *A*'s utterances and two which she fills
with feedback sounds but she does not actively take up the turn as she probably
would with a native speaker. This indicates a far greater tolerance of hesitation and
allowance for slower delivery, possible lexical search etc.

Thus, in some respects, the turn-taking in the conversation appears to be far less
smooth than in the estate agent's interview where there is little or no hesitation
between turns and where each of *A*'s responses is capped almost immediately by a
fresh question.

The estate agent, of course, also invited elaboration of *A*'s original request.

'*I*'d like to buy a house.'

It is the manner in which this takes place that is so different. There is much more
of the 'machine gun' style of talking (cf. Tannen, 1981) in his behaviour than in the
researcher's.

Peter Sayers has pointed out that the style of interacting used by the researcher
may not be 'good conversation' in any normative way but it may be closer to the
type of interaction used by counsellors in counselling sessions.

A final feature of the native speaker's behaviour in the conversation which merits
examination is one of relexicalization of the informant's speech. On several occasions,
A's words are either paraphrased or given a more accurate synonym as in the
following cases:

'electrical parts' is relexicalized as 'wiring',
'jobs around the central heating' as 'repairing in the power circuit',
'the carpet er the + pavement' becomes 'floorboards' and 'welled' becomes
'willing'.

These phrases introduced by the native speaker interlocutor are then usually appro-
priated by the informant and integrated into his repertoire.

Such overtly pedagogic behaviour on the researcher's part, supportive though it is, in its own way casts *A* in a subordinate role. Nevertheless, the fact that *A* has in most cases signalled his uncertainty of the lexis means that these paraphrases are a response to a request for help. By contrast, in the estate agent's office, no relexicalization is provided. It is not necessary, and *A* does not imply that he needs help. This is perhaps because he has no need, or possibly because he feels he cannot ask for help.

S, in his conversation with two researchers, one a native English speaker and one a native Italian speaker, talks about a typical day for him – 'this is my life'. He describes how he often plays cards with his friends and they talk about their hopes for the future. He is thinking of setting up a business in Italy where his brother runs a hairdresser's shop.

In this interaction he creates a very different 'ecosystem' from the one in the estate agent's. In the conversation which lasts more than seven minutes, he holds the floor entirely except for one request for clarification and one summing up comment, respectively, from each of the two interactants. His utterances are marked by many of the features of unplanned discourse (Tarone, 1983; Ochs, 1979) identified in other SL learners. He relies heavily on such universal discourse principles such as: things happen in the sequence in which they are told unless marked otherwise. He also code-switches freely into Italian for many connectives, discourse markers and occasionally for specific lexical items.

He is listened to, attended to, with his interlocutors providing appropriate feedback and only once checking his meaning throughout the conversation. The only occasion on which the smooth flow of *S*'s conversation is disrupted, is when one of the interlocutors uses a typical native-speaker strategy to show conversational co-operation. At an obvious turn-transition point, she comments:

(17) *E*   so while you play cards you discuss + business
         I see <laughs>
     S   ? I play?

This kind of summarizing and commenting rolled into one often marks smooth native-speaker conversation but causes awkward moments, disjuncture or interruption in native/non-native speaker interaction. In fact, it is as if *S* neither required nor expected anything more than minimal feedback such as 'mm' and 'yes' and found anything more, disruptive.

What the learner may have learnt

The conversation provides *A* with an opportunity to take time, search for grammatical and lexical items which, if he does not provide them, the researcher provides. Here, he learns a good deal of lexis, possibly grammar, but is not forced to become a better communicator in interactive terms.

It is difficult to assess what *S* learnt from this interaction with the two researchers. It certainly provided him with an opportunity to talk freely and in a relaxed way without 'let or hindrance'. And it is important that all adult acquirers have this opportunity. He does check from time to time that his listeners are with him:

(18) *S*   go in the house the my friends for coffee play the cart speak ?no? the money the job

However, he does not explicitly seek help when searching for a lexical item but code-switches into Italian. We could, broadly, say from the two contexts described here that in Canale's (1983b) terms he has a high level of sociolinguistic and strategic competence for the particular contexts of each interaction, but does not attend very much to his discourse and grammatical competence. In this he is quite typical of a number of long resident minority ethnic workers who are fluent but inaccurate, and his competence is very similar to the Japanese learner, Wes, studied by Schmidt (1983).

Conclusion

In this paper we have begun to explore the notion of context in the particular circumstances of minority ethnic workers acquiring a second language. We are interested in them both as learners and as minority ethnic workers having to get things done and negotiate a less disadvantaged social identity for themselves. We are also interested, as our three levels of contexts suggests, with short-term goals (Did they get what they wanted? Did they learn anything specific from the encounter?) and longer-term goals (How will this encounter affect motivation, interactional knowledge and how they are perceived by the majority community?).

A good example of the tension between short-term and long-term goals is *A*'s encounter with the estate agent. The interaction proceeds smoothly but it is unlikely that the identity of minority ethnic workers as being in some way socially more inferior or less competent has been challenged. In a sense, they both collude in making this an unequal encounter. So *A* may acquire interactional knowledge (and some useful knowledge of the world) and indeed he may have chosen to take on the role of receiver of information. But if it was not a conscious choice or if he continues to present only this face in institutional encounters, then he will only acquire the kind of interactional knowledge which is likely to maintain his disadvantaged position in society. By contrast, the conversation creates an active learning environment for him.

Different learners, it seems, develop different competences and need different contexts for further development. *A* has a wider vocabulary than *S* and the conversation described here captures some of the learning processes he uses. *S*'s lexical repertoire is much more limited but his strategic and sociolinguistic competence help him to negotiate a more equal relationship in gatekeeping encounters. *S* develops his strategies through such encounters, but would benefit from the kind of pedagogic conversations that *A* helps to create. *A*'s talks with strangers are not unsuccessful but he could benefit from learning from second language speakers like *S* how a more equal relationship could be interactionally accomplished.

Notes

1. In this paper we use minority ethnic workers and second language speakers interchangeably. The purpose is to remind the readers that the groups with whom we are working are doubly disadvantaged in British society.
2. For a full description of the ESF project, including a rationale for the research and detailed descriptions of the key areas of investigation see: *Second Language Acquisition by Adult Immigrants, A Field Manual* edited by Clive Perdue. Newbury House Publishers, 1984.
3. For a full discussion of how language works as an invisible agent for maintaining power structure see: *Critical & Descriptive Goals in Discourse Analysis* by Norman Fairclough. Lancaster Papers in Linguistics no. 1. To appear in *Journal of Pragmatics* 9, Summer, 1985.
4. The appeal to the personal may, in fact, be directly related to inequality in interaction and not necessarily to native/non-native interacting. Exploratory work on female/male discourse suggests that women use more personal argument in an unequal encounter – negotiating with a male boss – than in an all-female meeting of equals. (*Humanistic Approaches to Improving Communication between Men and Women*. Linguistic Society of America Workshop, Georgetown University, July 1985.)

The Notion of 'Competence' and the Patois Speaker

VIV EDWARDS

VIV EDWARDS

Department of Applied Linguistics, Birkbeck College

Introduction

Important changes have taken place within the West Indian community in the last ten years which are reflected in the speech patterns to be found in this community. The 1950s and 1960s were decades in which new arrivals formed a large proportion of the Afro-Caribbean population. Legislation enacted during the 1960s, however, had the effect of reducing immigration to a trickle. By 1975 virtually all black children entering school had been born in Britain. Whereas older siblings and cousins belonged to a generation which included both British and Caribbean born children, those born from 1970 onwards could have very little contact with recent arrivals from the West Indies. The black community remains extremely heterogeneous, drawing as it does on both British born and Caribbean born people from many different territories. Yet it is important to recognize that the current generation of children and adolescents marks the transition from 'West Indian' to 'British black' and all that this entails.

Throughout the 1960s and early 1970s the main focus in education was the continuing influence of 'Patois', the most common community term for distinctively Caribbean speech. Children had been expected in the early days of migration to adjust rapidly to British English but reports of Patois influence on speech, reading and writing were common. It was against this background that the present research project was conceived. (1) Some 45 British born black people between the ages of 16 and 23 were recorded in Dudley, West Midlands, in the summer of 1983. We drew on approximately equal numbers of men and women, and in all cases their parents had come from Jamaica. The young people were recorded in friendship groups in a variety of situations: in a formal interview with a white researcher; in a formal interview with a black researcher; in informal racially-mixed conversation; in informal black conversation; and on their own, without the presence of a researcher. In this way we succeeded in sampling a wide range of speech from extremely formal to extremely informal. We were also able to monitor the effect of the ethnic composition of the group on speech patterns.

We considered three different linguistic measures: the overall frequency of Patois features (Edwards, 1986); the different patterns of Patois usage (Edwards, 1985); and the various levels of competence in Patois which existed within the sample. For the purposes of the present paper, I will focus on the last of these three measures.

A note on 'competence'

The language behaviour of British black people appears to differ from that of West Indians in a number of important ways. There are strong indications, for instance, that the British black situation is closer to that of a bilingual community than to the post-creole community which operates in the Caribbean (cf. De Camp, 1971). In a British context we are dealing with polar varieties far further removed from one another than the basilectal and acrolectal varieties (or broad Patois and standard) which characterize Caribbean speech. 'Patois' and 'English' in a British context differ systematically not only in segmental phonology, but also in aspects of voice set, such as pitch, tempo, loudness and timbre. Grammatical differences are also more clearly demarcated in a British setting: although the 'mesolectal' or intermediate forms which cannot unambiguously be assigned either to the basilectal or to the standard do occur, there is a strong preference in British black speakers for basilectal forms (cf. Wright, 1984; Edwards, 1986).

The argument for treating the British Black community as bilingual would appear to be strengthened by the prevalence of the code-switching behaviour which characterizes stable bilingual communities world wide. With very few exceptions, recognizably British black speech does not entail the sustained use of Patois features of phonology and grammar, but rather the variable use of such features as part of code-switching behaviour.

In the present discussion we are concerned with intra-individual differences in the ability to use Patois as part of this code-switching behaviour and the word which most readily comes to mind for this phenomenon is 'competence'. This non-technical use of competence clearly departs from the Chomskyan definition which has caused increasing frustration among linguists working with variable language data over the years. Hymes (1979:41) sums up the dissatisfaction of many in this field thus:

> The abilities of individuals are both more and less than was implied by Chomsky's notion: more in that they comprise more than grammar, often more than a single variety or indeed language; less, in that it is in the nature of the social division of labor and the contingency of experience that the systematic potential of the language as a whole exceeds the command of any one person. It seems to me desirable to reinstitute the term 'competence' in the study of individual differences.

The use of competence in the present discussion should therefore be understood as referring to individual language abilities, and not to the Chomskyan competence/performance dichotomy.

Patois competence scale

The speakers in the study behaved in a variety of ways. Some used Patois to some extent in all situations, others only in conversation with other Black people and still others only in the privacy of conversation with friends. In considering the question of language abilities, however, we are concerned with *whether* and not *how often* or *in which situations* a Patois feature is used. An inventory of twenty of the most common features of Patois (see Appendix A) was constructed, and each speaker assigned one point for each feature which was found on at least one occasion during recording.

Competence scores varied between 12 and 20, and speakers' own comments showed a keen awareness of the range of Patois competence which is to be found in the

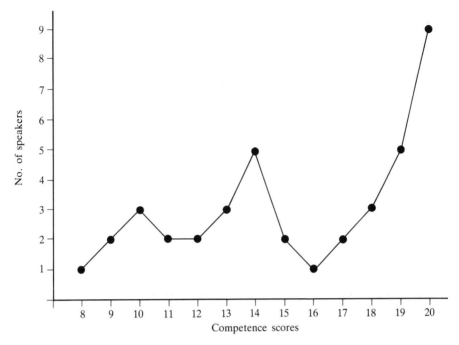

FIGURE 1   *Distribution of competence scores*

British Black community. Estimates of community usage were high, although there was also acknowledgement of young people who could not – or would not – speak Patois. Speakers also discussed their own personal competence in Patois. Some young people explained that they were not comfortable in English, while others lamented their limited proficiency in Patois. However, all claimed to speak Patois 'often' or 'sometimes'.

When the Patois features are arranged from most to least frequently occurring along the horizontal axis and the speakers from highest to lowest scorers along the vertical axis, some very interesting patterns emerge which can be seen in Table 1 on the following page. First, all of the speakers used certain Patois features at some point during recording, although the extent of this Patois competence varies considerably from speaker to speaker. Approximately one-third of the young people emerge (see section A) as highly competent Patois speakers using the whole range of features making up the competence scale. In the region of a quarter of the sample (see section C), in contrast, use very few Patois features and can only be described as having limited competence in Patois. The remaining speakers (see section B) are distributed between these two poles.

Equally striking, these Patois features are not distributed at random amongst the speakers. Preliminary analysis suggested that they might be broken into three bands. One band (section 1) consists of those features which are found in the speech of all the young people in the sample; another band (section 3) contains only those features found in highly competent speakers; and a third (section 2) is made up of the features

TABLE 1
Patois Competence Scale

Group	speaker nos.	dentals	/o/	3rd person present -s	plurals	simple past	mi	im	dem	do + neg	adjectival verbs	focus	questions	infinitives	continuatives	other pronouns	locating verb	'-dem' plurals	psychic state verbs	equating verb	past marker
A	43	X	X	X	X	X	X	X	X	X	X	X	X	X	X	X	X	X	X	X	X
	44	X	X	X	X	X	X	X	X	X	X	X	X	X	X	X	X	X	X	X	X
	40	X	X	X	X	X	X	X	X	X	X	X	X	X	X	X	X	X	X	X	X
	34	X	X	X	X	X	X	X	X	X	X	X	X	X	X	X	X	X	X		X
	11	X	X	X	X	X	X	X	X	X	X	X	X	X	X	X	X	X	X		X
	15	X	X	X	X	X	X	X	X	X	X	X		X	X	X	X	X	X	X	X
	41	X	X	X	X	X	X	X	X	X	X	X	X	X	X	X	X	X	X	X	X
	33	X	X	X	X	X	X	X	X	X	X	X	X	X	X	X	X	X	X	X	X
	16	X	X	X	X	X	X	X	X	X	X	X	X	X	X	X	X	X	X	X	X
	23	X	X	X	X	X	X	X	X	X	X	X		X	X	X	X	X	X	X	X
	29	X	X	X	X	X	X	X	X	X	X		X	X	X	X	X	X	X	X	X
	18	X	X	X	X	X	X	X	X	X	X	X	X	X	X	X	X	X	X	X	X
	4	X	X	X	X	X	X	X	X	X	X		X	X	X	X	X	X	X	X	X
	12	X	X	X	X	X	X	X	X	X	X	X		X	X	X	X	X	X	X	X
	24	X	X	X	X	X	X	X	X	X	X	X	X	X				X	X	X	X
B	31	X	X	X	X	X	X	X	X	X	X	X	X	X	X	X	X			X	
	7	X	X	X	X	X	X	X	X	X	X	X	X	X	X	X			X	X	
	13	X	X	X	X	X	X	X	X	X	X	X	X	X	X	X		X	X		
	32	X	X	X	X	X	X	X	X	X	X	X	X	X	X	X		X	X		
	45	X	X	X	X	X	X	X	X	X	X	X	X	X	X	X	X	X	X		
	28	X	X	X	X	X	X	X	X	X	X	X	X	X	X	X	X		X		
	6	X	X	X	X	X	X		X	X	X	X		X	X	X	X	X			
	10	X	X	X	X	X	X	X	X	X	X	X			X	X	X				
	14	X	X	X	X	X	X	X	X	X	X	X	X		X	X		X			
	42	X	X	X	X	X	X	X	X	X	X	X	X	X	X	X		X			
	19	X	X	X	X	X			X	X	X	X	X	X	X	X					
	1	X	X	X	X	X		X	X	X	X	X		X	X	X			X		
	9	X	X	X	X	X		X	X	X	X	X		X	X	X	X				
	3	X	X	X	X	X		X	X	X	X	X	X		X	X				X	
	2	X	X	X	X	X		X		X	X		X		X				X	X	
	8	X	X	X	X	X	X	X	X	X	X	X	X	X	X						
C	26	X	X	X	X	X	X	X	X	X	X				X	X		X			
	17	X	X	X	X	X	X	X	X						X	X		X			
	26	X	X	X	X	X	X	X	X		X		X		X			X			
	38	X	X	X	X	X	X	X	X		X	X	X	X							
	30	X	X	X	X	X	X	X	X	X	X	X		X							
	35	X	X	X	X	X	X		X		X	X	X				X		X		
	20	X	X	X	X	X	X		X										X		X
	21	X	X	X	X	X	X	X	X		X			X							
	27	X	X	X	X	X	X	X	X	X	X										
	36	X	X	X	X	X	X	X	X		X					X					
	39	X	X	X	X	X	X	X	X	X											
	37	X	X	X	X	X	X								X	X					

| | | 1 | | | | | | | 2 | | | | | | | | 3 | | | | | |

found in the speech of proficient and intermediate speakers. It thus seems reasonable to assume that empty cells in blocks A2, A3 and B3 can be attributed to shortage of speech data, whereas empty cells elsewhere reflect patterns which exist in the poplation as a whole.

The parallel between these British black speakers and second language learners is clear. Some of the features included in the competence scale such as *seh* after psychic state transitive verbs and the use of *did* as a past tense marker are more variable than others. By the same token, certain young people, such as speaker number 20, show more idiosyncratic variation than others. Nonetheless there can be little doubt that Patois competence is achieved by the acquisition of groups of features rather than by one feature at a time, and that there is a definite order to this acquisition.

Language acquisition order

This possibility was explored further by using the Ordering–Theoretic method first developed by Bart and Krus (1973) and applied to the study of acquisition in second language learning by Dulay, Burt and associates (e.g. Dulay, Burt and Krashen, 1982) on the present data. Each feature was assigned a value of 1 if the speaker had acquired it and 0 if it had not been acquired. All structures were then ordered in relation to one another, giving four possible patterns:

1.1 Both structures have been acquired
1.0 The first named structure has been acquired, the second has not
0.1 The first named structure has not been acquired; the second structure has been acquired.
0.0 Neither structure has been acquired.

The hierarchy is determined by establishing which pairs of features consistently show the 1.0 pattern across speakers. The proportion of 'disconfirming' patterns with a 0.1 pattern is calculated for a given pair of structures, and one construction is said to precede another if 5 per cent or fewer disconfirming cases are found. Two structures are considered to form an unordered pair when they show only a small percentage (usually seven per cent or less) of disconfirming cases in *both* directions; or when there are seven per cent or less disconfirming cases in one direction and the proportion of disconfirming cases in the opposite direction is not twice as large.

Table 2 below displays the ordering relationships obtained on applying the Bart and Krus methodology to the data. The resultant Stair Matrix confirms the impressions of the Patois Competence Scale of Table 1: Patois features are not distributed at random, but are acquired in a set order across a population of speakers. The Stair Matrix is able to differentiate more finely between the various features which make up the Patois Competence Scale, so that we find six acquisitional groups rather than

TABLE 2
Stair matrix for the Patois data

	dentals	/o/	3rd person present -s	plurals	simple past	mi	im	dem	do + neg	adjectival verbs	continuatives	focus	questions	infinitives	other pronouns	psychic state verbs	'-dem' plurals	locating verb	equating verb	past marker
dentals						+	+	+	+	+	+	+	+	+	+	+	+	+	+	+
/o/						+	+	+	+	+	+	+	+	+	+	+	+	+	+	+
3rd person present -s						+	+	+	+	+	+	+	+	+	+	+	+	+	+	+
plurals						+	+	+	+	+	+	+	+	+	+	+	+	+	+	+
simple past						+	+	+	+	+		+	+	+	+	+	+	+	+	+
mi						+	+	+	+	+		+	+	+	+	+	+	+	+	+
im												+	+	+	+	+	+	+	+	+
dem												+	+	+	+	+	+	+	+	+
do + neg												+	+	+	+	+	+	+	+	+
adjectival verbs												+	+	+	+	+	+	+	+	+
continuatives												+	+	+	+	+	+	+	+	+
focus																+	+	+	+	+
questions																(7)	+	+	+	+
infinitives																			+	+
other pronouns																			+	+
psychic state verbs																			+	+
'-dem' plurals																			(7)	+
locating verb																			(7)	+
equating verb																				
past marker																				

+ denotes 5% or fewer disconfirming cases
7 denotes 7% disconfirming cases

the three broad bands of features which emerge in Table 1. The first band corresponds to the first of the acquisitional groups in the Stair Matrix, whereas the other two bands can each be subdivided into two further groups.

Competence and social network

The present speakers all share the experience of having been born and lived in Britain all their lives. Their individual responses to this experience, however, are necessarily very different. The young people on whom the study is based come from a wide range of educational backgrounds. Some went to schools for the educationally sub-normal; others have O and A-levels; one young man is a student at a Polytechnic. Some left schools without any qualifications and have no plans for further training; others are studying at evening classes or are on full-time 'Access' courses which may enable them to go on to higher education.

Similarly, the young peoples' attitudes towards mainstream white society vary enormously. Although they all tended to be highly critical of the police and media treatment of black people, their views on other points of contact between black people and mainstream white society, such as schools and teachers, ranged from extremely hostile to uncritical.

The social network relationships of the young people were also very different. Some of the speakers had grown up on a council estate where there were very few black people, and had attended a school which was overwhelmingly white. Others lived in an area of extremely dense ethnic minority settlement, and had gone to schools where there was a high proportion of black pupils. A particularly important factor in determining the social networks of the young people was whether or not they were in employment. All speakers reported that at least two of their three closest friends were black. Those who were unemployed were thus very likely to spend their time in the company of other unemployed black friends, whereas those who had jobs generally found themselves in a minority position in the work place and had far more social contact with white people.

Finally, the sex of speaker is another potentially important variable, but a close examination of the composition of the sample makes it clear that it is unlikely to exert a statistically significant effect on Patois speech independently of the other variables considered. Although there was an excellent spread of academic achievement for both males and females, the females were concentrated among the high achievers and the males among the underperformers, thus reflecting trends which have been reported for black students elsewhere (cf. Driver, 1980). The same spread was found in attitudes towards mainstream white society, but, again, female speakers were concentrated among the least hostile and male speakers among the most hostile. Similarly, although there were many young women with dense black social networks and many young men with diffuse networks, male networks tended to be denser than female ones.

Of all the background variables which were considered, only social network was found to have a statistically significant effect on Patois competence (significance level: < 0.1). The 'blacker' the social relations of the speakers, the greater their competence in Patois was likely to be. This finding must surely go a long way in dispelling the popular stereotype of the typical Patois speaker as an angry, male underachiever. The sample included various young people who had done well in school and felt reasonably positive about life in a predominantly white society but were perfectly competent Patois speakers. It also included a number of young women who fell in this same category.

Discussion

It would seem that the rather confused picture of the current state of Patois usage in Britain can be attributed mainly to the failure to ask pertinent questions. For the greatest part, researchers have sought to determine how many young people use Patois, without any real appreciation of what precisely is involved in speaking Patois. If we define Patois in terms of the usage of certain marked features such as uninflected nouns and verbs (all di *book*; John *walk* home) then the present study would suggest that all young British black people speak Patois on at least some occasions. If, however, we decide that Patois speakers need to be able to use the full range of features normally associated with West Indian speech, then only a third of the young people we recorded would fall into this category.

The most important factor in deciding what constitutes Patois usage must surely be the symbolic function of recognizably black speech features. Close examination of the ways in which young British blacks use these features leaves no doubt that they signal group solidarity and assertion of the speakers' black identity or wish to identify with black people (Hewitt, 1982; Edwards, 1985). These ends can be achieved just as effectively by the use of a small number of Patois features as they can by the use of the full range. For this reason, it seems reasonable to define the Patois speaker as anyone who uses distinctively black features, irrespective of the range.

The preference for the broader rather than the narrower definition of Patois speech should not detract, however, from the fact that language abilities in Patois within the British black community are highly variable. Patois competence was found to be very closely related with the social networks of the speakers in the present study, in such a way that those whose networks included most black people were also the most competent Patois speakers.

The picture which emerges thus challenges conventional wisdom in a number of important respects and raises various questions about the acquisition of this variable competence. Many people assume, for instance, that there is a simple split between home and school, whereby Patois is used in family situations and 'English' elsewhere. Neither the speech recorded in the present study nor young black people's own accounts of their language use lend any weight to this position. While it is acceptable for older people to use Patois to their juniors there is a strong expectation that younger people should reply in English. Speakers frequently reported their parents' prescriptive attitude towards Patois usage, and sometimes showed considerable amusement at what they perceived to be parental inconsistency.

> Dem shout if we talk dis kind of Patois language. Dey say, 'Listen to dem how dem talk bad'. A night den she was watching television . . . 'But una can't turn di television up pon di other side, na?' And den we turn back to her and says, 'Look who's talking!' Den she start saying, 'Well, then, that's where we grew up, dat's where we learn fi talk'. I say, 'We kids pick it up from you, so what's wrong with that?

Exposure to Patois in the home will almost certainly ensure a receptive competence (cf. Troike, 1967) on the part of British black speakers. The opportunities of young people to actually use Patois, however, will vary enormously according to their individual circumstances. Those who associate mainly or exclusively with other black people will clearly have more opportunity to develop their productive skills than those who live, work and socialize with a high proportion of white people. While the frequency with which British black speakers use Patois is related to factors such as education and attitudes towards mainstream white society (Edwards, 1986), levels of competence are not. Some of the most competent Patois speakers in the present sample had performed well at school and were relatively uncritical of the dominant white society.

The different patterns of features which occur in young black peoples' speech suggest that many young black people are behaving essentially as second language learners. It seems likely that Patois is acquired in a range of different ways within the British black community. Some speakers would seem to learn Patois in infancy and maintain their proficiency into adolescence and adulthood. Others appear to learn Patois in infancy, lose this facility in childhood and selectively reacquire it in adolescence. Since the present study deals only with speakers in the 16–23 age range, this position can only be speculative and a great deal more work clearly remains to be done.

Note

1. The present paper is based on work undertaken as part of the Economic and Social Research Council funded project, 'Patterns of Language Use in a British Black Community'.

Appendix A: Patois features in the competence scale

1. *Dentals*
   /t.d/, e.g./tik, dat/ – thick, that
2. *Vowels*
   /o/, e.g./fon/ – fun
3. *Third person singular present tense verbs*
   John *swim* fast, Kevin *eat* a lot
4. *Plurals*
   six *car*
5. *Simple past tense*
   Winston *see* di boy; Beverley *walk* away
6. *First person singular pronoun*
   mi feel happy
7. *Third person singular pronouns*
   im put im coat away
8. *Third person plural pronouns*
   dem like di baby; look at *dem* hat
9. *Negatives*
   Di boy *no* see it – the boy doesn't see it
10. *Adjectival verbs*
    Di man *happy* – the man is happy
11. *Continuatives*
    John *a* come – John is coming
12. *Focus*
    A John do it – *John* did it/it was John who did it
13. *Questions*
    Mary *a* go home? – Is Mary going home?
    Harvey see di man? – Did Harvey see the man?
14. *Infinitives*
    John aks *fi* see it – John asked to see it
15. *Other pronouns*
    Unu want it – you (plural) want it
    Give me *fi-dem* book – give me their books
16. *Psychic state transitive verbs*
    Tony tell me *seh* im no know – Tony told me he didn't know
17. *'-dem' plurals*
    Give me di book – *dem*
18. *Locating verb*
    Mary *deh* a yaad – Mary is at home

19. *Equating verb*
   Patrick *a* di winner – Patrick is the winner
20. *Past markers*
   Roy did ready in di morning – Roy was getting ready in the morning

Section Five:

VARIABILITY AND PEDAGOGIC ISSUES

In this section we will look at a number of pedagogic issues from the perspective provided by research into SLA variability. We are concerned therefore, with the contribution which this branch of SLA research can make to language teaching and testing.

Not all researchers feel ready to apply the results of SLA research. Many feel that the research which has taken place to date does not provide us with either a full enough description of what happens during SLA nor with clear-out explanations of how it happens. There is no generally agreed theory of SLA which can be used as a basis for pedagogic prescriptions. Some researchers, therefore, recommend caution. They point out that much more research needs to take place in order to establish to what extent the findings already available are generalizable to other contexts. Other researchers, however, have not been so reticent; they have felt able to make recommendations about both *what* should be taught and *how* it should be taught. In particular, Krashen (1981) has used his understanding of SLA research to identify what he refers to as 'the fundamental fact' of language pedagogy (namely, that successful classroom acquisition will take place if there is plenty of comprehensible input which the learners are disposed to attend to).

We are aware of the dangers of premature attempts to implement the findings of SLA research. We believe, however, that there is less danger of the advice researchers provide leading to a bandwagon effect than some researchers believe. Teachers in our experience have a healthy scepticism regarding what researchers can do for them. Their teaching is based on tradition and practical experience in the classroom; teachers tend to teach as they were taught and to rely on what has worked for them in the past in their different teaching situations. Confronted with new ideas, teachers may or may not choose to act on them. If they do, it will be to try them out in their teaching. The extent to which the ideas become incorporated into teachers' daily practice will have less to do with whether they are based on sound research than with whether they work with their students. We would argue that this is exactly as it should be.

There is another reason why SLA researchers should be prepared to apply their findings now rather than later. It is a mistake to believe that a point will be reached some time in the future when a generally agreed theory of SLA, based on substantial and solid research will become available. Theory-construction is a never-ending affair. At each stage of development new hypotheses will be projected to be either incorporated or rejected in the light of the available evidence. There is no final-state theory. Who is to decide when a theory is powerful enough to warrant applications? How will this be decided? Even more to the point, we should not expect that SLA research will ever lead to the evolution of a *single* theory. Instead we should anticipate

159

that the current position, where multiple theories, models, frameworks and principles compete for attention, will be maintained. Applying the results of SLA research, therefore means examining how the various aspects of language teaching might be made more relevant and efficient by attending to what we know, at any point in time, about how learners learn a language. It also means being prepared to undertake this using the multiple perspectives provided.

SLA researchers should also recognize that their research will only provide one input out of many into the formulation of language teaching theory and practice. As Stern (1983) has shown us pedagogic concepts are drawn from a variety of fields – linguistics, sociology, psychology and education. SLA researchers should not be so presumptuous to imagine that the concepts which their field provides will necessarily weigh more than those of the other fields.

Lightbown (1985) has argued that the role of SLA research is in teacher *education* rather than teacher *training*. That is, it is best used to help teachers develop appropriate expectations about what learners are likely to do rather than to suggest what techniques teachers should use. We agree that SLA research has a special role to play in sensitizing teachers to how learners learn – for instance, to make teachers aware of the inevitability of errors in the learning process and to make them think carefully about error-correction. But we also feel that SLA research should contribute to the ongoing discussion of key issues to do with syllabus design (cf. Pienemann, 1985) and also the nature of language teaching materials and general methodology. These contributions should not take the form of 'formulas', 'recipes' or 'prescriptions' but of 'ideas' and 'arguments' which can be weighed, and if considered worthwhile, tried out.

It is in this spirit that the articles in this section have been written. The authors are interested in exploring how educationalists can take account of the effect that context has on the use and acquisition of a second language. They do not seek (and certainly do not expect) to have their suggestions implemented without further discussion. Rather they wish to contribute to the ongoing debate regarding such issues as the teaching of basic reading skills to L2 learners (Wallace), the choice of syllabus and methodology (Ellis) and the sampling of language behaviour in testing (Skehan).

The inherent variability of language learner behaviour is a fact of enormous importance for language teaching and testing. Where teaching is concerned the key issue is how the kinds of language behaviour which are typically present in a language classroom relate to the kinds of language behaviour which will be required of the learner outside the classroom. After all, learners are not being taught an L2 solely for use in the classroom. The basis of all language teaching is that the learners are being equipped to use the L2 in other contexts. Likewise where testing is concerned, the key issue is whether the kinds of language behaviour sampled by a language test correpond to the kinds of language behaviour which will occur in naturally-occurring situations. A test is only valid if the results it provides have *predictive* value. In both cases, therefore, the issue is the relationship between the language behaviour elicited in a pedagogic context (teaching or testing) and that which occurs in the situational contexts outside the language classroom in which the learner will find himself. What researchers have discovered about the nature of context-induced variability can provide a number of insights about this crucial relationship.

Wallace looks at the reading behaviour of L2 learners, describing it as 'a particular kind of language acquisition'. In general, SLA research has examined learner *production* and has paid scant attention to *reception*. Thus the basis for examining the variability of L2 use has been data derived from spoken or written tasks. There is, however, no reason why this variability should not be investigated using data derived from listening or reading tasks. Indeed, it can be argued that researchers broaden their data base in this way in order to examine how such variables as medium and modality affect language use and learning. Wallace, however, is less concerned with contributing to interlanguage theory, as this is currently stated, and more with examining how various contextual factors influence the early *reading* behaviour of L2 learners. She examines both intratextual factors (i.e. the linguistic properties of the text and the topic of the reading material) and situational factors (i.e. the effect of the teacher's interactional 'style') on how the learners read aloud. She shows that this behaviour can vary greatly according to how these factors shape individual teacher–reader interactions. For example, an L2 reader may be able to read aloud a word in one context but fail to do so in another, because he is unable to make it mean anything. For Wallace, the effectiveness of reading instruction is determined by the extent to which the teacher impedes or facilitates learner behaviour by the way she shapes the learning context through her choice of reading material and through the way she interacts with the learner. Wallace's paper, then, is about how teachers can manipulate the context in the classroom to create the conditions for the kind of reading behaviour conducive to learning.

The paper of Ellis is concerned with broader issues – the form that a language syllabus should take and the choice of teaching methodology. His paper is a contribution to the ongoing debate regarding whether teaching should be focused on linguistic form (i.e. on *accuracy*) or whether it should instead be concerned with providing opportunities for unfocused language use (i.e. for *fluency*). This is a debate of major importance in language pedagogy today. Variability research has an obvious contribution to make to this debate in that it provides a principled way of explaining why the ability a learner acquires to use a linguistic form accurately in one context does not guarantee the ability to use it accurately in other different contexts. Thus, variability research can help us to a much more refined understanding of what we mean by *accuracy* and *fluency*. It can also help us to see that the pedagogic choice is not a binary one; not only can teaching incorporate both accuracy and fluency work but it can do so in a principled manner. It should be noted that the kinds of conclusions regarding pedagogy that Ellis comes to is in accordance with the conclusions which others arguing from non-SLA standpoints have come to (cf. Brumfit, 1983).

In accordance with his previously published work, Ellis views SLA variability from within a Labovian framework. He reviews a number of studies of SLA variability which have taken place using Labov's methodology and on the basis of these puts forward eight propositions comprising what he calls 'a variability perspective' on SLA. He then uses these to consider the relevancy of language teaching. This involves an examination of syllabus construction, materials and classroom methodology. The essence of Ellis' argument is that *formal* instruction involving a product syllabus, focused language teaching materials and a methodology leading to planned discourse in the classroom will influence the learner's careful style, but will not directly influence his more vernacular styles. However, providing there is opportunity for using the L2 in unplanned discourse, derived perhaps from the use of unfocused materials based on a process syllabus, the learner will develop a vernacular style, both directly from input received in this type of language use and indirectly as language forms initially only available in a more careful style are 'pulled' through the stylistic continuum into more informal styles. Ellis also makes a number of proposals regarding how the effects of linguistic context can be taken into account in designing a product syllabus and focused materials. For Ellis, then, the relevancy of language teaching is relative to kinds of language use (defined in terms of the degree of planning required) the learner needs to master. He points out that such a view is very different to that adopted by Krashen, who adopts a much more absolutist stance in arguing that focused instruction should have very little place in classroom teaching.

The last paper in this section considers testing from the point of view of SLA variability research. Skehan, like other authors in this book, is critical of Labov. In particular he suggests that we need to be more precise about what 'attention to speech' involves. He proposes that an information processing model might help us to do this. In this model the language user is credited with a 'workspace' in short term memory. There are a number of factors competing for his attention – sociolinguistic, planning and interactional. But because there is limited space not all can be attended to. Variability arises as a result of the factors the language user chooses to prioritize in any single situation. Skehan also refers to the work of Selinker and Douglas (1985). They propose that interlanguage knowledge is structured in terms of *discourse domains*, defined as internally created 'slices' of an individual's life. For example, a learner might create a domain for 'cooking' or for 'critical path schedules' (an academic subject). This framework has clear relevance to testing, particularly ESP testing (cf. Selinker and Douglas, forthcoming). Skehan uses these frameworks to discuss what he sees as the principal issue in testing, namely how to sample language behaviour in such a way that generalizations can be made on the basis of test performance about performance in non-test situations. Skehan's main proposal is that the best approach might be to try to identify the performance factors that influence language behaviour in different domains and to incorporate an understanding of these into test design. Skehan concludes by pointing out that SLA researchers interested in variability can benefit from the work of language testers by attending to what the latter have to say about validity and reliability when they design their data elicitation instruments.

It is interesting to note that there is no consensus in the papers by Ellis and Skehan (or indeed in the book as a whole) about which model or framework of variability to use as a basis for observations about teaching or testing. In one or the other of these papers reference is made to the work of Labov (and, of course, Tarone), to Bialystok and Sharwood-Smith, to Hatch and to Selinker and Douglas. This plethora of models is characteristic of SLA research in general. The lack of consensus might be thought of as problematic when it comes to considering the relevancy of variability research to language pedagogy. However, we do not believe that this need be so. This is because, as we pointed out earlier, the authors of these papers have not so much set about trying to *apply* the results of SLA research as to use them to *gain insights* of value to language pedagogy. Their starting points have not been what the research has to say but their understanding of a number of key issues of current interest to educationalists concerned with language pedagogy. These issues have been explored in the light of what the research shows about SLA variability.

We can conclude by restating the major pedagogic issues which these papers have considered. There are perhaps two. The first concerns *pedagogic relevancy*. Here the question is how the teacher can ensure that the language behaviour which occurs in the classroom leads to learning which can be used in language behaviour in non-classroom situations. Or, from the point of view of testing, how the tester can ensure that the language behaviour which is sampled in a test shows evidence of the kind of abilities which will be required in non-test situations. The second issue concerns *pedagogic efficiency*. Here the question is how the teacher can create relevant contexts in the classroom which will ensure that learning takes place efficiently (i.e. rapidly and successfully). Or, how the tester can devise tests which test relevant language abilities economically and reliably. These are general issues and discussion of them will make use of concepts taken from a number of different disciplines. The study of SLA variability can be considered to have something special to offer to the debate because it is concerned directly with the relationship between language use and context.

Variability and the Reading Behaviour of L2 Readers

CATHERINE WALLACE

Ealing College of Higher Education

I should like in this paper to discuss what can be discovered from the learner's variable reading behaviour that might help us improve our strategies for teaching L2 reading. Second Language Acquisition studies have largely investigated SLA as speech or writing behaviour. Reading behaviour also merits attention, and I shall here focus on this one particular kind of L2 language behaviour, taking the situation where L2 learner reader is reading aloud to a teacher.

Introduction

There are two ways in which looking at the learning to read process is relevant to second language acquisition studies. Firstly, we are provided with another kind of data – apart from speaking or writing data – for interlanguage studies. This data can shed light on interlanguage development, as in those cases, for example, where learners are observed in reading aloud to render written texts in their current interlanguage. Secondly, we can observe L2 reading as an acquisition process – a particular kind of language acquisition; that is, the move into the written medium. I shall be looking at the second of these in the rest of this paper. In doing so, I shall consider some variables which can facilitate or impede the learning to read process for L2 readers.

The background to this paper is my observation that both text and teacher are frequently working against the learner in her acquisition of L2 reading. In talking of the acquisition of L2 reading, I should like to consider two kinds of contextual variability, variability within the text and variability within the situation in which learner reads aloud to teacher in a one-to-one teaching situation. In other words, when we talk of the context of reading we may mean either the textual context or the immediate situational context in which the reading event occurs. I shall suggest that certain kinds of variable within the text may lead to varying reading behaviour on the part of the learner. Similarly, variables within the situation will result in varying reading behaviour. I shall discuss intratextual variability under Text and Topic, that is, firstly how might particular features of texts trigger off apparently inconsistent learner reader behaviour, and, secondly, how can a writer's selection and organization of topic of subject matter facilitate or hinder a learner's ability to draw on relevant background knowledge. The aspect of the situation that I shall focus on is the teacher, more particularly how teacher-behaviour affects learner-behaviour.

In thus looking at the variables of text, topic, and teacher, I am suggesting a need to see learning to read behaviour as interactional not only with the text, but, in the case of early reading aloud, with the teacher. This involves us in looking qualitatively at the learning to read situation. Miscue Analysis has been very influential in offering a way to evaluate a learner's reading errors or miscues qualitatively. Goodman and Burke (1973) offered a framework for describing reader miscues in linguistic terms, as graphophonic, syntactic or semantic, depending which features of the text readers directed their attention at. However, miscue analysis has been used as a tool to assess the learner reader's strategies rather than as a means of assessing the teaching/learning situation itself. Ultimately, I suggest, we need ways of evaluating not merely the nature of the learner's miscues but the nature of the whole interaction between teacher, learner and text.

It may appear to many of us obvious that reading behaviour is variable. So why the need to stress this as a factor in learner reading (L1 or L2)? There *is* a need, I believe, in the light of the continuing adherence, not always explicit, and in spite of the interest in more qualitative ways of assessing learners, to the concept of reading age. Learners are said to 'have' a reading age, much as they have blue eyes. What is more, this is not assessed by teachers, who have, over time and in different situations, observed individual childrens' reading behaviour, but by tests. One of the most recent and comprehensive studies of childrens' reading (Schools Council Project, *Extending Beginning Reading*, 1981) talks of the child's 'actual' reading age' as measured by Schonell's graded word reading test of 1948. Alongside the 'actual' reading age we have 'Teacher's estimate'. Teachers are classified as over- or under-estimators of the childrens' reading ability. The clear implication is firstly, that tests know best, and secondly, that at any one point learners 'have' a reading age which takes no account of contextual variables of any kind. Other researchers concede that children can 'make a jump' over their normal level of competence, with highly motivating material (cf. Harrison, 1980). But again the use of the word 'normal' suggests that such children will soon sink back to some kind of rightful and expected place much below the 'brighter' children in the class. Why not turn this around and say that many children may perform well below their competence because the style and content of the texts are unattractive and inaccessible and the situations in which they read aloud to an adult in school ill-designed to motivate them. None of us reads effectively when interest is low and purpose absent, which must for many children often be the case in classrooms.

Of course, much depends on one's view of reading. Some would see learning to read as necessarily involving the acquisition of particular skills or sets of skills; others as primarily a kind of language behaviour where the learner, in searching and predicting text, depends more on her knowledge of the syntactic and semantic features of English than on possession of a specific skill such as the ability to match up phonemes and graphemes. It will be clear that I am considering reading as language behaviour. In this case it is plausible to start with the premise that reading behaviour, like all language behaviour, is inherently variable, and that educators, rather than wishing to test or assess learners, might best consider what those variables are which affect a learner reader's performance on any one occasion.

Data collection and subjects

The subjects mentioned here are eight learner readers, four adults and four children, in the fairly early stage of learning to read in a second language.[1] The four adults were my own learners. The two older adults, who possessed only minimal literacy in English, were taught in the context of a local literacy scheme. The teenagers were taught at a College of Further Education. Of the four children the older two, Maqsood and Sarla, were given extra help with their reading by myself every week for 10 weeks. They were two of a number of children selected by the school's specialist language teacher, as needing some extra help with their reading. The two youngest children were taught in a familiar classroom context, in one case by a specialist ESL teacher; in the second by both an ESL and a class teacher.

Some brief notes about the learners are included here:

		Length of time in Britain
Joyce:	Thai, 40+, very reduced English. Some L1 literacy.	12 years
Peter:	Anglo-Indian, 40, L1 English, but speech shows considerable reduction of structure. No literacy at start of classes.	12 years.
Ranjit:	Indian Sikh, 19, L1 Punjabi. Literate in Punjabi	2 years.
Yasmeen:	Pakistani Muslim, 19, L1 Urdu. Literate in Urdu.	1½ years.
Maqsood:	Pakistani Muslim, 10, L1 Urdu. (English near native in day-to-day spoken contexts).	5 years
Sarla:	Indian Hindu, 11, L1 Gujerati (English shows clear non-native features).[2]	5 years.
Balwinder:	Indian, 8, L1 Punjabi.	Born in Britain
Manjula:	Indian, 8, L1 Gujerati.	Born in Britain

The data were selected from many hours of teacher–learner interaction and the reading of more learners was taped and transcribed than is directly referred to here (though some of this additional data is used to illustrate Figure 1).

In the case of the four older readers most lessons were taped, apart from the very earliest. The tape-recorder thus became accepted as a feature of lessons. Transcripts were prepared that included reading aloud, interaction around the text, and conversation of varying degrees of intimacy. Lessons with Joyce, for instance, took place in Joyce's kitchen over gin and tonics and cigarettes and this is at times reflected in the tenor of the accompanying conversation!

The two older children, Maqsood and Sarla, were likewise always taped beyond the earliest 'settling down' sesssions. The two younger children Balwinder and

Manjula were taped by their own teachers in a school situation where the tape-recorder, though not a habitual feature of the one-to-one reading aloud situation, would nonetheless be fairly familiar in class work.

Text-induced variability

In the case of the first sense of context that I have taken, I should like to consider some of the textual features that can be observed to trigger-off variable reading ability in individual learner readers. One way of illustrating an apparent variability of competence is in the matter of reading words. Put simply, why can a reader read a word on one occasion and not on another? I make the point because the conventional way (certainly implicit in many reading schemes) of trying to predict a reader's success in getting meaning from a particular text is to consider the number of words which are new for the learner. On the face of it, defining reading as 'knowing the words' is a commonsense view. Certainly, so-called 'Look and Say' approaches to the teaching of reading make this assumption. Words are introduced on flashcards prior to reading on the understanding that the learner then 'knows' the words contained in the reading primers and is therefore equipped to embark on meaningful reading.

However, most teachers are aware that learners may 'know' a word in one context but not in another. Learners may stop dead at a familiar word and one which, phonically, is readily decodable. Joyce had no difficulty with the word 'hand' in this context:

(1) 'She put her hand on Harry's arm',

nor a little later in the same text,

(2) 'She put out her hand again'.

Joyce 'knew' the word, one might therefore say, but later in the same text she had difficulty with the item in this context:

(3) 'Harry felt for the clock and looked hard at it. The hands shone up at him.'

It is not simply the fact that 'hand' and 'arm' collocate more readily than 'hands' and 'clock' but that 'hands' in (3) is elliptically introduced (the hands *of the clock*). Thus the difficulty of the polysemous introduction of the word 'hand' is compounded by unclear reference (i.e. the hands *of what* or *whose* hands) Joyce's variable response to the word 'hand' shows how difficulties with meaning may override graphic knowledge.

While teachers and writers of material for young learner readers are likely to be aware of the phenomenon of polysemous content words in texts, rather less attention has been paid to learners' varying ability to deal with function words, the apparently 'simplest', certainly most frequent items of language in either written or spoken texts. Peter, a total beginner to reading at the age of 40, observes, 'It's the little words I can't get. I can get all the big ones'. The little word which caused difficulty for Peter in his text extract is the word 'one':

(4) 'In one film a man jumps from a horse, In another film one falls from a car, In another one falls from the top of a mountain.'

While Peter read 'in one film' with little difficulty, the subsequent anaphoric reference caused great confusion.

It is not simply that function words have no lexical meaning but that early learner readers are not aware of the referring function of certain items of language, such as 'one', 'own' or 'the' in some contexts. It is not reading the words which is at issue but acquiring an understanding of the way in which reference is used in written texts.

The varying collocation in the above example (i.e. 'one film' vs. 'one falls'), within a few lines of text, was another of Peter's difficulties. Learner readers are particularly dependent on high-frequency and predictable collocations. Texts can then be economically chunked and processed more readily. The way in which items are collocated throughout a text creates expectations on which leaner readers are particularly dependent. For example, Maqsood had read the word 'beer' a number of times in the text from which 5 comes.

		Teacher
(5) Text:	Harry stamps upstairs	
Maq:	Harry stamps upstairs	
T:	He hates Linda	
M:	He hates Linda	
T:	He hates Gran	
M:	He hates Gran	
T:	He hates beer	
M:	He hates . . . *What's this?*	Well, you got that before. 'He hates Gran, he hates . . .?
	Beer?	Do you think that's a strange thing to say?
	Yes, he can't hate beer because it ain't a living thing	

Clearly there was no sense in which Maqsood did not know the meaning of 'beer'. The difficulty seems to be that expectations of an association with animateness (set up by the words 'Gran' and 'Linda') was defeated.

In the case of L2 readers in particular a difficulty may be created by culture specific collocations. For instance, Ranjit could not predict: 'cups and . . . . .' in text.[6]

		Teacher
(6) Text:	The clattering of utensils made a lot of noise	
Ranjit:	The clattering of —— made a lot of noise	UTENSILS – pots and pans
T:	as plates, cups and saucers were all ——	

R: as plates, cups and s —   guess, 'cups and s —' ? what goes
                                       with cups? Let's ask Armindo
A: *Saucers*
R: *Saucers? What is saucers?*   Cups and saucers go together.
                                       Don't you have saucers, just cups?
R: *Yes, but we don't call them like*
     that. We call them plate.   Ah, you don't have a special word?

From this exchange between teacher and learners, it seemed that there is no equivalent collocation for 'cups and saucers' in Ranjit's mother tongue, Punjabi, in which
a translation for saucers would be something like 'small plates'.

Incidentally it is often more reflective readers who balk in the way that Maqsood
and Ranjit do here, simply because they cannot 'make the text mean' (to quote
Meek *et al.*, 1983). Skilled decoders, on the other hand, can frequently be observed
to plough on regardless, seeing it as their business merely to render what is on the
page.

We might compare Ranjit's difficulty with 'cups and saucers' with his response to
the word 'tubewell' later in the same text:

                                       Teacher
(7) T: The men always bathed in front of
          the tubewell
     R: The men always bath . . .
          (hesitates . . . *what is this*)
          bath . . . bathed in front of the
          tube – well – tubewell (said
          quickly with recognition)   So what did they do?
     R: *The men always bathed in front of*
          the tubewell. It's a water pump   Is this a picture?
     R: *No, that's a handpump. A tubewell*
          is a erm . . . it takes water from the
          ground with a motor

Here Ranjit's manner of handling the word 'tubewell' – at first hesitantly, then with
a flash of recognition – reveals the 'making it mean' process. Ranjit is able to draw
on his background knowledge of the topic (village life in the Punjab) to predict the
word 'tubewell'. Put simply, he knows what the text is about. What's more, he then
quite spontaneously offers me a description of a tubewell, as a kind of pump. The
text at this point presents a familiar situation to Ranjit for which he has a schema
into which 'tubewell' can readily be accommodated. A number of researchers into
L2 reading have talked of the implications of schema theory for ESL reading comprehension (notably Carrell, 1983 and elsewhere). I will here simply give Widdowson's
(1984) definition of schemas as 'cognitive constructs which allow us to organize
information in long-term memory and which provide a basis for prediction'.

With L2 learners there may be, especially in the case of what we might call culture-
specific knowledge, either a total lack of knowledge of the topic or of familiarity

with the situation, so that no schema is triggered; or there may be a mismatch whereby new items in the text cannot be accommodated within the schema which the preceding part of the text has activated.

An example of the former is given in (8):

(8) Text: Gran can remember the war and the power cuts
    Sarla: Gran can remember the war and the power cuts

    T: So she makes sure that 'that Hitler' will never put her in the dark again
    S: So she makes sure that . . . that . . . that Hit. . . .

An adult native speaker at least would readily identify the topic (i.e. what we are talking about at his point) as World War II. Sarla struggles through what is linguistically a simple passage well within her general reading competence. She finally balks at 'that Hitler'. She has no schema which would relate 'war', 'power cuts' and 'Hitler'. Indeed, most of the other children in the group, including native speakers of the same age, had only a very hazy idea that Hitler was someone bad and foreign.

An example of the second case – of not being able to accommodate incoming information into the existing schema – is in (9) below:

Teacher

(9) Text: I've also got too much iron in my blood
    Yasmeen: I – ve also got too much iron in my blood

    T: I have to have injections for that daily
    Y: I have to have in – in – oh yeh injection   IN . . .? good, you know what they are, don't you?

    Y: *Yeh injection yeh I know* 'for that daily'
    T: Sometimes I have to have a pump
    Y: Sometimes I have to have a pum – *what*?

    T: To get rid of the iron
    Y: To get right off the iron

    Y: *I don't know – what's this?*   Iron, well iron is what you have in your body. In your blood you have iron. It gives you strength. Now she has too much iron in her blood so she has a pump to bring the iron out of her body.

T:	I have penicillin	You know what	
Y:	I have penicillin	penicillin is?	
Y:	*Yes medicine . . . yes, yes I know penicillin – injection or medicine*		
T:	Vitamin C and follic acid		
Y:	Vitamin C and foll? . . . Follis	Follic acid, just another medicine, 'cos she's ill.	

This text is about hospitals for which Yasmeen has a schema, that is she knows about injections, penicillin and so on and even though these words were new to her in written English she read them with little hesitation. However, she balked at the word 'pump'. This, I suggest, is because she cannot readily attach a meaning to the word which would make it fit the schema. Schematic anticipation is frustrated.

When writers flout schematic anticipation in this way the teacher is on hand in one-to-one reading aloud. When the schema fails Yasmeen turns to the teacher. Where the interaction with the text breaks down the interaction with the teacher comes into its own.

Teacher-induced variability

This brings us to consider the teacher's role in the three way interaction between text, teacher and learner. Teachers too can either impede or facilitate a reader's progression through the written text. While a whole range of variables in the situation – who is reading to whom, where, when and why – will clearly affect learner reader behaviour and will interact with each other, here I should like to focus on the 'to whom' factor – the teacher. Firstly, how do early readers reading aloud to a teacher see their respective roles? Even the physical proximity of teacher to learner, whether side by side, for instance, or face to face, will affect the nature of the interaction: does the learner read aloud to the teacher, with the teacher only interrupting when the text fails to make sense? Or does the teacher also have access to the text and intervene when the learner reads something other than what is on the page? Do they take it in turns to read?

Reflecting on our own teaching style can be instructive. Judith Graham, as described in Meek *et al.* (1983) observed herself in a video playback of a lesson with her student Jamie. She was turning the pages of the book for him. Instances of teacher control of this kind show how reluctant we often are to offer our learners autonomy as readers. For many children in school, reading aloud to teacher consists of coming to the front of the class to read. As Southgate *et al.* (1982) point out, teachers in a busy class may be simultaneously hearing a child read while attending to other childrens' spelling queries, for instance. Children may thus be encouraged in the view that reading aloud is to be done as quickly as possible without pause for comment, query or reflection.

Teachers will reveal through verbal and non-verbal behaviour a view about the reading and learning to read process and of their own and the learner's role in the interaction. One kind of behaviour is the use of question types, for instance. Barnes (1969) investigated this feature of classroom interaction in monolingual classrooms. More recent researchers (cf. for example, Long and Sato, 1983) have looked at forms and functions of questions in ESL classrooms. It is clearly a feature of teacher/ learner interaction which is readily observable in one-to-one teaching situations. In the data I examined, consisting of eighteen reading sessions (eighteen different learners, five teachers) I found that teacher questions, whether retrospective/checking questions or cues/prompts were broadly classifiable as either text-centred or learner-centred. It should be added, however, that this is not a clear dichotomy as questions which involve making inferences or suppositions about the text (cf. Davies and Widdowson, 1974) must also be partly directed at the learner's knowledge of the world.

Figure 1 suggests a way of looking at the data. It will be seen there for instance that text can be treated as predominantly substance or sense, by which I mean that the surface characteristics of texts (usually the look or sound of words or parts of words) can be focused on or the meaning of parts or the whole of texts; in particular how parts relate to other parts and the parts to the whole. The learner's knowledge of the world or of the system of English can be variously appealed to or teachers might ask 'strategy' questions. By strategy questions I mean those questions which invite readers to reflect on their own typical reading behaviour or their use of particular strategies in this instance. Strategy questions are important in that through them learners are helped not simply to carry out the reading process but to be aware of the process itself as reflected in their own reading behaviour.

In the data I looked at there were few instances where the reader was required to draw on her knowledge of the language system other than at the level demanded by questions such as 'What's that word mean?', and knowledge of the world questions were rarely developed so as to offer learners a bridge between personal experiences and those described by the text. There were only a very few instances of strategy questions, requiring learners to introspect on their own strategies. In fact some

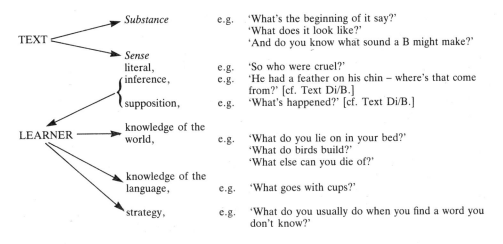

FIGURE 1   *Teacher questions, directed at texts or learners*

teachers asked very few questions at all on the content of the learner's reading, confirming Southgate *et al.* (1982) who, looking at all aspects of classroom reading in great detail, note: 'only rarely was it observed that a teacher asked either a direct or open-ended question of a child on the content of his oral reading'.

In short there is noticeably very little interaction between teacher and learner on many occasions of one-to-one reading aloud. Where teachers do ask questions they occasionally produce no response at all from a child. So unused are some children, it would seem, to being invited to participate in any discussion around the text that they may well perceive some teacher questions as non-questions, especially closed yes/no questions such as 'Do you know what that means?'

Even more striking is the apparant reluctance of learners themselves to ask questions or offer comment. For L2 learners in particular, the opportunity is lost to develop insights into the nature of the system of English (as well as features of stories and the reading process itself) by engaging with the teacher in a shared exploration of written texts.

The teacher's typical linguistic and other behaviour will lead learners to assign to her a role, likely to be interpreted in various ways. So teachers may be perceived as primarily participators, interrogators or correctors. The role and general style of the teacher will affect:

(a) the range of roles open to the learner; is she allowed to ask questions, offer comment, disagree?
(b) the learner's attitude to the reading lesson;
(c) the learner's view as to what reading is.

All these taken together will have an effect on the reader's general reading behaviour. A teacher's consistent use of particular question types or cues, for instance, will indicate her perception of the nature of the interaction. In turn learners will make some assessment of what is going on, for example 'she is teaching me to read', 'we are sharing a story', 'she is listening to me read', 'she is correcting my pronunciation of English'.

As a case in point we might consider Manjula, who was taped reading aloud successive parts of the same story to two successive teachers. Manjula is aged 8 years old, her L1 is Gujerati and although her spoken English is very good she has been attending an ESL class during the year. Teacher *A*'s behaviour showed a high degree of consistency. She did not ask Manjula any questions at all about the story; on two occasions she checked out the meaning of words or phrases. Otherwise, her teaching strategy was to repeat in a slow, careful, clearly articulated style, parts of the text read by Manjula or to ask her to repeat chunks of text, even though these had been rendered in a manner quite acceptable to most users of English. One such teacher intervention follows 'the old bear' in (10). At this point the teacher intervenes with 'Can you say that'? Manjula does so, carefully articulating the phrase.

It is not surprising that Manjula's rendering of the text following this kind of intervention is very carefully articulated so that 'catch you' is pronounced as /kætʃ ju:/ rather than /Kætʃuː/ and 'eat you' as /iːt ju:/ rather than /iːtʃuː/. Heavy aspiration is given finally on items such as 'not' and 'up' to produce [notʰ] and [ʌpʰ].

(10)   *Manjula*   *Teacher A*
          One day Ugly Boy came running
          into the house. He said
          'Grandmother, I am hungry.
          I am going out to pick some
          nuts. I am not afraid of the old bear'
                                                    the 'old' bear
                                                    Can you say that?
                         the old bear
          But his grandmother cried 'Oh, my
          boy, you must not!
          The wicked bear will catch you.
          She will eat you up'

It seems likely that Manjula has acquired a view of reading, influenced by Teacher *A*'s behaviour, as recitation or 'practising pronunciation'; at the same time she is accommodating to the teacher's own over-articulated style during the lesson. The resulting style is quite different from any other oral medium, including story reading in most contexts, and quite different from Manjula's own typical spoken English. As soon as Teacher *B* takes over, Manjula's reading begins to change. This can be illustrated by her articulation of the word 'bear'. In similar phonetic contexts it shifts along a continuum from [bɛər] to [bɛət] to [bɛə]. At the same time fluency and pace develop. Manjula's pronunciation of English is near native but it may well be that Teacher *A* is responding to her as an ESL pupil. She did not, I observed, behave in the same way with the one native speaker of the group.

A different kind of interaction was that between Di and Balwinder. Balwinder read the text in Figure 2 without any intervention from her teacher. She made few miscues most of which maintained the sense of the text fairly well. Her most interesting departure from the text is in the last two lines:

The lion and the rooster

1. When the rooster came along the path
2. Old Lion's mouth curled in a smile
3. as he called Friend Rooster 'Come and talk
4. for a while. I am old and tired. I can't get about
5. much these days. Won't you stop for tea with me'.
6. The rooster answered 'Oh lion your
7. eyes have a hungry look. I'll keep on going.
8. The sun is warm and the path is long'.
9. The lion said 'Just stop for a little while. I have
10. everything ready'. 'Well just for a minute, friend
11. lion. I don't want to be here too long'. 'Oh
12. this won't take long', Old Lion said
13. as he led the rooster into his cave.
14. Later Old Lion nodded in the sun. He
15. wiped a feather from his chin and said
16. 'I'll miss Friend Rooster. But
17. it was nice to have him for tea'.

FIGURE 2

T. I'll miss Friend Rooster. But
B. I'll miss Friend Rooster. But
T. It was nice to have him for tea
B. It was nice to have tea with him

This was the ensuing conversation between Di and Balwinder.[3]

Di What's happened?
B. Miss, he had some tea with the rooster, miss and . . . (   ) he have it for just a minute and. . . .
Di What's he done here (referring to line 14)
B. he nodded . . . went to sleep
Di and he had a feather on his chin. Where's that come from?
B. From the Rooster Miss
Di How did it get there?
B. . . .
Di Can you read this bit again?
B. 'He wiped a feather from his chin and said I'll miss Friend Rooster but it was nice to have tea' – he gave him a feather from his body Miss
Di Mmm. What does it mean when it says 'I'll miss him'?
B. He'll miss his friend
Di Why, where's he gone?
B. He's gone . . . Miss, the lion?
Di No the rooster
B. Miss he's gone somewhere else
Di It says here: 'But it was nice to have him for tea'
B. He's gone to have tea somewhere else
Di Do you think so?
B. Yes Miss
Di Right, you read the next bit and we'll see (B. reads the next section of the story which describes a similar encounter, this time between Friend Goat and Old Lion. The outcome is the same as that between Lion and Rooster.) Di stops B. at this point: 'he led Goat into his cave'.
Di Whats he doing here then?
B. Miss he, the lion led the goat to his cave
Di What did he do there?
B. Miss he gave some tea to the goat
Di Do you remember at the very beginning it said he didn't want to go out and get his food. He didn't want to go out hunting. Why was that?
B. Because he was too old
Di So where's he getting all his tea from
B. From his friends' houses Miss
Di Is he? Where does it say that?
B. From his friends' *caves*
Di But he hasn't been anywhere has he? Read the next bit very carefully and see if you can see what's happening

B. 'Later Old Lion was warming himself in the sun. I'll miss Friend Goat he said
    as he plucked a tuft of black hair from his mane. But it was nice to have tea
    . . . for . . . tea . . . (does not complete)
B. *continues:"* Much
Di Could you read that bit again?
B. 'But it was nice to have tea . . . it was nice to have him for tea'. He had him
    for tea Miss
Di Mmm. So what did he do?
B. He gave him some tea
Di (repeating very slowly) He 'had' him 'for' tea
B. Oh! He ate him up!
Di And what happened to rooster?
B. He ate him up as well!

We see the teacher encouraging Balwinder to relate meanings across the text – to
use inference. Di aims to help Balwinder maximize the information given in the text
and to draw on her relevant knowledge of the world, for example that roosters have
feathers. Asking questions at word or sentence level will not reveal the kind of
difficulty Balwinder has here. One needs rather to task the one key question which
pulls the meaning of the whole text together. This is just what Di does here with her
question 'What's happened?', which leads Balwinder and herself into the lengthy but
finally fruitful shared exploration of the text.

Conclusion

In conclusion, I should like to suggest that texts can help the ESL learner reader by
employing predictable, fully structured language. Learner readers who lack the same
level of English language competence as their L1 peers may be helped by a greater
redundancy in texts, so that for instance, it becomes particularly important to spell
out cohesive ties and avoid elliptical reference. This may result at times in some
sacrifice of 'naturalness' but will ease the L2 reader into the new medium.

   In terms of the content or topic of texts, we need to be alert to the possibility of
there being a mismatch of schemas especially in the case of highly culture-specific
texts. This can occasionally be turned to advantage through a sharing, and comparing
of culturally based perceptions and interpretations of the events, behaviour and
phenomena described in texts. But most important I believe is the need to consider
the whole context of reading aloud. The event becomes not so much a recitation *to*
teacher as an interaction *with* both teacher and text. The interaction is a three-way
one in that the learner uses the teacher as a resource where necessary; the teacher
mediates in the reader's interaction with the text, and the text becomes the occasion
for an interaction between learner and teacher.

Notes

1. The exception is Peter, whose L1 was English, but whose speech showed considerable reduction of structure.
2. Sarla was beginning to learn to read in Gujerati. None of the other children was literate in the Mother Tongue.
3. Note on transcription: brief pause ''
    long pause '''
    transcription unclear ( )
    slow careful enunciation '.

Contextual Variability in Second Language Acquisition and the Relevancy of Language Teaching

ROD ELLIS
Ealing College of Higher Education.

Introduction

The purpose of this paper is to address the question: 'How can we take account of what is known about the nature of contextual variability in second language acquisition (SLA) in language teaching?' In general, theories of SLA have paid scant regard to the variability of interlanguage systems (Beebe and Zuengler, 1983), while language teaching has tended to treat learning as the acquisition of a homogeneous competence enshrined as a grammar of target language norms. My concern, then, is to argue both for a model of SLA that gives due recognition to language-learner language variability and for an approach to language teaching based on the acquisition of a heterogeneous competence.

The question that motivates this paper has arisen as a result of research that shows the effects of language pedagogy to be far from straightforward. Two examples of this research will serve to illustrate this point. Schumann (1978b) attempted to give instruction in English negatives to Alberto, a Spanish speaking subject learning English in the United States. His reason for giving this instruction was to discover whether the apparent 'pidginization' of Alberto's English could be overcome. Prior to the instructional experiment, Alberto's negatives were primarily of the 'no $+V$' type. The instruction covered a seven-month period, during which both elicited and spontaneous negative utterances were collected. The elicited utterances showed a marked development (64% correct as opposed to 24% before instruction). The spontaneous utterances, however, showed no significant change (20% correct as opposed to 22% before instruction). Schumann concluded that the instruction influenced production only in test-like situations, while normal communication remained unaffected. The second study was carried out by Perkins and Larsen-Freeman (1975). They investigated the effects of two months' instruction on twelve Venezuelan undergraduates in the United States. Two tasks were used to collect data: (1) a translation task and (2) an oral description task based on a non-dialogue film. On (1) the morpheme orders before and after instruction differed significantly but on (2) there was no significant difference. The researchers concluded that where spontaneous oral performance was concerned the instruction did not influence development.

To explain their results, then, these researchers drew a distinction between the kind of careful language elicited, for instance, by translation tasks and the kind of spontaneous language use associated with unplanned oral production. They noted that the instruction they provided influenced the former but not the latter. The results are intuitively appealing, given that, as teachers, we are familiar with the problem of 'backsliding', where students perform a particular structure accurately in the context of controlled language practice but fail to do so in free practice or in communication outside the classroom. The problem is an important one because it raises one of the central questions of language pedagogy, namely the relationship between what Brumfit (1984) has called 'accuracy' and 'fluency' activities.

One answer to this question can be found in Krashen's (1981) Monitor Model of SLA. This rests on the now well-known distinction between 'acquisition' and 'learning'. Krashen postulates specific conditions for the use of 'learnt' knowledge (i.e. there must be sufficient time and the learner must be focused on form) and argues that if these conditions are not met the learner will only be able to call on 'acquired' knowledge. Thus in spontaneous communication 'learnt' knowledge is not available for monitoring. Krashen argues that acquired and learnt knowledge are entirely separate. Thus he sees no relationship between the development that arises from 'accuracy' and 'fluency' teaching, as each contributes to a distinct kind of competence. But such a position is not acceptable to many teachers who operate a methodology based on distinguishing 'skill getting' and 'skill using' (Rivers and Temperley, 1978), and who see, therefore, 'accuracy' training as a preparation for eventual 'fluency'. Yet Krashen's views on the relevancy of instruction are compatible with the results of the research undertaken by Schumann and Perkins and Larsen-Freeman.

The question we need to consider is whether Krashen's explanation is the only one and whether it is the best one. In this paper I want to explore how an alternative theotetical framework for SLA, based on the notion of contextual variability, can account for the reseach findings. In particular I want to argue that such a framework can provide a principled basis for inter-relating 'accuracy' and 'fluency' work.

The paper falls into two principal parts. In the first part I review some research into contextual variability in SLA and develop a framework for a 'variability perspective' on SLA. In the second part of the paper I explore the relevance of this 'variability perspective' for three areas of language pedagogy – syllabus design, language teaching materials and classroom practice. In the conclusion I return to a consideration of the relationship between 'accuracy' and 'fluency' teaching.

Some major issues: a look at the research

Earlier I stated that theories of SLA have ignored interlanguage variability. This is not entirely correct, however. There have been a number of studies of contextual variability in SLA and at least one major theoretical statement (Tarone, 1983). A good starting point, then, is to briefly survey the major research findings.

SLA researchers have been aware for some time that data collected using different instruments reveal different linguistic properties. Lococo (1976) for instance, found major differences in the percentage of errors in prepositions, adjectives and determiners produced by university students enrolled in an elementary Spanish course, according to the kind of task used to collect the data. Similar results have been reported by Larsen Freeman (1976) and Bahns and Wode (1980). In particular differences occur as a result of whether the data reflect spontaneous language performance or elicited language.

Given that the performance data of L2 learners differ according to task, the question arises as to whether these differences are systematic or haphazard. Tarone makes a strong case for systematicity. She reviews a number of studies of variability in SLA and argues that they provide clear evidence of style-shifting. That is, L2 learners can be credited with a variable capacity and draw on particular variants according to the degree of attention they are paying to linguistic form. Style-shifting occurs along a continuum ranging from a 'careful' to a 'vernacular' (or 'casual') style. The careful style is most evident in grammatical intuition data and the vernacular style in spontaneous oral communication.

There are a number of further points to make about style-shifting in SLA. First, it needs to be emphasized that the evidence shows that L2 learners possess a number of styles, not just two, as in the acquisition/learning dichotomy. This suggests that the Monitor Model may not constitute an adequate account of the nature of interlanguage systems. Contextual variability is not an either–or phenomenon; it is a continuous phenomenon.

Second, the research provides strong evidence to suggest that when tasks are ordered according to the degree of attention to linguistic form they require, accuracy levels in the use of specific linguistic forms vary continuously, with the highest levels evident in the learner's careful style and the lowest levels in the vernacular style. It has been suggested that it is the careful style that is most permeable to the influence of target language forms.

Third, it has been shown that the careful style is also the style that is most influenced by the learner's first language (L1). Beebe (1980), for instance, found that Thai learners used /r/ variably depending on whether they were conversing or listing words. But the nature of the variability was complex. When /r/ occurred finally the customary pattern of style-shifting was observed. That is, the learners performed more accurately in their careful style than in their vernacular style. However, initial /r/ showed the opposite effect, with the vernacular style displaying more accuracy than the careful style. The reason for this, Beebe suggests, was that the learners were transferring a prestige /r/ variant, which differed from target language /r/, in this position when they were focused on form. Schmidt (1977) reports the same effect for the th-variable in Arabic learners of English. Thus the careful style is also permeable to the influence of the L1 when the native language forms have prestige value in the L1.

Fourth, whereas the pattern of style shifting in interlanguage phonology appears to be fairly predictable, style shifting in interlanguage grammar appears to be more complex, subject to the interplay of additional factors. Tarone (1985) found that the type of discourse affected the levels of accuracy of certain morphological structures and could produce a different effect than the expected one. Tarone found that the learners in her study used the third person singular verb morpheme -s as expected (i.e. with greatest accuracy in the careful style and lowest accuracy in a casual style). However, the pattern of use for two other structures – direct object pronoun and articles – was the opposite. Tarone explains this by postulating that the task used to tap the vernacular style also required the production of cohesive discourse. Thus the learners' use of direct object pronouns and articles (but not of the third person singular morpheme) was motivated by the need to make their discourse textually cohesive and this need over-rode the normal pattern of style-shifting. Fakhri (1984) also found that discourse factors influenced the use of linguistic forms. In this case it was not the type of discourse that counted but pragmatic considerations. Her subject made variable use of the pro-drop rule according to her perceived need to keep the reference clear. These studies indicate that contextual variability in grammar is a complex affair, influenced not only by style-shifting but also by discourse and pragmatic factors.

Another factor that can influence the general pattern of style-shifting in interlanguage grammar is the nature of the linguistic rule. Ellis (forthcoming) found that not all structures manifest style-shifting or manifest it to the same degree. Apart from the fact that some structures may have been thoroughly acquired in the sense that they are used categorically in all styles, other structures, which are still in the process of being acquired may not be subject to style shifting. Ellis found that whereas an easily learnt structure such as regular past tense style shifted in a highly regular fashion, a structure such as irregular past tense, which is not easily learnt, did not style shift at all. The absence or presence of style shifting, therefore, appears to be dependent on the nature of the forms in question.

So far my review of the major issues concerning variability in interlanguage has considered the systematic variability that arises from style-shifting. However, contextual variability also occurs as a function of linguistic context. That is, systematic variation arises as a result of internal as well as external factors. Dickerson (1975), for instance, found that Japanese learners of English varied in their use of /z/ according to the linguistic environment of the sound. The precise phonetic quality of /z/ changed according to the adjacent consonants and vowels. SLA can be characterized as the gradual movement towards categoricality as the learner masters the use of variants in one linguistic context after another.

What is the relationship between external factors responsible for style shifting and internal factors responsible for incremental learning across different linguistic contexts? Downes (1984), writing about sociolinguistic variation in natural languages, proposes that stylistic variability is primary. He argues that there is a prior probability of a rule applying determined by extralinguistic factors. This leads to style shifting. Probabilities can then be assigned to various internal linguistic environments. There has, however, to the best of my knowledge, been no study investigating whether this is the case in interlanguage.

Finally, we need to acknowledge that not all variability is systematic (i.e. describable in terms of intra- and extralinguistic factors). If interlanguage is to be treated as a natural language (Adjemian, 1976) we can expect considerable non-systematic variability. As Downes puts it, 'heterogeneity is the normal state of language'. Systematic variability only arises when speakers make selections from the 'pervasive fluctuation'. Thus systematic variability is a reflection of linguistic *change*. Non systematic variability is present before change is initiated and serves as the resource for change. It is this view of variability that Ellis (1985b) proposes as a basis for understanding the role of variability in SLA. Because of the permeability of interlanguage systems new forms are constantly entering but in the first place are used together with existing forms in free variation to perform the same range of language functions. At some later point the learner tries to maximize his linguistic resources by eliminating free variation. At this point we will observe systematic variability according to the situational and linguistic contexts of use. At a still later stage, systematic variability may for some learners, at least, give way to the categorical use of chosen variants (which may or may not be identical with target language norms). This process of development is shown diagramatically in Figure 1. It should be noted, however, that this is not intended as a model of overall interlanguage development (i.e. the stages do not correspond to stages in the vertical development of SLA taken as a whole). Rather it shows how new interlanguage forms, which may appear at different developmental points, evolve.

This review of the major issues involved in viewing interlanguage as a variable system points to the pervasiveness of different kinds of variability in language-learner language and also suggests the significance of variation as a mechanism for change in the process of SLA. At this point it is useful to step back from the research and formulate an overall framework for considering variability in SLA. This I now attempt in the form of a series of propositions, based both on the foregoing research and sociolinguistic theory.

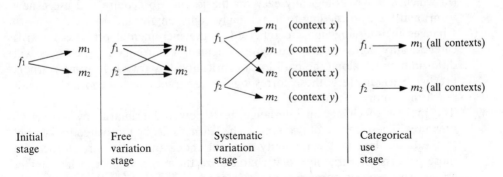

f = form
m = meaning
'context' refers to both situational and linguistic contexts

FIGURE 1   *The changing pattern of variability in SLA*

A general framework for variability in SLA

The following propositions are an attempt to define a framework for viewing SLA as a variable phenomenon. They should be viewed as hypotheses rather than absolute facts. They are our 'best bets' from what we currently know about variability in SLA.

(1) All interlanguage systems are heterogeneous. At any single stage of develop-

ment, including the terminal stage, at least some forms will exist in free variation.

(2) Systematic variability occurs when the learner selects specific forms and begins to use them in accordance with extralinguistic and intralinguistic factors. This variability will be evident in all levels of interlanguage (phonology, lexis and grammar).

(3) Stylistic variability is a reflection of the degree of explicitness/implicitness with which knowledge of linguistic variants is represented in the learner's interlanguage. The learner operates a stylistic continuum such that different variants are manifested with different frequencies in different styles. These styles range from the careful to the vernacular and arise as a product of the degree to which the learner is focused on form.

(4) New linguistic forms can enter the learner's interlanguage in any style, but the careful style is especially prone to invasion. In contrast the vernacular style is relatively stable. One of the principal ways in which change takes place in interlanguage is through the spread of selected variants from the careful style towards the vernacular style.

(5) When new linguistic forms enter the learner's interlanguage they will not do so in all linguistic environments at once. Environments can be ordered according to their 'weight', with learning occurring first in 'heavy' environments (in which it is psychologically easy for the learner to acquire and use a new form) and then proceeding to increasingly 'light' environments.

(6) Changes in interlanguage are reflected in the incremental progress towards categoricality across styles and across linguistic environments. Learners will differ in how far along the path to categoricality they travel. In some learners prestige 'variants' (e.g. those corresponding to target language norms) will not reach their more casual styles.

(7) The process of change in interlanguage is powered primarily by normative pressures. These can be of two kinds. The learner may be motivated to 'belong' to the target language community and will endeavour, therefore, to acquire those patterns of variability that characterize the target dialect of his contact group. This type or normative pressure can be labelled 'social'. Alternatively the normative pressures can derive from the authority and status inherent in institutional structures. These will be influential either when group structure is weak so that 'social' pressures are minimized or when the context of learning does not involve contact with the target language community, as, for instance, in classroom learning. The particular type of institutional normative pressure present in the foreign language classroom can be characterized as 'pedagogic'. Learning continues as long as the learner acknowledges either 'social' or 'pedagogic' normative pressures; it ceases when the learner is no longer open to such pressures. In this case the learner's interlanguage 'fossilizes' in whatever state of variability it has reached at that point.

(8) Change can also occur as a result of structural pressures that arise in an interlanguage system through the introduction of new variants. The learner is led to maximize the efficiency of his system in order to communicate effectively.

This induces a chain reaction effect on existing resources once these are augmented. Whereas the normative pressures referred to above can be viewed as 'external', the kind of structural pressure that occurs as a result of these normative pressures, can be seen as 'internal'. The constant flux of interlanguage systems is the result of this internal pressure.

These eight propositions comprise what I call a 'variability perspective' on SLA. It is now time to consider the relevancy of language teaching in the light of this perspective.

The relevancy of language teaching

It is possible to identify a clear thread in many of the current attempts to apply models of SLA to language teaching. It is this. Language teaching should attempt to create in the classroom conditions which exist in 'natural' language learning (Hughes, 1983). In its strongest form this has led to the claim that formal language instruction involving the presentation and practice of target language rules has no place in successful language learning. In other words, for language teaching to be relevant it must only provide opportunities for authentic communication. In this part of the paper I want to dispute this claim. I shall endeavour to show that the 'variability perspective' outlined in the previous section provides a principled basis in SLA theory for 'accuracy' work as well as 'fluency' work. I shall consider three areas of language pedagogy – syllabus design, language teaching materials and classroom practice – and argue in each case for a balanced approach incorporating both 'accuracy' and 'fluency'.

(1) **Syllabus design**. A syllabus for language teaching will consist of a statement of the content that is to be taught. This content can be specified in two different ways. It can consist of an itemization of *linguistic* features. These may be presented either directly as a list of language forms or indirectly as a list of functions and semantico–grammatical categories together with their linguistic exponents. Both a structural and a notional syllabus provide a linguistic content, differing only in how the linguistic material for learning is organized. Thus they are both *product* syllabuses, because they are both characterized by a content consisting of the linguistic products to be learnt. The alternative to this kind of syallabus is a *process* syllabus (also referred to as a procedural or task based syllabus). In a process syllabus no attempt is made to specify the linguistic features to be taught. Instead the content of the syllabus is specified as a list of activities or tasks to be performed by the learners under the guidance of the teacher. A process syllabus, in fact, will not have the appearance of a language syllabus at all, but will resemble the syllabus of a content subject such as science or geography. An example of a process syllabus is that used in the Bangalore Project (see Johnson, 1982). Examples of the kind of content found in this syllabus are 'making the plan of a house', 'choosing routes from a map' etc.

There are two major questions we need to ask about these two methods of specifying the content of a syllabus. (1) Is it possible to make a principled choice between them, i.e. to argue that one is more likely to lead to successful classroom learning than the other? (2) If no principled choice is possible, how can the two methods be jointly used to produce an integrated syllabus involving both product and process elements? I shall address these questions from the variability perspective.

The assumption that underlies a process syllabus is that 'form is best learnt when the learner's attention is on meaning' (Prabhu, 1982; cited in Brumfit, 1984). We find a similar claim in Krashen and Terrel (1983): 'Language is best taught when it is used to transmit messages not when it is explicitly taught for conscious learning'. Also Breen (1983) argues for 'greater concern with the capacity for communication . . . with a focus upon means rather than predetermined objectives'. The justification for these claims comes from SLA theory, in particular Krashen's Monitor Model. The learner is credited with an in-built syllabus of his own which dictates the route of acquisition and which cannot be altered by pedagogic attempts to structure the linguistic content of learning from the outside. All that is required is the opportunity to engage in meaningful communication. But the theory of SLA that protagonists of a process syllabus draw upon takes no account of variability and its role in acquisition. Instead it views the learner's competence as homogeneous and learning as a series of more or less discrete stages.

A variability model of SLA lends greater support to a product syllabus. Recall that it is the learner's careful style that is most permeable. Recall also that new rules arise as the result of normative pressures, one source of which is the authority of institutional structures (i.e. in the case of the classroom, the teacher). The careful style is characterized by close attention to form. Here, then, are grounds for arguing that the process of change in interlanguage can be directed by supplying the learner with the norms of the target language, presented as a series of items to be carefully practised. This is exactly what is intended by a product syllabus. The learner is systematically introduced to the formal structures of the target language which are given normative status by authority of the syllabus. A variability perspective, therefore, provides a warrant for a product syllabus. Such a syllabus can serve two functions. First, it can provide a basis for developing the learner's careful style (which in the case of learners who have no need or wish to engage in spontaneous language use will be sufficient in itself). Second, it can serve as a basis for fostering variable structures in the learner's interlanguage by introducing new variants, which, later on, given the right conditions, can spread through the stylistic continuum and so become available for use in more casual styles.

Our knowledge of the nature of variability in SLA, however, suggests that not all grammatical structures are candidates for style-shifting and, the corollary of this, not all structures can enter into the learner's careful style as explicit knowledge. Structures that are regular are easy to formulate, thus easy to teach and easy to learn. Faerch and Kasper (forthcoming), for instance, found that a Danish learner of L2 English and L2 German found it easier to apply conscious knowledge in a translation task (which tapped the careful style) for German than for English. They speculate that this was because this kind of knowledge was more comprehensive in this subject's German interlanguage because German has many low-level rules that are obligatory, frequent, easy to formulate and thus easy to teach. It may be, therefore, that we need to restrict the items in a product syllabus to those that are learnable as explicit knowledge. Pica (1985) lends support to such a view. Her research shows that whereas instruction appears to be successful in the case of structures where there is form-function transparency (e.g. plural -*s*), it has no effect on structures which are complex (e.g. article *a*). We need to know more about those structures that can be influenced by instruction. We also need to discover more about what structures exhibit variability, because it is in precisely these areas that instruction should help most (Hyltenstam, 1985). With these provisos, a variability model of SLA provides a solid rationale for a product syllabus.

It also provides a rationale for a process syllabus. The spread of knowledge along the stylistic continuum requires the opportunity to engage in a range of language styles, including the vernacular. This is precisely what a process syllabus aims to provide. It presents the learner with a series of tasks the main purpose of which is to motivate communication. We can hypothesize that this fosters interlanguage development in a number of ways. First, the learner will be motivated to eliminate free variation in order to increase the efficiency of his communication. Thus free variation will give way to systematic variation. Second, he will have the opportunity of 'trying out' the variants of his careful style in more casual styles. Third, he will be encouraged to explore new linguistic environments for existing variants i.e. learn how to use them in increasingly 'light' linguistic contexts. The process by which new forms advance along the stylistic continuum is a complex one. It is doubtful whether this process can be structured from the outside. Therefore, a process syllabus has value because it provides the learner with the 'space' for his variable system to grow and to reshape. A process syllabus is the best bet for encouraging the movement towards categoricality.

Swan (1985) comments 'learning a language is not the same as using a language'. I believe that learning is very closely related to using but that nevertheless the point that Swan is getting at is correct. Swan, as I understand him, wants to make a distinction between the 'learning' that occurs as a result of teaching directed by a product syllabus with 'using' what has been learnt in natural communication. In the context of variability theory the same idea can be expressed more neatly; learning to perform in a careful style is not the same as learning how to perform in a vernacular style. It is, however, as Swan argues, a good start. The point I wish to emphasize is that different kinds of use result in different kinds of learning.

The variability perspective, then, lends support to both a product and a process syllabus. The question arises as to how they can be combined into a single integrated syllabus. One possibility is to arrange a tight integration, where specific 'products' are linked to the performance of specific tasks in the process component of the syllabus. This will produce a 'spiral syllabus' of the kind proposed by Brumfit (1980) – see Figure 2 (a). Although this arrangement is appealing, it is not, I think, feasible. This is because it is impossible for syllabus designers to predict which linguistic forms introduced as explicit knowledge will actually be called upon when the learner is required to perform in casual styles. It is the learner himself who must determine how his variable system will develop. The 'spiral syllabus', therefore, seems less appropriate than the 'parallel syllabus', in which there are two separate strands, one for 'products' and the other for tasks, each graded and sequenced separately. In such a syllabus the principal decision will be to decide what proportions of teaching time to allocate to the product and process strands. This decision will need to be informed by a number of factors, including the general goal of the syllabus (e.g. whether to develop a full stylistic range in the learner or whether to focus on developing a mono-stylistic competence, careful or vernacular) and the age of the learner (e.g. young children may not have developed the cognitive capacity to acquire a careful style and so would benefit from a syllabus heavily weighted in favour of the process component).

(2) **Language teaching materials**. One way of viewing language teaching materials is as devices for implementing a syllabus. It follows, then, from what has already been argued, that we require materials of two basic kinds. First, materials are needed to introduce the learner to the norms of the chosen target language variety, that is, to present and practise specific linguistic items derived from the product component of the syllabus. We can refer to these as 'focused materials'. Second, materials are needed to enable the learner to develop his

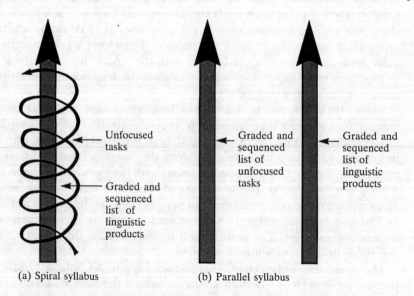

FIGURE 2   *Two ways of 'integrating' product and process in syllabus design*

variable interlanguage system. These will facilitate the dispersal of variants throughout the stylistic continuum. This kind of materials will consist of 'unfocused activities' based on the process component of the syllabus.

Where focused materials are concerned, one decision to make is how to deal with meaning. In structural materials the focus will be placed on linguistic forms and meaning will be handled through contextualization. In functional and notional materials the focus will be placed on meaning and linguistic form will be handled by selecting exponents of specific functions and notions. I do not wish to enter into the pros and cons of these two approaches to focused materials. Probably, as Swan (1985) argues, we need both. Essentially, however, both approaches serve the same basic purpose. That is, their relevancy lies in the effects they achieve in developing the learner's careful style. They will enable the learner to consciously manipulate specific linguistic items for conveying specific meanings, when he is focused on form. There should, however, be no expectancy that focused materials of either type will in themselves foster the ability to use these items in spontaneous language use (i.e. the vernacular style). Their role in language pedagogy should be seen as that of laying a foundation of knowledge upon which the learner can himself act in the subsequent process of building a variable interlanguage.

A variability perspective on SLA does suggest one way in which focused materials can be refined. Traditionally language drills have been developed to practise selected formal features (and their meanings) with little regard for the linguistic environment in which these features are embedded. We might try to take account of the way the learner acquires new forms by systematically presenting them in different linguistic contexts, sequenced according to how 'heavy' or 'light' they are. This is likely to call for a cyclical approach in which items are initially presented in 'heavy' environments and then later reintroduced in 'lighter' environments. At the moment SLA research does not provide us with sufficient information to reliably determine how linguistic environments should be weighted, but there is nothing to stop the materials writer doing as he has always done and base his decisions on his own intuitions, informed by the general principle of incremental learning over different linguistic environments for which a sufficient warrant already exists in SLA research.

Unfocused activities are designed to stimulate what is often referred to as 'authentic communication' in the classroom. They are characterized by the following (based on Ellis, 1982):

(1) A non linguistic outcome (e.g. drawing a picture, making a model, solving a problem)
(2) a concern for message rather than channel.
(3) A gap of some kind (opinion, information, personal feelings) which has to be bridged.
(4) A need to negotiate meanings in order to achieve the outcome.
(5) Learner control over the resources (verbal or non-verbal) that are used.

When the learner performs in unfocused activities he will not, in the first instance, be able to access forms in his careful style. Thus, analysed knowledge learnt through drills will not be readily available. He will be forced back on those processes involved in using and internalizing a vernacular style. However, we can hypothesize that the communicative pressure that arises from using language in this way induces a 'pull' effect and so leads to the stylistic spread of new forms. The extent to which this takes place will be influenced by the extent to which the learner accepts the social norms implicit in the 'correct' target language forms. For unfocused materials to do their job the learner must be seen to be 'striving toward a norm', for it is this that 'will pull the learner's whole repertoire in the direction of variation similar to that found in the native speaker's use of the language' (Littlewood, 1981: 155). However, this striving should consist of a general orientation to the learning task rather than as a conscious attempt to apply target language norms in specific activities. The latter would simply result in further practice of the learner's careful style.

So far this discussion of language teaching materials has been based on the apparent dichotomy of focused and unfocused materials. However, these constitute a continuum rather than a dichotomy. Many pedagogic activities are intermediate. That is, they will meet some but not all of the five criteria listed above. It is tempting, therefore, to see a parallel between the stylistic continuum of interlanguage and the focused/unfocused continuum of language teaching materials. At one end there will be drills which influence the learner's careful style while at the other end there will be communication activities that influence the vernacular style. In between there will be a variety of activities corresponding to the range of styles between the poles of the continuum. We might go further and speculate that by sequencing activities according to their degree of focus, we can lead the learner along the stylistic continuum. In such a course, we would start with focused activities and then gradually introduce more and more unfocused activities. In this way the materials would reflect and support the process by which a variable interlanguage develops. Such a proposal is far from revolutionary. Arguably, it corresponds to well tried pedagogic practice.

The most important lesson to be learnt from a variability perspective on SLA is that the value of language teaching materials is relative. Different kinds of materials foster different kinds of learning. Potentially all materials are relevant. Irrelevancy occurs when the teacher or the learner seeks to achieve one kind of learning through the exploitation of materials which are only capable of fostering a different kind of learning.

(3) **Classroom practice**. Dickerson (1975) makes a number of general comments about the applications of a variability perspective on SLA to classroom practice. She writes:

> The knowledge that the learner operates a variable interlanguage system should be of practical value to the language teacher in such areas as teacher attitude, teacher expectations and the evaluation of student practice.

Dickerson argues that the teacher should expect variability in her students' perform-ance and should cease to be surprised that 'backsliding' occurs. Also the teacher should recognize that change is bound to be gradual. No matter how skilfully the teacher handles the presentation and practice of new items these will not be immedi-ately assimilated into the learner's system. Therefore the teacher should be prepared to acknowledge degrees of attainment. That is, she should not measure all learner productions against the norms of the target language but give credit for productions that display progress even though they are still 'deviant' in terms of the native speaker's grammar. Finally, Dickerson suggests that, because learner performance varies according to task, the teacher should avoid making comparisons between different kinds of task. The learner's progress needs to be measured with reference to performance in each style considered separately.

Perhaps the major aspect of classroom practice which a variability perspective can shed light on is classroom interaction. Any learning that takes place in the classroom arises in the course of interaction – between the teacher and the students, in pairs or groups of students or between students and texts. Interaction, then, is 'the funda-mental fact of language pedagogy' (Allwright, 1984a). In this view language teaching materials are not so much devices for implementing the syllabus as tools for generating classroom interaction. What does a variability perspective have to say about the relationship between classroom interaction and language learning?

The classroom has the potential for affording a range of interactional types (see Ellis, 1984a). These can derive from pedagogic activities (i.e. from the implemen-tation of different kinds of language teaching materials). They can also derive from classroom management and organization activities, providing that these are conducted in the target language. Also, if the target language functions as the medium of communication between students (as is likely to be the case in mixed ESL classes) there will also be interactions of a social nature. These various kinds of interaction can be classified according to whether they afford 'planned' or 'unplanned' discourse. The former is discourse that lacks forethought and that has not been organized prior to actual performance. It is most clearly evident in spontaneous oral communication. Planned discourse is discourse that has been organized before it is performed. This organization can occur at different levels – the overall framework of the discourse, the construction of sentence plans and the motor programme for performing the discourse. The two discourse types constitute the poles of an interactional continuum and they arise under different conditions of use. In unplanned discourse we find interchangeability of roles between the participants, informality, spontaneity and reciprocity. In planned discourse we find fixed roles, formality, rigidity and lack of reciprocity (cf. Lakoff, undated).

Now, the argument I want to advance is that different types of classroom interaction contribute the advancement of the learner's variable interlanguage system in different ways. The stylistic continuum is both the product and the reflection of participating in different types of discourse ranged along the planned/unplanned continuum. Participation in the kind of planned discourse that results from teacher-directed language drills leads to the acquisition of target language norms in the learner's careful style. Such discourse is likely to be characterized by the familiar three phase pattern (initiate – response – feedback) described by Coulthard and Sinclair (1975) and also by overt error correction. Its purpose is to enforce pedagogic norms. Participation in the more freely-structured discourse that results from unfocused activities requires the performance of a greater range of speech acts and induces the negotiation of meanings required for the development of a vernacular style. Thus, learning is linked to language use with different kinds of learning arising out of different kinds of language use. The development of a variable interlanguage rests on the availability of opportunities to take part in different kinds of classroom interaction.

We can conclude, therefore, that the relevancy of language teaching is, in the final analysis, to be found in ensuring a match between the interactional opportunities afforded the learner and the kind of competence the teaching is designed to create. As Ellis (1984b) comments:

> Because different kinds of knowledge and different processes of language use are involved in different discourse types, it cannot be expected that the acquisition of one style will facilitate the use of another style.

Conclusion

I began this paper by referring to research that showed that although formal instruction appears to have a beneficial effect on the language performance that is elicited by using instruments such as translation tasks, it does not appear to have any effect on spontaneous use. I noted that Krashen's Monitor Model provides an apparent explanation in terms of the distinction between 'acquisition' and 'learning'. I would like to conclude this paper by querying whether Krashen's explanation is the best one.

First, it should be clear that a variability model of SLA, such as that outlined in this paper, is also capable of explaining why formal instruction benefits only elicited performance. We can assume that the instruction provided by Schumann and Perkins and Larson-Freeman was of the kind that affected the development of the learner's careful repertoire. That is, that it consisted largely of focused activities leading to planned discourse. This repertoire would be available when the learners performed their careful style but would not be available for spontaneous language use in the vernacular style. Thus the effects of instruction would be observed when the learners' careful style was elicited but not when the data collection instrument required the vernacular style. This is exactly what the results of the two studies show.

Thus Krashen's Monitor Model and the Variability Model are both able to explain the research results. How, then, can we choose between them? One way is by taking a look at some further research into the effects of instruction on SLA. Long (1983b) has reviewed most of the available research dealing with this issue. His conclusion is as follows:

> Put rather crudely instruction is good for you, regardless of your proficiency level, of the wider linguistic environment in which you receive it, and of the type of test you are going to perform on.

In other words, instruction helps to speed up the rate of learning even if it does not effect the pattern of learning. Long argues that these findings are not easily accommodated by the Monitor Model unless the importance of 'learning' is upgraded. Now, this is precisely what a variability model does by suggesting that (1) formal instruction can benefit the development of the learner's careful style and (2) knowledge initially available in the learner's careful style can be 'pulled' into other more casual styles, providing that certain conditions are met. Classroom learners will outperform naturalistic learners on tasks that tap the careful style. They will also outperform them on tasks that tap other styles providing they have the opportunity to extend explicit knowledge towards and into the vernacular style. This opportunity can exist in the classroom when unplanned discourse occurs. For ESL learners (who were the subjects of most of the research Long looked at) this opportunity is also likely to exist outside the classroom. To put it another way, when learners are subject to pedagogical and social normative pressures, their interlanguages will be more permeable to change and thus will develop more rapidly.

The Monitor Model is a homogeneous competence model. Krashen sees no connection between 'acquisition' and 'learning'; monitoring is a feature of performance, not competence. Krashen has used the Monitor Model, which I believe to be fundamentally wrong, to argue the case for a language pedagogy directed at supplying comprehensible input through focusing on meaning in natural communication. In this scheme of things the formal teaching of the linguistic code is relegated to a position of almost zero importance. As Faerch (forthcoming) points out the blanket rejection of formal language teaching is both arrogant and contrary to the successful experiences of many teachers, who have used traditional grammar teaching methods. Nor, I have tried to argue, is the blanket rejection of grammar teaching warranted if account is taken of interlanguage as a variable system. A variability perspective treats the learner's competence as heterogeneous. Applied to language pedagogy, it stresses the dual contribution of formal and informal instruction, of accuracy and fluency. These can be fostered by a parallel syllabus incorporating both product and process elements leading to materials that vary in the extent to which they are 'focused' on language form and, through these, to a range of discourse types from the planned to the unplanned in the classroom itself. Not only is such a model of SLA better equipped to deal with the known facts of SLA, but the approach to language pedagogy which it supports is compatible with the experiences of countless successful teachers.

I would like to end with a few words of caution. The proposals for language teaching that I have put forward on the basis of a variability perspective for SLA are intended to stimulate thought – in particular regarding the relationship between 'accuracy' and 'fluency' activities. I am aware that our current knowledge of SLA – and this includes our knowledge of variability – is still sparse. Arguably it does not provide an adequate basis for making explicit recommendations. Hyltenstam (1985) suggests that SLA research is applicable to pedagogy on two levels; (1) a very specific and narrow level (i.e. where detailed proposals about syllabus design and teaching methodology are made) and (2) a more general level (i.e. where the teacher's general knowledge about SLA influences his daily practice in different ways). Hyltenstam argues that the results of SLA research are still too fragmentary to justify (1). It seems to me, though, inevitable that we should seek to apply our increasing understanding about how SLA takes place to language pedagogy, and that, there is nothing wrong with specific and direct proposals, providing that these are treated in the same way as other specific proposals based, for instance, on linguistic enquiry. That is, they should be viewed tentative, as *suggestions* rather than directions. It is in this spirit that I have advanced arguments for a pedagogical approach based on what we currently know about SLA variability.

Variability and Language Testing[1]

PETER SKEHAN

Institute of Education, University of London

Current approaches to language testing: the problem of sampling

The basic purpose of language testing is to sample language behaviour in such a way that generalizations may be made about the testee's likely performance in other (usually non-test) situations. Debates among language testers are therefore frequent on the methods of sampling that may be employed, on the ease of generalization to other situations, and on the range of situations that it is permissible to generalize to. In all these cases, the issue revolves around the way in which some sort of fairly arbitrary number scale, lying somewhere between the nominal type and the equal interval type, may form the basis for statements about how people will perform when confronted with real-life, or 'criterion' situations. One can identify three main phases in language testing in recent years, and, by way of general background, each of these will now be discussed.

The psychometric/structuralist phase is mainly associated with a view of language which sees it as analysable by means of a skills-by-levels matrix. One axis of the matrix consists of the four language skills while the other is concerned with putative *levels* of language, i.e. phonology, syntax, lexis etc. The intersection of these two axes produces something like sixteen to twenty-four cells, each of which may be measured (see, for example, the discussion in Davies, 1977). The cells so defined are thought to represent the essential building blocks of language so that one can gain an accurate picture of general language performance by sampling the matrix of cells as widely and as systematically as possible. By so doing one obtains a broad based measure of a general language capacity.

The integrative phase of language testing disputes the viability of sampling components of analysable building blocks of language, and instead proposes the need to examine extended chunks of language. Further, the integrative approach often focuses on the testee's capacity to utilize predictive skills in order to deal with redundancy in language. This capacity of prediction, thought to be basic for language processing, draws upon different aspects of the language system (syntactic, semantic, and pragmatic) to handle ongoing language comprehension and production. Efficient sampling is therefore achieved by ensuring that representative segments of language are reduced in redundancy and the candidate's ability to cope with these changes is measured. This fundamental, unitary, and pervasive capacity can then be the basis for (statistical) predictions of how the testee will operate in other situations.

Although different from one another in that the psychometric approach focuses on different components while the integrative approach emphasizes one underlying skill, the two approaches have in common that they seek to measure a general *linguistic* ability which is the foundation or base for other performance. However, both approaches have been attacked in recent years by proponents of communicative language testing, who claim that testing has to reflect real features of communication, such as time-pressure, interaction, purpose, relationships between participants, and unpredictability (Morrow 1977, 1979). It is felt, in other words, that measures of linguistic competence, such as those that may be produced by psychometric or integrative tests, will not be a sound basis for predicting how testees will perform when faced with real communicative situations. Consequently, a variety of techniques have been devised of both a direct and semi-direct nature which require candidates to interact with interlocutors, or achieve collectively some communicative aim, or answer questions in a structured interview, or make judgements about the appropriateness of possible responses etc. Such techniques, it is thought, will provide a better sampling basis for generalization although it must be said that the expansion of testing techniques so involved has not been accompanied by consensus as to how the different aspects of communicative behaviour relate to one another.

In addition to the more practical developments of actual assessment techniques, attempts have been made to provide a theoretical framework for language testing. Canale and Swain (1980) for example, propose that general communicative competence is composed of grammatical, sociolinguistic, discourse, and strategic competences. Within such a framework, the psychometric and integrative approaches to language testing can be seen as focusing on linguistic competence, while more recent attempts to produce more communicative tests have involved various degrees of emphasis on all four competences. Some tests highlight sociolinguistic factors such as relationships between participants and/or appropriateness of response, others emphasize the testee's sensitivity to discourse organization (often in an academic or ESP setting) and the ability to handle extended chunks of language. Finally, some tests may incorporate difficult one-way or two-way information gap tasks which bring into sharp relief the candidate's strategic ability in dealing with situations where communication is difficult and resourcefulness to get a message across is at a premium.

The implication of a model such as Canale and Swain's for language testing in that a much wider sampling of behaviour is necessary if we are to be able to generalize about a candidate's likely performance in new situations. It certainly implies that knowledge of someone's linguistic competence may not be revealing about his ability to function appropriately with different text types and when communication difficulties are encountered. Indeed, the model raises the possibility that competence in each of the four areas *may* develop separately. There has not been much published research as yet to explicate empirically the sort of inter-relationships that may hold between the different components of the model. However, an interesting, although anecdotal, account is provided in Schmidt (1963) of the longitudinal development of Wes, a Japanese learner of English in Hawaii. Wes manifested remarkably little grammatical development over a three-year period, and not much more sociolinguistic improvement. However, he did make considerably greater development in discourse and strategic competence, to the extent that he was able to engage in extensive and fairly effective interactions with native speakers by the end of the three-year period.

In other words, despite making relatively little improvement in grammar, Wes did manage to learn how to tie bits of language together to convey his intended meanings.

He also became more resourceful when communication breakdowns occurred, so that his interactions did not continue to impose a considerable burden on native speaker interlocutors, and the breakdowns which occurred resembled, for the native speaker interlocutors themselves, the sorts of breakdown that occur anyway in ordinary native speaker–native speaker interactions. The example of Wes demonstrates the possibility of exclusively grammatical competence based tests (and, in this case, sociolinguistic competence as well) not reflecting the considerable linguistic improvement he made in other areas of language functioning over the time period in question, and of the need to have a wider framework for evaluation of language performance.

However, it should he said that although models such as that of Canale and Swain extend our knowledge of the breadth of what is to be sampled, they still do not claim to provide us with anything close to a blueprint of how to set about constructing a comprehensive battery of language tests, nor as they provide us with the frame-work for an analysis of language elicitation tasks. This, however, brings us closer to the main theme of this chapter, which is to consider, against the general background of the discussion of language testing already provided, what the study of language variability can contribute to our understanding of how to sample language.

Models of variability; their implications for language testing

The task of relating language variability research to language testing is considerably facilitated by the discussions of different paradigms for studying variability provided by Tarone (1983) and Ellis (1985b). Tarone distinguishes between three such paradigms – homogeneous competence, dual competence, and a capability continuum – and to these Ellis adds a fourth, that of multiple competence.

Tarone's discussion of the homogeneous competence paradigm makes it clear that such an approach carries with it clear implications for language testing. The paradigm emphasises the competence which is homogeneous and which guides language behaviour generally. This would argue for a single dimension of language use, perhaps best assessed through the total score of a battery of tests generated by a skills-by-levels matrix, or alternatively by a single score taken from a representative integrative reduced redundancy test which loads highly on Oller's unitary competence factor (where Oller's terminology has a clear and direct relationship with homogeneous as used by Tarone). Further, the ideal data for the homogeneous competence paradigm would be intuitional data (and perhaps elicited language). This would be seen as reflecting most clearly an underlying competence without intrusion of performance errors. This, in turn, would seem to legitimize the indirect nature of many of the testing techniques associated with the psychometric and integrative eras, and suggest that since such techniques provide the most faithful route into an underlying homogeneous competence, they would be the soundest basis for generalization about language performance in a variety of contexts.

The dual knowledge paradigm also has clear implications for language testing. Krashen (1981) has argued that performance based on learning and acquisition will produce two different orders of accuracy, such that learning-based (and monitored) performance will favour accuracy with syntactic rules that are simple to understand

and easy to implement when time is available. He contrasts this with the 'natural order' which is revealed when performance is based on the acquired system. Krashen, in other words, posits two (*and only two*) distinct orders of acquisition (or, more properly, accuracy) which will be revealed according to the contexts in which data is obtained. He is suggesting, that is, that there are two basic types of testing situation. In one, when there is time available, a focus on form, and the opportunity to use easy rules, a certain type of performance will prevail. In the other, when none of the crutches for monitoring is available, the natural order will manifest itself. Krashen (1981) uses this analysis to account for discrepancies in test results which have been obtained by different investigators, and even suggests that the debate on the unitary competence hypothesis, i.e. that some investigators have reported one unitary factor while others have reported several, is resolvable to the extent that a multi-factor solution to language competence is found when there is opportunity for at least some monitoring, while unitary factors are found when tests truly tap acquisition. The implication is that tests should elicit performance based on acquisition if useful generalization to actual language use is to be made, while tests which elicit learned performance are likely only to be the basis for prediction about how well students will do in artificial, 'monitorable', situations.

In terms of testing, therefore, the dual competence appproach is similar to the homogeneous competence paradigm in proposing one test-type which is adequate as a basis for sampling. However, unlike a homogeneous competence which would accept intuitional and elicited data, the dual competence approach favours unmonitored, 'acquired' speech as the basis for sampling. However, it has to be said that the distinction, in principle, between the two competences is not easy to operationalize (cf. the discussion in McLaughlin, 1978), and Krashen has been severely criticized (see e.g. Skehan 1984a; Green, 1984) on his tendency to play fast-and-loose with actual tests which are sometimes assigned to the monitored category and sometimes to the acquired, with the assignment being variable but always protective of the Monitor model.

In terms of the study of variability, though, it is obviously the third and fourth paradigms which are more interesting for language testing. The capability continuum proposes that the capability (not competence, Tarone 1983:151) underlying performance constitutes a range of styles along a continuum, and that this continuum is mainly, if not exclusively, affected by the amount of attention that is paid to speech. The continuum nature of the range of styles connects with overlapping grammars at each point of the continuum by means of variable and categorical rules. The range of styles is bounded at one end by the vernacular, where least attention is paid to speech, which is the most stable, and which is least permeable by other rule systems. At the other extreme we have the formal style, where most attention is paid to speech, which is the least stable, and which is most permeable by the other rule systems. Finally, with the capability continuum, *acquisition* arises either from forms spontaneously produced in the (stable) vernacular, or through diffusion of new forms, which are originally produced in the formal style, but from which: 'In time, the adjustment can be expected to spread to less formal types of performance, and in the last instance, it will show up in informal oral production' (Hyltenstam, 1978:6).

The capability continuum is most interesting for language testing in terms of the linguistic data that it advocates collecting. Basically it proposes that the existence of a continuum of styles implies that data collection at any one point of the continuum will be inadequate, and that effective testing would involve sampling at various points if a complete picture of a learner's language performance is to be obtained. Consequently, there is a place for spontaneous data; for the collection of imitations; for elicited data; and intuitional judgements. Thus the whole range of the language tester's armoury is legitimized to the extent that it has a place along the style continuum and reflects the degree of attention paid to speech. Speakers will not be characterizable in terms of a single score but will have to be tested in a variety of situations. As Ellis (in press) has noted, the performance of individuals will vary significantly from one point of the continuum to another, such that the criterial used to discriminate between levels of performance will shift, cf. the different accuracy orders in his study for the past regular and past irregular depending on the degree of both language and content planning involved. In fact, Ellis proposes that the degree of speech planning is an important influence on performance and variability. Planning, in turn, is separable from degree of attention since it raises the issue of the amount of pre-speaking and situation preparation that may have been engaged in. This, in turn, raises that issue of the degree of organization of one's knowledge which, in turn, is likely to influence the ease of planning (Bialystok and Sharwood-Smith, 1985). We will return to this issue below. At the very least, however, it can be seen that different amounts of planning, either of content or language, will influence performance so that sampling behaviour will require that performance with varying opportunities for preparedness will be important to get a true picture of an individual's capability.

Finally, Tarone's discussion of the capability continuum suggests that tests of the extremes of the speech continuum may have special significance for acquisition. Tests of vernacular performance may reflect the emergence of spontaneously produced new forms. Alternatively, tests of the formal style may pick up first or early appearance of forms which will spread along the continuum as speakers learn to 'act on their knowledge' (Widdowson, 1975). This approach would be useful if also accompanied by painstaking charting as the new form moved along the continuum as it offers the possibility of identifying which aspects of the language system emerge spontaneously in the vernacular and which spread from the formal style. (See Pienemann, 1985 for interesting discussion on the features of language to which this might apply.) Such potential research would also constitute an interesting empirical test of the capability continuum. It might also provide information on aspects of the system which do not spread completely, or alternatively, those aspects of the system whose progress is halted by fossilization.

Perhaps finally in this section it is worth mentioning Tarone's discussion of the Observer's Paradox: that the very attempt on the investigator's part to elicit speech will alter the situation for the speaker and cause him to pay attention to language, hence influencing the results. Possibly language testers have been overly sanguine about the ease with which they can enter subject's lives and extract useful data. This problem can be seen very clearly when one takes account of the work of Beebe

(1980; Beebe and Zuengler, 1984) on the relevance for second language acquisition of Giles' speech accommodation theory. She shows how the speaker's psychological perception of an interlocutor may cause him to converge or diverge in terms of speech style. The most obvious manifestation of such accommodation is likely to be with accent (cf. Giles and Powesland, 1975; Giles, 1979). However, other features of speech may also be affected, such as *amount* of speech, as well as syntactic complexity – highly salient variables for the evaluation of speech performance (Beebe and Zeungler, 1984; Milanovic, 1985). Thus, choice of interviewer for oral interaction assessment may influence the results obtained. In view of the slender amount of research evidence currently available, it is difficult to know how significant this eventually may be. However, it is immediately obvious how important it is likely to be in ESL situations as well as those which have a multi-ethnic or cultural dimension, since in such cases interlocutor variables may be highly salient psychologically for the interviewee.

The fourth paradigm, multiple competence, was introduced by Ellis (1985b) following Selinker and Douglas (1985). It proposes that second language acquisition involves the construction of several interlanguages which are separate but overlapping in terms of role systems. Such systems are domain specific, so that we are left with the need to identify the areas of language use which have to be investigated separately. For language testing this requires that separate tests will be required for each significantly definable domain since the claim that is being made essentially is that it is hazardous to generalize language performance to new areas of discourse. Sampling therefore necessitates covering the relevant domains. In theory such an approach has obvious implications for the testing of English for Specific Purposes, an area where great difficulty has been experienced in arriving of appropriate levels of specificity (Criper, 1982; Skehan, 1984b), and the identification of distinctly separate domains.

Some problems in variability research

The four paradigms described above have provided an exceptionally useful framework within which to view the problem faced by the language tester in deciding how to obtain representative data. The homogeneous competence and the dual knowledge approaches are interesting but not very significant for variability, as Tarone (1983) has shown. The capability continuum and the multiple competences approaches are far more useful, and demonstrate the range of situations which need to be sampled if anything like a comprehensive picture of the individual's performance is to be obtained, and if the variability in performance is to be captured. This enlarged conception of the problem of sampling can only be beneficial for language testing.

However, there are some problems with contemporary approaches taken to the study of variability, and it is important to consider these also. In fact, it could well be that contempoary developments in language testing may help to clarify some of these issues such that variability and language testing may be ripe for crossfertilization.

The first problem is that currently variability and style shifting are mainly related to the amount of attention paid to speech. Attention is assumed to be continuous and to underlie a continuum of style. Ideally this perspective would require that it can be demonstrated that an operationalized measure of attention (and only attention) can be related systematically to variability and style-shifting. This problem is, in fact, similar to that faced by Krashen in terms of operationalizing the distinction between learning and acquisition (see above) except that now the problem is increased in scale since the gradations involved are no longer simply a dichotomy. Sato (1985) suggests that there is no objective way of determining how much attention is devoted to form in different tasks, and that consequently it would be more accurate to claim that the attention–variability connection can only be regarded as an assumption.

However, there may be reasons to believe that even such an assumption is not tenable. It may be preferable, in fact, to try and elaborate a more complex model of the role of attention, to do justice to the range of empirical data that is already available. Rampton (this volume) has shown that young speakers in multi-ethnic situations exploit the solidarity connotations of 'broken' English to achieve effects with other multilingual interlocutors. This is done in 'vernacular' speech situations in a conscious way which is clearly recognized by their hearers. In other words, even in a seemingly 'low-attention to speech' situation, such speakers apply some thought to the effects they can create by manipulation of sociolinguistic aspects of code. Trevise and Noyau (1984) similarly describe a Spanish speaker who is acquiring French in France. The speaker is integratively motivated. The main part of Trevise and Noyau's study emphasizes variable rules for French negation, relating them to conditions of elicitation. Contrary to prediction, however, one of their speakers produced the more vernacular form of negation (' – pas' as opposed to the more formal 'ne – pas') when more attention to speech was possible. When less attention was involved, she produced the 'ne – pas' form. A subsequent interview revealed that the learner in question, presumably because of her integrative motivation, was aware of the variability of the negation rule and its sociolinguistic dimension, and used the vernacular form even though less natural to her, whenever she had sufficient time to pay attention to form since she wanted to appear 'natural'.

Finally, we can draw attention to Beebe's work (Beebe, 1980; Beebe and Zuengler, 1984) applying Giles' speech accomodation theory to second language acquisition (Beebe and Giles, 1984). She has shown that second language speakers accommodate to their interlocutor. This may take the form of converging (i.e. becoming more like the speech of the interlocutor), or diverging (becoming less like it) depending on a complex set of factors such as integrative vs. instrumental motivation (Bourhis and Giles, 1977) and psychological orientation of the interlocutors towards one another (Thakerar, Giles and Cheshire, 1982). Earlier work by Giles emphasizes convergence and divergence mainly in terms of accent. However, Beebe and Zuengler (1984) have also shown that the amount of talk, its syntactic complexity, and content are affected by interlocutor accommodation. Thus it is possible for variability in language to occur towards or away from vernacular styles independently of degree of attention paid to speech, since one assumes the various types of accommodation consume similar amounts of attentional resources. More generally, the research by Rampton, Trevise and Noyau, and Beebe has demonstrated that sociolinguistic factors may be salient even in what are often regarded as low-attention situations like the vernacular. Speakers may perceive the 'vernacular' as a desirable conversational style and invest additional attention in approximating what they perceive it to be.

Perhaps the real source of all this difficulty is the need to be more precise about what attention consists of. The capability continuum seems to assume a fairly uni-dimensional approach with degree of attention related to fairly superficial aspects of the task. It may be better to work towards models of attention more grounded in cognitive psychology. It has been proposed for example, that attention involves the co-ordinated functioning of different memory systems. In particular, speech planning may involve the assembly, in short-term memory (Hatch, 1980), of units or chunks of language from long-term memory which are accessed with different time delays prior to their execution as speech. Short term memory is limited in capacity, and therefore the assembly of speech units prior to their execution poses capacity problems – the limits of the system may be regularly stretched as new elements enter. Hatch (1980), following Atkinson and Schiffrin (1968) and Baddeley (1976) suggests that one has to take account, within STM, of both a memory store as well as control processes, with the memory component working flexibly with the control processes and indeed being controlled by them. Speech requiring extensive memory use would limit the flexibility and scope of control processes that are usable while speech involving more complex decisions would use up space and mental resources which would otherwise be available for memory. Further, the control processes themselves would be varied, so that in addition to handling the problem of a memory vs. control processes tradeoff, different and competing demands on attentional resources would arise if different aspects of long-term memory had to be accessed, and/or if some aspects of production e.g. phonology, were more salient. The model, therefore, looks upon STM as a workspace and a bottleneck, vital for speech production and comprehension, but constraining such processes because of STM characteristics. If a lot of material has to be retained in STM, there is little scope for control processes to devote themselves to focusing on form. If very little material has to be remembered (possibly because the speaker chooses to use 'simplified', undemanding language), there will be more scope for control processes to operate and for there to be a focus on form.

The model, however, has clear implications for the study of variability and style shifting. It can accommodate the existing uni-dimensional research, such as that reported in Dickerson and Dickerson (1977) and Fasold (1984), fairly easily. One would normally expect word list reading to involve minimal memory demands and so to allow considerable attentional resources for phonological factors. In turn, dialogue reading would require more extensive use of memory, and also access to more suprasegmental conventions of language processing which do not make extensive demands of attentional resources, but definitely more than those implicated in word-list reading. Vernacular speech, on the other hand, may require a much greater degree of planning (Ochs, 1979), with more elements occupying short-term memory space during half-completed plans, and extensive control operations to marshal all the resources that are being used. In addition, more attention would have to be devoted to interpretation of the speech contribution of the interlocutor. Consequently, there is likely to be less spare capacity to devote to variably used aspects of the language system.

The advantage of the flexible workspace approach to attention becomes clearer when we examine the inconsistencies in variability data mentioned earlier, i.e. the results of Rampton, Trevise and Noyau, and Beebe. Control and attentional resources may be committed by the speaker to ensure sociolinguistic effectiveness, so that the desire to demonstrate integrativeness with the target language society may consume the requisite attention (cf. Trevise and Noyau), or alternatively the need to manipulate simultaneously solidarity to ingroups as well as distancing from outgroups (Rampton) may override factors generally associated with vernacular speech. However, sociolinguistic factors are not the only factors which may re-prioritize the allocation of attentional resources. Speech planning may also be important, as Ellis (in press) has demonstrated, such that the micro decisions made during speech production may be more viable in some situations for language learners than in other contexts (planning factors will be discussed more fully below). Similarly, the demands made by the interaction itself may require attention, as in the case of the speech accommodation studies reviewed above, where interlocutors are, in some sense, deliberately matching or mismatching their speech to achieve a certain effect.

In other words, simply focusing on attention on the speech continuum and equating it with formality may fail to capture the way in which sociolinguistic and psycholinguistic factors may be important in the vernacular and actually require more attention if interlocutors are to be sensitive to one another. An information processing model allows a greater concern with these additional speech planning factors over and above that resulting from an attention-equals-formality perspective. It does this by drawing on the idea of control processes operating within the flexible workspace of primary memory to prioritize attention. If socio- and psycholinguistic factors are paramount, then they can consume considerable attention so that interlocutors can ensure that they are coming across correctly, whether through 'hedged boasts' (Rampton) or accommodations to their interlocutors (Beebe and Zuengler) or 'riskier' uses of the past tense (Ellis).

The major disadvantage with this changed perspective on the functioning of attention is that it is more intuitively satisfactory than it is experimentally testable. It re-analyses attention so as to accommodate discrepant results from the capability continuum approach but as a result it is close to allowing any pattern of results, since a post-hoc account of the priorities for attentional resources can always be found. This problem will be deferred until the last section of this paper, when, even, if a solution is not proposed, the relevance of language testing techniques to the problem is discussed.

So far in this section, we have looked at the problem of attention in variability research. A second general area where the capability continuum may require some expansion relates to the *content* of the speech involved. Recently, Selinker and Douglas (1985) have proposed that the task–style variability studied by Tarone is a subset of 'context' variability which is based on domains of discourse. In other words, speakers will be able to operate differently in different areas – Selinker and Douglas, for example, contrast the performance of an ESL learner first when he is speaking about crtitical path schedules (a technical subject), and second, about Mexican cooking.

The discussion by Selinker and Douglas has a clear relationship with developments in English for Specific Purposes (as pointed out above). Selinker and Douglas, and many ESP writers, suggest that performance in circumscribed areas is describably different from performance in other areas. In ESP this has led to the prospect of designing more efficient courses, while for Selinker and Douglas the implication seems to be the dangers of generalizing from one domain to another, when, in fact, domain differences will make this impermissible. Consequently, language testers, (e.g. Carroll, 1980; Weir, 1983), when they produce tests for separate areas, will need to justify the choice of areas that they make, and how performance on a given test from a specific domain can be the basis for judgements about the probable performance in other areas.

There are, however, similar problems for Selinker and Douglas as there are for needs analysis based ESP course designers (Munby, 1978). First of all there is the need to identify discourse domains. If we are to expect different performance in different domains, then it is important to be able to identify what constitutes a domain, and how domains are to be distinguished from one another. This is related to the issue within ESP of what makes for specific areas, and what levels of specificity one should aim at. Within ESP many have argued that the pursuit of specific purpose language is misguided, and that specific domains which make different demands on features of the language code are hard to find. Certainly within language testing the attempts to find appropriately restricted domains which can be tested have been severely criticized (Criper, 1982; Skehan, 1984b) for lacking any theoretical motivation.

It is argued here that it would be more useful to ask what influences the performance one may observe in different domains. This would allow general features of language processing to emerge which are implicated to different degrees in different domains. One approach to such a general framework is provided by Bialystok and Sharwood-Smith (1985) when they propose the existence of knowledge-based as well as control-based influences on performance. Knowledge-based influences, in their model, refer to the degree of analycity of the linguistic system. These are related, in the case of the language learner, to the extent of organization within this domain. Control-based influences implicate processing constraints which are designed to cope with the underlying knowledge base in the context of actual performance conditions.

It is proposed here that the range of Bialystok and Sharwood-Smith's model should be widened to include more than simply linguistic factors. It should also include knowledge of and degree of analycity of, different subject areas (or domains). This, in turn, would implicate the accessibility of the different areas, since some will be relatively diffuse and at low stages of analycity, while others will be more organized, and have established 'pre-packaged' organization. When well-analysed areas are the basis for speech, the organization of the area concerned will require less processing attention, and liberate attentional resources for potential use elsewhere. When more diffuse areas are concerned, part of the effort of production will involve the actual process of reorganizing the knowledge base, or at least coping with its lack of structure. As a result, more attentional resources will be required, in the form of control processes in STM having to work harder at retrieving and organizing information.

This analysis allows us to reinterpret Selinker and Douglas' proposal of discourse domains in terms of domains with different knowledge structure. Such domains as are well-organized, whether because of extensive previous analysis, extensive previous use, or simply inherent ease, will be susceptible to less demanding planning and will be the basis for more fluent communication. Domains which are more diffuse (either conceptually, for native speakers, or linguistically, for language learners, or both, for language learners talking about a complex subject, e.g. critical path schedules) will be more demanding to speak about, such that planning processes will consume considerable attentional resources. The extended analysis of a knowledge-based system provides a framework within which the various types of speech planning can fit, so that conceptual problems (Selinker and Douglas) and linguistic problems (Ellis) can be seen to be similar in the difficulties they pose.

In effect, therefore, the model of memory functioning outlined in the previous section has been widened to clarify the relationship between short-term and long-term memory. The previous discussion was in terms of capacity limitations within STM and the tradeoff between short-term memory storage and control processes. The present discussion has tried to clarify some of the ways control processes have to operate upon the contents of long-term memory when the structure and organization of such long-term memory material may be at various degrees of organization, analycity, and accessibility.

Language testing and variability

The preceding section has discussed two general problems in the study of variability. First, it has examined difficulties associated with equating style shifting and variability with amount of attention, and second, the role of the content of speech, drawing on Bialystok and Sharwood Smith's recent discussion of knowledge-based and control-based influences on performance. In this final section, it will be argued that techniques associated with language testing may now be useful to variability researchers in attempting to operationalize the more general models of speech performance that are involved, and to make predictions of language performance rather than provide post-hoc 'explanations'.

Language testers have been obsessed for many years with the twin goals of reliability and validity, and have developed an armoury of techniques for investigating the extent to which tests possess these desirable qualities. At times, language testers may seem to have been beguiled by mere numbers to the exclusion of reality. However, this labour may have been productive in terms of techniques developed. The concern with reliability, for example, has demonstrated the importance of consistency of measurement and of the elimination of error. In the present context, it may be that variability researchers too could benefit from running standard checks to establish the reliability of the measurements they are using. Otherwise inconsistent results are likely to occur simply because of the fickle behaviour of error variance and then become the basis for invalid generalizations.

More relevantly, however, in terms of the first problem discussed above, that of deciding how to operationalize the question of the amount of attention paid to speech, one recognizes the 'validation problem'. One needs to establish that tests which purport to require a particular use of attentional resources do, in fact, require such use. They must be demonstrated to do so stably and in contrast to other tests which are meant to require different use of attentional resources. Some of the techniques used recently to validate oral proficiency tests may be relevant. For example, convergent-discriminant approaches may help to establish systematic relationships between tests, even, possibly allowing investigation of how socio-linguistic factors may lead to different use of attentional resources and different patterning of results.

The most interesting connection between variability studies and language testing, however, is probably with the issue of the organization of and structure of knowledge domains. Language testers can recognize here the 'dimensions of language' problem, and see Bialystok and Sharwood-Smith's proposal of knowledge-based and control-based influences as the beginning of two-dimensional model of language structure. As such, the model becomes testable, since tests should be generated to occupy the four quadrants defined by Bialystok and Sharwood-Smith's two dimensions. The tests which are then produced on the basis of theory can then be subjected to factor analysis to investigate whether the underlying pattern of relationship confirms that predicted by theory.

Indeed it is striking how models of language performance proposed by language testers seem to embrace similar considerations. Cummins (1983), for example, distinguishes between the dimensions of cognitively-demanding/cognitively-undemanding and context-embedded/context-disembedded, while Canale (1983a), going beyond the earlier four competences framework (Canale and Swain, 1980), discusses three dimensions of language proficiency – a basic level, a communicative level, and an autonomous language proficiency, concerned with more disembedded uses of language. It seems that such discussions of language proficiency by testers have a similar status to those of variability theorists in that many insights are looking for corresponding empirical data. It is proposed that the techniques of language testing may be able to help us decide if the insights can be operationalized objectively, and whether the dimensions of language performance posited in the two cases are largely the same. If so, the concept of variability may be usefully expanded, and further aspects of variation in behaviour accounted for as systematic.

Note

1. The author would like to thank Ben Rampton for reading an earlier draft of this paper, and making extensive comments on it.

Section Six:

CONCLUSION

Concluding Comments

RICHARD ALLWRIGHT

University of Lancaster

Since these comments come at the end they may properly be called 'Concluding Comments', but they will not, and probably could not, constitute 'conclusions', because that would imply that the foregoing papers had all been leading in some particular and concerted direction towards closure of some sort. What I suggest we have is not 'closure' so much as a clear indication of heterogeneity, of lively research activity that is pursuing a great variety of goals in an equally great variety of ways. Any attempt to suggest overall consensus, to bring everything that is going on under some collective umbrella would seem to be not merely falsely optimistic but also both dangerously misleading and ultimately harmful. The field is not yet ready for a narrowing down of perspectives. We are still at the stage when a great range of perspectives is needed, when we need to encourage anyone with sufficient interest in the area to devote research energies and resources to it to work strictly from his or her own special viewpoint, rather than knuckle under to some premature claim that somehow we already know what lines of enquiry to pursue and how to pursue them.

What follows, then, is a personal statement of a personal viewpoint, one that may commend itself to others, but not, I hope, one that will appear to be demanding exclusive attention for itself. I write as a classroom researcher, and that means essentially as someone who has long been looking inside classrooms for clues to an understanding of language learning and teaching. In the last twenty or so years of language classroom research we have gone through a great variety of perspectives, starting with what now can be seen to have been hopelessly ambitious global hopes, and then retreating to look at almost any aspect of classroom behaviour that caught our fancy, without too much regard to what contribution we might be making to the underlying, but as yet very dimly perceived, theoretical issues. It is arguable, I believe, that that was a necessary stage in the research effort, rather than a time-wasting diversion. It is also the stage described above as characteristic of current work in the area of concern in this volume – the relationship between 'variability' and 'context' and between both of these and language learning. In classroom research, though, we may have done enough of the relatively random preliminary work to feel justified in thinking of ourselves as now coming out the other side, ready to adopt a more 'theoretical' perspective and pursue it wholeheartedly. My point in making such suggestions here is that they relate well to the issues of 'context' and 'variability'.

So, how does the perspective of classroom research relate to the notions of 'context' and 'variability'? The most obvious thing to say here is that the classroom is the setting for both the 'situational' and the 'contextual' types of variability distinguished by Tarone in her opening address, but for Tarone the central issue is always the variability in the behaviour of the individual, whereas for classroom researchers, and some of the other contributors to this volume, the central issue may be more how learner behaviour in general varies according to the setting in which it occurs. (There is also the interest in how learner behaviour sometimes varies in spite of an unvarying setting, as in Towell's study, and sometimes remains constant in spite of a varying setting, as in Weinert's.)

When we use the term 'learner behaviour', of course, we may mean at least two different things. From the sociolinguistic perspective we may be interested in behavioural variations whether or not they are linked to linguistic development, but from the primarily pedagogic perspective of language classroom research we are likely to be interested almost exclusively in variations in learning. (For the moment, at least, it seems preferable to use such terms as 'development' and 'learning' without intending technical meanings, and therefore crucial distinctions, for them.) We want to know, to put it crudely, what the relationship is between what teachers teach and what learners learn. For us the language classroom represents an especially interesting context for linguistic development in that although whatever happens there is likely to be primarily motivated by a desire on the part of the teacher to determine what linguistic development takes place, increasingly we are having, as researchers and as teachers, to face up to the possibility that whatever does in fact determine linguistic development in classroom language learners is largely independent of the deliberate teaching acts that are so carefully planned and conscientiously implemented in the classroom (see again Weinert's study).

For this researcher, at least, the clue to eventually understanding this puzzling situation may lie in what is probably a misleading assumption behind much of the work in the area. This is the assumption that what the learners actually get in the classrooms is best seen simply as the implementation of the teacher's plan. It seems more useful to me to see the language classroom as a social setting in which the sum total of classroom language learning opportunities is locally determined. This context itself determines, in some sense (see Lyons' definition of 'context', as cited in the Introduction), the language that is used there. That language then constitutes the input immediately available to the learners who happen to be present (accepting, for now, what is to me an unhelpfully narrow conception of 'input'), which in turn constitutes the sum total of learning opportunities presented by the classroom context. I could go on to claim that these learning opportunities themselves will determine the course of linguistic development for classroom language learners, but that would be an unereasonably strong claim to make in the light of recent research, rather we might simply claim that the sum total of learning opportunities sets logical limits to the linguistic development that it can conceivably make possible (unless we are willing to believe that the 'creative construction' process is so powerful that it can be relied upon to fill any and all gaps in the input). What all this amounts to is the point that taking the concept of context more seriously has enabled classroom researchers to break free from the limitations of their hitherto too 'pedagogic' view of what happens in language classrooms. The question 'why don't learners learn what teachers teach?' (see Allwright, 1984b) can now be looked at quite differently. Instead of having to react to it in terms of an apparent failure of the teaching to have any significant effect on learning, we can now see it in terms of our failure as researchers to realize that the planned teaching is only one part of the input available to classroom language learners, even without the four walls of the classroom. At the same time our general experience as classroom researchers tells us that a purely linguistic notion of input is unreasonably narrow. As soon as we adopt the perspective of thinking in terms of 'learning opportunities' instead of 'teaching points' we can see that learning opportunities do not just consist of linguistic 'items'. They also include various forms of guidance about the language being learned, from simple error correction to lengthy explanations of linguistic phenomena. These also are parts of the context, and parts of the context that are typically attended to particularly carefully by the learners, if they are bothering to attend at all to what is going on.

We are now ready to import into this perspective some 'theoretical' background to more precisely 'motivate' our research effort. We can hope to throw light, in the classroom context, on the 'theory-based' claim that the notion of comprehensible input is the key to our understanding of second language acquisition, in or out of the classroom. This claim has been explored in a number of studies, but it has not been put to the test in any clear way. It is relatively easy to show that different sorts of classroom activities lead to different quantities of 'conversational adjustments', but quite another matter to demonstrate that these different quantities are themselves causally related to linguistic development. In any case, as soon as we look at ordinary classroom data we see much more going on than just conversational adjustments being made, and we begin to think more naturally in terms of the 'quality' of classroom interaction rather than of the mere quantity of conversational adjustments, in line with the earlier comments about the need to broaden the scope of the term 'input', in the light of classroom data.

Mere mention of a term like 'quality of interaction', however, is asking for trouble, especially if it appears to carry with it the implication that we already know what we mean by 'quality'. In a sense all we know is that we should expect it to be a highly complex matter, and that we should prepare ourselves for an exhaustive enquiry that takes into account at least the range of perspectives represented in this volume – the sociolinguistic, the linguistic, the pedagogic, and that from work in second language acquisition. Following Ellis's lead we might expect input variability to be a major contributory factor, but I would suggest (no doubt *with* Ellis) that we should not expect it alone to provide us with all the explanations we need of the phenomena of classroom language learning. Finally, we have also to be wary of imagining that all the answers are to be found in the immediate 'context' of classroom language learning anyway. However far studies of the classroom context take us we must expect that there will be phenomena that resist explanation in contextual terms. As yet we do not know, and can hardly even guess, just how far studies of context will in fact take us, but we do know already (from preliminary research being conducted at Lancaster, but also from common experience) that what learners get from lessons can be remarkably idiosyncratic and mysterious. We have learners claiming, for example, to have learned words from a particular lesson in spite of the fact that there is no trace of those words in the classroom transcript. Perhaps they are merely mistaken, but until we can be sure of that, we must surely assume both that a narrow conception of 'context' is unlikely to be misleading, and that even the broadest conception of 'context' (if it is to remain meaningful) will be unable to account for everything of interest to us in our attempt to properly understand classroom language learning.

These 'concluding comments' have been motivated by a desire to relate the themes of this volume to my own concerns as a language classroom researcher. I have not, however, felt any strong need to spell out those themes as I see them. Rather I have taken them for granted as a heterogeneous collection of concerns that will already be familiar to the reader. I have also taken heterogeneity as their key feature, and tried to show that this heterogeneity is an important strength. At the same time, however, I have attempted to show that this heterogeneity is something that is timely as far as language classroom researchers are concerned, because it offers just the variety of perspectives that is needed to throw light on the 'theoretical' issue now under investigation by them.

Bibliography

Abrahams, R. (1976) *Talking Black*. Rowley, Mass.: Newbury House.

Adjemian, C. (1976) 'On the nature of interlanguage systems', *Language Learning,* **26**, 297–320.

Allwright, D. (1984) 'The analysis of discourse', in Davies, A., Criper, C. and Howatt A. (eds).

Allwright, R. (1980) 'Turns, topics and tasks: patterns of participation in language learning and teaching', in Larsen-Freeman, D. (ed.),

Allwright, R. (1984a) 'The importance of interaction in classroom language learning', *Applied Linguistics,* **5**(2): 156–71.

Allwright, R. (1984b) 'Why don't learners learn what teachers teach? – The interaction hypothesis', in Singleton, D.M., and Little D.G. (eds), *Language Learning in Formal and Informal Contexts*, pp. 3–18. Dublin: IRAAL.

Ammerlaan, A. (1984) 'A process-oriented approach to lexical strategies in referential communication'. Unpublished Master's Thesis, Nijmegen University.

Atkinson, J.M. and Drew, P. (1979) *Order in Court*. Macmillan.

Atkinson, J.M. and Schiffrin, R. (1968) 'Human memory: a proposed system and its control processes', in Spence, K.W. and Spence, J.T. (eds), *The Psychology of Learning and Motivation: advances in research and theory*. Vol. 2. New York: Academic Press.

Baddeley, A.D. (1976) *The Psychology of Memory*. New York: Basic Books.

Bahns, J. and Wode, H. (1980) 'Form and function in L2 acquisition', in Felix, S. (ed.), *Second Language Development*. Tübingen: Gunter Narr.

Barnes, D. (1969) 'Language in the secondary classroom', in Barnes D., Britten, J. and Rosen, H. (eds), *Language, the Learner and the School*. Harmondsworth: Penguin Education.

Bart, W. and Krus, D. (1973) 'An ordering theoretic method to determine hierarchies among items', *Educational and Psychological Measurement,* **33**: 291:300.

Bartlett, F.C. (1932) *Remembering*. Cambridge: Cambridge University Press.

Bateson, G. (1972) *Steps to An Ecology of Mind*. New York: Ballantine.

Beebe, L.M. (1977) 'The influence of the listener on code switching', *Language Learning,* **27**(2): 331–9.

Beebe, L.M. (1980a) 'Sociolinguistic variation and style-shifting in second language acquisition', *Language Learning,* **30**(1): 433–47.

Beebe, L.M. (1980b) 'Measuring the use of communication strategies', in Scarcella R., and Krashen S. (eds).

Beebe, L.M. (1981) 'Social and situational factors affecting the communicative strategy of dialect code switching', in Fishman, P. (ed.), *Unguarded and Monitored Language Behaviour, IJSL,* **32**.

Beebe, L. and Zuengler, J. (1983) 'Accommodation theory: an explanation for style shifting in second language dialects', in Wolfson, N., and Judd, E. (eds), *Sociolinguistics and Language Acquisition*, Rowley, Mass.: Newbury House.

Beebe, L.M. and Giles, H. (1984) 'Speech accommodation theories: a discussion in terms of second language acquisition', *IJSL,* **46**: 5–32.

Bell, A. (1984). 'Language style as audience design', *Language in Society,* **13**: 145–204.

Bellugi, U. and Klima, E. (1979) *The Signs of Language*. Cambridge, Mass.: Harvard University Press.

Bentlage, A. (1985a) 'Aspects of referential communication in a second language'. Unpublished MA thesis, Nijmegen University.

Bentlage, A. (1985b) 'Referring in a second language: some aspects of naming and describing', *Toegapaste Taalwetenschap in Artikelen* **23**: 15–25.

Bentlage, A., Bongaerts, E. and Kellerman, E. (forthcoming) 'Referential strategies in second language performance', in Gass, S. (ed.), *Studies in Second Language Acquisition* (Special issue on lexis).

Bialystok, E. (1983) 'Some factors in the selection and implementation of communication strategies', in Faerch, C. and Kasper G. (eds), pp. 100–18.

Bialystok, E. (1984) 'Strategies in interlanguage learning and performance', in Davies, A., Criper, C. and Howatt, A. (eds).

Bialystok, E. and Fröhlich, M. (1980) 'Oral communication strategies for lexical difficulties', *Interlanguage Studies Bulletin,* **5**: 3–30.

Bialystok, E. and Sharwood-Smith, M. (1985) 'Interlanguage is not a state of mind: an evaluation of the construct for second language acquisition', *Applied Linguistics,* **6**(3): 101–117.

Blom, J.P. and Gumperz, J.J. (1972) 'Social meaning in linguistic structure: code switching in Norway', in Gumperz, J.J. and Hymes, D. (eds), *Directions in Sociolinguistics. The Ethnography of Communication*, pp. 407–34. Holt Rinehart and Winston.

Bolinger, D. (1972) *Intonation*. Harmondsworth: Penguin.

Bordieu, P. (1977) *Outline of a Theory of Practice*. Cambridge: Cambridge University Press.

Bourhis, R. and Giles, H. (1977) 'The language of intergroup distinctiveness', in Giles, H. (ed.), *Language, Ethnicity and Intergroup Relations*. London: Academic Press.

Breen, M. (1983) 'Prepared comments on Keith Johnson's "Syllabus design: possible future trends" ', in Johnson, K. and Porter, D. (eds), *Perspectives in Communicative Language Teaching*. London: Academic Press.

Brown, G. (1985) 'A frequency count of 190,000 words in the London–Lund English conversation'. *Journal of Behavioural Research Methods, Instrumentation and Computation*, **16**: 501–531.

Brown, G. and Yule, G. (1983) *Discourse Analysis*. Cambridge: Cambridge University Press.

Brown, P. and Levinson, S. (1978) 'Universals in language usage: politeness phenomena', in Good, E.N. (ed.) *Questions and Politeness: strategies in social interaction*, pp. 56–289. Cambridge: Cambridge University Press.

Brown, P. and Levinson, S. (1979) 'Social structure, groups and interaction', in Scherer, K.R. and Giles, H. (eds), *Social Markers in Speech*, pp. 291–341. Cambridge: Cambridge University Press.

Brown, P. and Fraser C. (1979) 'Speech as a markers of situation', in Scherer, K. and Giles, H. (eds), *Social Markers in Speech*. Cambridge: Cambridge University Press.

Brown R. (1973) *A First language*. Cambridge, Mass.: Harvard University Press.

Brumfit, C. (1980) *Problems and Principles in English Teaching*. Oxford: Pergamon Press.

Brumfit, C. (1984) *Communicative Methodology in Language Teaching: the roles of fluency and accuracy*. Cambridge: Cambridge University Press.

Canale, M. (1983a) 'On some dimensions of language proficiency', in Oller, J.W. (ed.), *Issues in Language Testing Research*. Rowley, Mass.: Newbury House.

Canale, M. (1983b) 'From communicative competence to communicative language pedagogy', in Richards, J.C. and Schmidt, R.W. (eds), *Language and Communication*. London: Longman.

Canale, M. and Swain, M. (1980) 'Theoretical bases of communicative language teaching and testing', *Applied Linguistics*, **1**(1): 1–47.

Candlin, C.N. (1983a) 'Discourse patterning and the equalizing of interpretive opportunity, in Smith, L. (ed.), pp. 125–146, *op. cit.*

Candlin, C.N. (1983b) Preface in Faerch, C. and Kasper, G. (eds).

Carrell, P.L. (1983) 'Some issues in studying the role of schemata, or background knowledge, in second language comprehension', *Reading a Foreign Language*, 1(2).

Carroll, B.J. (1980) *Specifications for an English Language Testing Service*. London: British Council.

Chomsky, (1965) *Aspects of the Theory of Syntax*. MIT Press.

Cicourel, A. (1974) *Cognitive Sociology: language and meaning in social interaction*. New York: Free Press.

Clark, H. and Havriland, S. (1977) 'Comprehension and the given/new contract', in Freedie, R.O. (ed.), *op. cit.*

Cole, P. and Morgan, J. (1975) *Syntax and Semantics, Vol. 3: Speech Acts*. New York: Academic Press.

Cook, V.J. (1975) 'Strategies in the comprehension of relative clauses,' *Language and Speech*, **18**(3): 204–212.

Cook, V.J. (1977) 'Cognitive processes in second language learning', *IRAL*, **15**(1): 1–20.

Cook, V.J. (1985) 'Chomsky's universal grammar and second language learning', *Applied Linguistics*, **6**(1): 2–18.

Corder, S.P. (1967) 'The significance of learners' errors', *IRAL*, **5**(4).

Corder, S.P. (1974) 'Error analysis', in Allen, P. and Corder, S.P. (eds), *Techniques in Applied Linguistics. The Edinburgh Course in Applied Linguistics*, Vol. 3. Oxford: Oxford University Press.

Corder, S.P. (1978) 'Language learner language', in Richards, J. (ed.), *Understanding Second and Foreign Language Learning: Issues and Approaches*. Rowley, Mass: Newbury House.

Corder, S.P. (1981) *Error Analysis and Interlanguage*. Oxford: Oxford University Press.

Coupland, N.J.R. (1981) The social differentiation of functional language use: a sociolinguistic investigation of travel agency talk, PhD dissertation, UWIST.

Criper, C. (1982) 'Reaction to the Carroll paper (1)', in Anderson, J.C. and Hughes, A. (eds), *Issues in Language Testing*, ELT Document No. 111. London: British Council.

Cummins, J. (1983) 'Language proficiency and academic achievement', in Oller J.W. (ed.), *Issues in Language Testing Research*. Rowley, Mass.: Newbury House.

Davies, A. (1977) 'The construction of language tests', in Allen, J.P.B. and Davies, A. (eds), *The*

Edinburgh Course in Applied Linguistics, Vol. 4: Testing and Experimental Methods, pp. 38–104. Oxford: Oxford University Press.

Davies, A. and Widdowson, H.G. (1974) 'Reading and writing', in Allen, J.P.B. and Corder, S.P. (eds), *Edinburgh Course in Applied Linguistics*, Vol. 3. Oxford: Oxford University Press.

Davies, A., Criper, C. and Howatt, A.P.R. (1984) *Interlanguage*. Edinburgh: Edinburgh University Press.

De Camp, D. (1971) 'Towards a generative analysis of a post-Creole continuum', in Hymes, D. (ed), *Pidginization and Creolization*, pp. 349–70. Cambridge: Cambridge University Press.

Deulofeu, J. and Taranger, M.C. (1984) 'Relations entre le linguistique et le culturel: Microscopie de quelques malentendus et incomprehensions', in Noyau, C. and Porquier, R. (eds.), *Communiquer dans la Langue de l'Autre*, pp. 99–129. Saint Denis: Presses Universitaires de Vincennes.

Dickerson, L. (1974) Internal and external patterning of phonological variability in the speech of Japanese learners of English: towards a theory of second language acquisition. PhD dissertation, University of Illinois.

Dickerson, L. (1975) 'The learner's interlanguage as a system of variable rules', *TESOL Quarterly, 9*: 401–7.

Dickerson, W. and Dickerson, L. (1977) 'Interlanguage phonology: Current research and future directions', in Corder, S.P. and Roulet, E. (eds), *The Notions of Simplification, Interlanguages and Pidgins: Actes de sixième Colloque de Linguistique Applique de Neufchatel*, pp. 18–30.

Dittmar, N. (1980) 'Ordering adult learners according to language abilities', in Felix, S. (ed.), *Second Language Development*. Tübingen: Gunter Narr.

Dorian, N.C. (1982) 'Defining the speech community to include its working margins', in Romaine, S. (ed.), *Sociolinguistic Variation in Speech Communities*. London: Edward Arnold.

Downes W. (1984) *Language and Society*. London: Fontana.

Dressler, W.U. and Wodak, R. (1982) 'Sociophonological methods in the study of sociolinguistic variation in Viennese German', in *Language in Society*, II, 339–70.

Driver, G. (1980) 'How West Indians do better at school (especially the girls)', *New Society*, 17 January, pp. 111–4.

Dulay, H. and Burt, M. (1973) 'Should we teach children syntax?' *Language Learning, 23*: 245–58.

Dulay, H., Burt, M. and Krashen, S. (1982) *Language Two*. Oxford: Oxford University Press.

Edmondson, W., House, J., Kasper, G. and Stemmer, B. (1984) 'Learning the pragmatics of discourse: a project report', *Applied Linguistics, 5*(2), 113–27.

Edwards, V. (1985) 'Patterns of language choice and communication intent in a British Black Community.' Paper given at the International Conference on Languages and Dialects in Contact, Birkbeck College. To be published simultaneously in *Polyglot* and *CIRB*, Quebec, Serie-B.

Edwards, V. (1986) *Language in a British Black Community*. Clevedon, Avon: Multilingual Matters.

Ellis, R. (1982) 'Informal and formal approaches in communicative language teaching', *ELT Journal*, **36**(2): 73–81.

Ellis, R. (1984a) *Classroom Second Language Development*. Oxford: Pergamon Press.

Ellis, R. (1984b) 'The role of instruction in second language acquisition', in Singleton, D.M. and Little D.G. (eds), *Language Learning in Formal and Informal Contexts*. Dublin: IRAAL.

Ellis, R. (1984c) 'Can syntax be taught?: a study of the effects of formal instruction on the acquisition of WH questions by children', *Applied Linguistics, 5*(2): 138–55.

Ellis, R. (1985a) 'Teacher–pupil interaction in second language development' in Gass, S. and Madden, C. (eds), *Input in Second Language Acquisition*. Rowley, Mass: Newbury House.

Ellis, R. (1985b) 'Sources of variability in interlanguage', *Applied Linguistics, 6*(2): 118–31.

Ellis, R. (1985c) *Understanding Second Language Acquisition*. Oxford: Oxford University Press.

Ellis, R. (1987) 'Contextual variability in second language acquisition and the relevance of language teaching' (this volume).

Ellis, R. (forthcoming) 'Interlanguage variability in narrative discourse: style shifting in the use of the past tense', *Studies in Second Language Acquisition*.

Ellis, R. (forthcoming) 'The effects of linguistic environment on the second language acquisition of grammatical rules', Paper given at BAAL 1986.

Erickson, F. (1982) *The Counsellor as Gatekeeper*. New York: Academic Press.

Faerch, C. and Kasper, G. (1980) 'Processes and strategies in foreign language learning and communication', *Interlanguage Studies Bulletin* 5: 47–118.

Faerch, C. (1985) 'Meta talk in FL classroom discourse', *Studies in Second Language Acquisition, 7*(2): 184–99.

Faerch, C. and Kasper, G. (eds) (1983a) *Strategies in Interlanguage Communication*. London: Longman.

Faerch, C. and Kasper, G. (1983b) 'On identifying communication strategies in interlanguage production', in Faerch, C. and Kasper, G. (eds) (1983a), *op. cit.*

Faerch, C. and Kasper, G. (1983c) 'Plans and strategies in foreign language communication', in Faerch, C. and Kasper, G. (eds).

Faerch, C. and Kasper, G. (forthcoming) 'One learner–two languages: Investigation types of interlanguage knowledge', in Blum-Kulka, S. and House-Edmondson, J. (eds), *Interlingual and Intercultural Communication*. Tübingen: Gunter Narr.

Fairbanks, K. (1983) Variability in interlanguage. Unpublished manuscript, ESL Program, University of Minnesota.

Fairclough, N.L. (1985) 'Critical and descriptive goals in discourse analysis', *Journal of Pragmatics,* **9**.

Fakhri, A. (1984) 'The use of communicative strategies in narrative discourse: a case study of a learner of Moroccan Arabic as a second language', *Language Learning,* **34**(3). 15–37.

Fasold, R. (1984) 'Variation theory and language learning', in Trudgill, P. (ed.), *Applied Sociolinguistics.* London: Academic Press.

Felix, S. (1978) *Linguistische Untersuchungen zum natürlichen Zweitsprachenerwerb.* Munich: Wilhelm Fink.

Felix, S. (ed.) (1980) *Second Language Development.* Tübingen: Gunter Narr.

Felix, S. (1981) 'The effect of formal instruction on second language acquisition', *Language Learning,* **31**(1), 87–112.

Felix, S. (1982) *Psycholinguistische Aspekte des Zweitsprachenerwerbs.* Tübingen: Gunter Narr.

Felix, S. (1984) 'Maturational aspects of universal grammar', in Davies, A., Criper, C. and Howatt, A.P.R. (eds).

Felix, S. and Hahn, A. (1985) 'Natural processes in classroom second language learning', *Applied Linguistics,* **6**(3), 223–38.

Ferguson, G. (1983) 'The consequences of errors: a study of some judgements of error gravity in a sample of written compositions'. Unpublished MSc assignment, University of Edinburgh.

Ferrar, H. (1967) *A French Reference Grammar,* 2nd edition. Oxford: Oxford University Press.

Fillmore, C.J. (1979) 'On fluency', in Fillmore, E.H., Kempler, D. and Wang W.S.Y. (eds), *Individual Differences in Language Ability and Language Behaviour.* New York: Academic Press.

Fishman, P. (1983) 'Interaction: the work women do', in Thorne, B. Rowley, Mass.: Newbury House, Kramarae, C. and Henley, H. (eds), *Language, Gender and Society.*

Fowler, R. and Hodge, B. (1979) *Language and Control.* London: Routledge & Kegan Paul.

Fraser, B., Rintell, E. and Walters, J. (1980) 'An approach to conducting research on the acquisition of pragmatic competence in a second language', in Larsen-Freeman, D. (ed.), *op. cit.*

Freedle, R.O. (ed.) (1979) *Discourse Production and Comprehension.* Norwood, NJ: Ablex.

Furnborough, P., Jupp, T. Munns, R. and Roberts, C. (1982) 'Language disadvantage and discrimination: breaking the cycle of majority group perception', *JMMD* 3(3): 247–268.

Gaies, S. (1983) 'The investigation of language classroom processes'. *TESOL Quarterly,* **17**(2), 205–18.

Gal, S. (1979) *Language Shift.* New York: Academic Press.

Garfinkel, H. (1967) *Studies in Ethnomethodology.* Englewood Cliffs, NJ: Prentice-Hall.

Gass, S. and Madden, C., (eds) (1985) *Input in Second Language Acquisition.* Rowley, Mass.: Newbury House.

Gatbonton, E. (1978) 'Patterned phonetic variability in second language speech: A gradual diffusion model', *Canadian Modern Language Review,* **34**(3): 335–47.

Giddens, A. (1977) *Studies in Social and Political Theory.* London: Hutchinson.

Giles, H. (ed.) (1977) *Language, Ethnicity and Intergroup Relations.* New York: Academic Press.

Giles, H. (1979) 'Ethnicity markers in speech', in Scherer, K. and Giles, H. (eds), *Social Markers in Speech.* Cambridge: Cambridge University Press.

Giles, H. (1980) 'Accommodation theory: some new directions', in de Silva, S. (ed.), *Aspects of Linguistic Behaviour.* York University Press.

Giles, H. and Powesland, P. (1975) *Speech Style and Social Evaluation.* New York: Academic Press.

Giles, H. and St-Clair, R (eds) (1979) *Language and Social Psychology.* Oxford: Blackwell.

Giles, H. and Saint-Jacques, B. (eds) (1979) *Language and Ethnic Relations.* Oxford: Pergamon Press.

Glucksberg, S., Krauss R. and Higgins, E. (1975) 'The development of referential communication skills', in Horowitz, F. (ed.), *Review of Child Development Research,* **4**: 305–45.

Goodman, K.S. and Burke, C.L. (1973) 'The Goodman taxonomy of reading miscues', in Gollasch, F.V. (ed.) (1982) *Language and Literacy: the selected writings of Kenneth S. Goodman, Vol. 1: Process, Theory, Research.* Boston, Mass.: Routledge & Kegan Paul.

Goffman, E. (1971) *Relations in Public.* New York: Harper & Row.

Goffman, E. (1974) *Frame Analysis.* New York: Harper & Row.

Gregg, K.R. (1984) 'Krashen's Monitor and Occam's Razor', *Applied Linguistics,* **5**(2): 79–100.

Grice, H.P. (1967) 'Logic and conversation', reprinted in Cole, P. and Morgan, J. (eds). (1975), *Syntax and Semantics. Vol. 3*. New York: Academic Press.

Grice, H.P. (1975) 'Logic and conversation', in Cole, P. and Morgan, J. (eds), *Syntax and Semantics. Vol. 3: Speech Acts*. New York: Academic Press.

Grosjean, F. and Deschamps, A. (1975) 'Analyse contrastive des variables temporelles de l'anglais et du francais', *Phonetica, 31*: 144–84.

Gumperz, J.J. (1982a) *Discourse Strategies*. Cambridge: Cambridge University Press.

Gumperz, J.J. (ed.) (1982b) *Language and Social Identity*. Cambridge: Cambridge University Press.

Gumperz, J.J. (1984) *Communicative Competence Revisited*. Berkeley: University of California.

Gundel, J. and Tarone, E. (1983) 'Language transfer and the acquisition of pronominal anaphora', in Gass, S. and Selinker, L. (eds), *Language Transfer in Language Learning*. Rowley, Mass.: Newbury House.

Habermas, J. (1970a) 'On systematically distorted communication', *Inquiry, 13*: 205–18.

Habermas, J. (1970b) 'On communicative competence', *Inquiry, 13*: 360–75.

Hakuta, K. (1974) 'Prefabricated patterns and the emergence of structure in second language acquisition', *Language Learning, 24*, 287–98.

Halliday, M.A. (1978) *Language as a Social Semiotic*. London: Edward Arnold.

Harrison, C. (1980) *Readability in the Classroom*. Cambridge: Cambridge University Press.

Hatch, E. (1978) 'Discourse analysis and second language acquisition', in Hatch, E. (ed.), *Second Language Acquisition: a book of readings*. Rowley, Mass.: Newbury House.

Hatch, E. (1980) 'Conversational Analysis: an alternative methodology for second language acquisition studies', in Shuy, R. and Schnukal, A. (eds), *Language Use and the Uses of Language*. Georgetown University Press.

Hester, H. (1985) 'Learning from children learning', in Brumfit, C., Ellis, R. and Levine J. (eds), *English as a Second Language in the U.K.* ELT Documents 121. Oxford: Pergamon Press.

Hewitt, R., (1982) 'White adolescent Creole users and the politics of friendship', *Journal of Multilingual and Multicultural Development, 3*: 217–32.

Hinnenkamp, B. (1980) 'The refusal of second language learning in interethnic contexts', in Giles, H., Robinson and Smith (eds), *Language Social Psychological Perspectives*, pp. 179–84. Oxford: Pergamon Press.

Hitch, G. (1980) 'Working memory', in Claxton, G. (ed.), *Cognitive Psychology,* Methuen.

Huang, J. and Hatch, E. (1978) 'A Chinese child's acquisition of English', in Hatch, Ed (ed.), *Second Language Acquisition*. Rowley, Mass.: Newbury House.

Hudson, R.A. (1980) *Sociolinguistics*. Cambridge: Cambridge University Press.

Hudson, R.A. (1981) 'Some issues on which linguists can agree', *Journal of Linguistics, 17*: 333–43.

Huebner, A. (1983) *Longitudinal Analysis of the Acquisition of English*. Karoma Publishers.

Hughes, A. (1983) 'Second language learning and communicative language teaching', in Johnson, K. and Porter, P. (eds), *Perspectives in Communicative Language Teaching*. New York: Academic Press.

Hyltenstam, K. (1978) 'Variability in interlanguage syntax', *Phonetics Laboratory Working Papers 18*, pp. 1–79. Department of General Lingustics, Lund University, Sweden.

Hyltenstam, K. (1985) 'L2 learners' variable output and language teaching', in Hyltenstam, K. and Pienemann, M. (eds), *Modelling and Assessing Second Language Acquisition*, Multilingual Matters 18.

Hymes, D. (ed.) (1964) *Language in Culture and Society*. New York: Harper & Row.

Hymes, D. (1974) *Foundation in Socio-linguistics*. University of Pennsylvania Press.

Hymes, D. (1979) 'Sapir, Competence and Voices', in Fillmore, C., Kempler, D. and Wang, W. (eds) *Individual Differences in Language Ability and Language Behavior*, pp. 33–46. New York: Academic Press.

Hymes, D. (1980) *Language in Education: ethnolinguistic essays*. Language and Ethnography Series. Washington: Centre for Applied Linguistics.

Johnson, K. (1982) *Communicative Syllabus Design and Methodology*. Oxford: Pergamon.

Johnson, K. and Porter, D. (eds) (1983) *Perspectives in Communicative Language Teaching*. Oxford: Pergamon Press.

Kachru, B. (ed.) (1982) *The Other Tongue: English across cultures*. Oxford, Pergamon Press.

Kasper, G. (1979a) 'Communication strategies: modality reduction', *Interlanguage Studies Bulletin, 4(2)*, 266–83.

Kasper, G. (1979b) 'Errors in speech act realization and use of gambits', *Canadian Modern Language Review, 35*: 395–406.

Keenan, E. (1974) 'Conversational competence in children', *Journal of Child Language, 1*: 163–183.

Kellerman, E. (1977) 'Towards a characterisation of the strategy of transfer in second language learning', *Interlanguage Studies Bulletin, 2*: 58–145.

Kellerman, E. (1985) 'U-Shaped behaviour in advanced Dutch EFL learners', in Gass, S. and Madden, C. (eds).

Kellerman, E., Ammerlaan, A., Bongaerts, T. and Poulisse, N. (1986) 'System and hierarchy in L2 compensatory strategies', in Scarcella, R., *et al*. (eds).

Klein, W. and Dittmar, N. (1979) *Developing Grammars: the acquisition of German by foreign workers.* Heidelberg: Springer Verlag.

Krashen, S. (1976) 'Formal and informal linguistic environments in language learning and language acquisition', *TESOL Quarterly*, **10**: 157–68.

Krashen, S. (1977), 'The monitor model for adult second language performance', in Burt, M., Dulay, H. and Finocchiaro, M. (eds) *Viewpoints on English as a Second Language.* New York: Regents.

Krashen, S. (1981) *Second Language Acquisition and Second Language Learning.* Oxford: Pergamon Press.

Krashen, S. and Terrel, T. (1983) *The Natural Approach: language acquisition in the classroom.* Oxford: Pergamon Press.

Krauss, R., and Weinheimer, S. (1966) 'Concurrent feedback, confirmation, and the encoding of referents in verbal communication', *Journal of Personality and Social Psychology*, **4**: 343–46.

Krauss, R., and Weinheimer, S. (1967) 'Effect of referent similarity and communication mode in verbal communication', *Journal of Verbal Learning and Verbal Behaviour*, **6**: 359–63.

Labov, W. (1969) 'Contraction deletion and inherent variability of the English copula', *Language* **45**: (4).

Labov, W. (1970) 'The study of language in its social context', *Studium Generale*, **23**, 30–87.

Labov, W. (1972) *Sociolinguistic Patterns.* University of Pennsylvania Press.

Lakoff, R. (undated) 'Expository writing and the oral dyad as points on a communicative continuum'. Mimeograph. Berkeley: University of California.

Lange, D. (1979) 'Negation in natürlichen Englisch–Deutschen Zweitsprachenerweb: Eine Fallstudie', *IRAL* **17**(4):331–48.

Larsen-Freeman, D. (1976) 'An explanation for the morpheme acquisition order of second language learners', *Language Learning*, **26**: 125–34.

Larsen-Freeman, D. (ed.) (1980) *Discourse Analysis in Second Language Research.* Rowley, Mass.: Newbury House.

Le Page, R.B. (1980) 'Projection, Focusing, Diffusion', *York Papers in Linguistics*, York University.

Le Page, R.B. and Tabouret-Keller, A. (1982) 'Models and stereotypes of ethnicity and language,' *JMMD*, **3**(3): 161–92.

Levinson, S. (1983) *Pragmatics.* Cambridge: Cambridge University Press.

Lightbown, P.M. (1983) 'Exploring relationships between developmental and instructional sequences in L2 Acquisition', in Seliger, H. and Long M. (eds), *Classroom Oriented Research in Second Language Acquisition.* Rowley, Mass.: Newbury House.

Lightbown, P. (1984) 'The relationship between theory and method in second language acquisition research', in Davies, A., Criper, C. and Howatt, A. (eds).

Lightbown, P. (1985) 'Great expectations: second language acquisition research and classroom teaching', *Applied Linguistics*, **6**: 171–89.

Lightbown, P.M. and d'Anglejan, A. (1985) 'Input and acquisition for second language learners in and out of classroom', in Gass, S. and Madden, C.G. (1985) *Input in Second Language Acquisition.* Rowley, Mass.: Newbury House.

Littlewood, W. (1981) 'Language variation and second language acquisition', *Applied Linguistics*, **11**(2): 150–58.

Long, M.H. (1983a) 'Linguistic and conversational adjustment to non-native speakers', *Studies in Second Language Acquisition*, **5**(2):177–93.

Long, M.H. (1983b) 'Does second language instruction make a difference? A review of the research', *TESOL Quarterly*, **17**(3): 359–82.

Long, M.H. and Sato, C. (1983) 'Classroom foreigner talk discourse: forms and functions of teachers' questions', in Seliger, H. and Long, M. (eds) *Classroom Oriented Research in Second Language Acquisition.* Rowley, Mass.: Newbury House.

Long, M.H. and Sato, C. (1984) 'Methodological issues in interlanguage studies: An interactionist perspective', in Davies, A., Criper C. and Howatt A.P. (eds).

Lund, R. (1985) The formal accuracy of college German students with the finite verb on a communicative production task and linguistic awareness tasks. PhD dissertation, Curriculum and Instruction, University of Minnesota.

Lyons, J. (1969) *Introduction to Theoretical Linguistics.* Cambridge: Cambridge University Press.

Lyons, J. (1977) *Semantics*, Vols 1 and 2. Cambridge: Cambridge University Press.

McLaughlin, B. (1978) 'The monitor model: some methodological considerations', *Language Learning*, **28**(2): 309–32.

McLaughlin, B. (1980) 'Theory and research in second language learning: an emerging paradigm', *Language Learning*, **30**(2): 331–50.

Meek, H., Armstrong, S., Austerfield, V., Graham, I. and Plackett, E. (1983) 'Achieving literacy: longitudinal studies of adolescents learning to read, Routledge & Kegan Paul.

Mehan, H. (1979) *Learning lessons: social organization in the classroom*. Harvard University Press.

Meisel, J. (1980) 'Linguistic simplification', in Felix, S. (ed.).

Milanovic, M. (1985) 'Communicative language testing: profiles and certification'. Paper presented at the TESOL Convention, New York.

Miller, G. and Johnson-Laird, P. (1976) *Language and Perception*. Cambridge, Mass.: Belknap Press.

Milroy, L. (1980) *Language and Social Networks*. Oxford: Blackwell.

Milroy, L. (1984) 'Comprehension and context: Successful communication and communication break-down', in Trudgill, P. (ed.), *Applied Sociolinguistics*. New York: Academic Press.

Mittner, M. (1984) 'Strategies discursives, variabilité et situations de communication', in Extra, G. and Mittner, M. (eds) *Studies in Second Language Acquisition by Adult Immigrants*. Tilburg University Press, 83–112.

Mougeon, R. *et al.* (1979) 'Acquisition of English prepositions by monolingual and bilingual (French/English) Ontarian Students', in Eckman, F. and Hastings, A. (eds.), *Studies in First and Second Language Acquisition*. Rowley, Mass.: Newbury House.

Morrow, K. (1977) *Techniques of Evaluation for a Notional Syllabus*. London: Royal Society of Arts.

Morrow, K. (1979) 'Communicative language testing: revolution or evolution?' in Brumfit, C.J. and Johnson, K. (eds), *The Communicative Approach to Language Teaching*. Oxford: Oxford University Press.

Munby, J. (1978) *Communicative Syllabus Design*. Cambridge: Cambridge University Press.

Ochs, E. (1979) 'Planned and unplanned discourse', in Givon, T. (ed.) *Syntax and Semantics. Vol. 12: Discourse and Semantics*, pp. 51–80. New York: Academic Press.

Ochsner, R. (1979) 'A poetics of second language acquisition', *Language Learning*, **29**(1): 53–80.

Oller, J.W. (1979) *Language Tests at School*. London: Longman.

Olson, D. (1970) 'Language and thought: aspects of a cognitive theory of semantics', *Psychological Review*, **77**: 257–73.

Parrish, B. (1985) 'A new look at articles,' M.A. Plan B Paper. English as a Second Language, University of Minnesota.

Pavesi, M. (1984) 'The acquisition of relative clauses in a formal and informal setting: Further evidence in support of the markedness hypothesis', in Singleton, D.M. and Little, D.G. (eds), *Language learning in Formal and Informal Contexts*. Dublin: *IRAAL*.

Perdue, C. (1986) '*Devenir bi-lingue, parler bi-lingue*', in Lüdi, G. (ed.), *Devenir Bilingue, Parler Bilingue*. Tübingen: Gunter Narr.

Perdue, C. (ed.) (1984) *Second Language Acquisition by Adult Immigrants: a field manual*. Rowley, Mass.: Newbury House.

Perkins, K. and Larsen-Freeman, D. (1975) 'The effect of formal language instruction on the order of morpheme acquisition', *Language Learning*, **25**(2): 237–43.

Pica, T. (1983a) 'The role of language context in second language acquisition', *Interlanguage Studies Bulletin*, pp. 101–23.

Pica, T. (1983b) 'Adult acquisition of English as a second language under different conditions of exposure', *Language Learning*, **33**(4): 465–97.

Pica, T. (1984) Procedures for morpheme data analysis in second language acquisition research. Paper presented at the TESOL Convention, Houston, Texas.

Pica, T. (1985) 'Linguistic simplicity and learnability: Implications for language syllabus design', in Hyltenstam, K. and Pienemann, M. (eds), *Modelling and Assessing Second Language Acquisition*, Multilingual Matters 18.

Pica, T. (1985) 'The selective impact of classroom instruction on second language acquisition', *Applied Linguistics*, **6**(3).

Pienemann, M. (1984) 'Psychological constraints on the teachability of languages, *Studies in Second Language Acquisition*, **6**(2).

Pienemann, M. (1985) 'Learnability and syllabus construction', in Hyltenstam, K. and Pienemann, M. (eds), *Modelling and Assessing Second Language Acquisition*. Clevedon, Avon: Multilingual Matters.

Poulisse, N., Bongaerts, T. and Kellerman, E. (1984) 'On the use of compensatory strategies in second language performance', *Interlanguage Studies Bulletin*, **8**: 70–105.

Poulisse, N., Bongaerts, T. and Kellerman, E. (1986) 'The use of retrospective verbal reports in the analysis of compensatory strategies', in Faerch, C. and Kasper, G. (eds), *Introspection in Second Language Research*. Clevedon: Multilingual Matters.

Prabhu, N. (1982) 'The communicational teaching project', South India, mimeo. Madras: The British Council.

Rampton, B. (1985) Stylistic variability and not speaking 'normal' English: some post-Labovian approaches and their implications for the study of interlanguage. Paper presented at the Ealing Conference on Contextual Variability and Second Language Acquisition.

Rampton, M.B. (forthcoming) Language use in a multilingual British neighbourhood. PhD thesis, University of London, Institute of Education.

Raupach, M. (1983) 'Analysis and evaluation of communication strategies', in Faerch, C. and Kasper, G. (eds) (1983a), *op. cit.*

Raupach, M. (1984) 'Formulae in second language speech production', in Dechert, H.W., Möhle, D. and Raupach, M. (eds), *Second Language Productions*. Tübingen: Gunter Narr.

Richards, J.C. (1979) 'Rhetorical and communicative styles in the new varieties of English', *Language Learning*, **29**: (1).

Richards, J.C. and Sukwiwat, M. (1983) 'Language transfer and conversational competence', *Applied Linguistics*, **4**(2): 113–25.

Rivers, W. and Temerley, M. (1978) *A Practical Guide to the Teaching of English*. Oxford: Oxford University Press.

Roberts, C. (1985) *The Interview Game*. London: BBC Publications.

Rosansky, E.J. (1976) 'Methods and morphemes in second language acquisition research', *Language Learning*, **26**(2): 409–25.

Rosch, E. (1977) 'Human categorization', in Warren, N. (ed.), *Advances in Cross-cultural Psychology*, Vol 1. New York: Academic Press.

Rosen, H. and Burgess, T. (1980) *Language and Dialects of London School Children*. London: Ward Lock Educational.

Sacks, H., Schegloff, E.A. and Jefferson, G. (1978) 'A simplest systematics for the organization of turn-taking for conversation', in Shenkein, J. (ed.).

Sato, C. (1985) 'Task variation in interlanguage phonology', in Gass, S. and Madden, C. (eds), *Input in Second Language Acquisition*. Rowley, Mass.: Newbury House.

Scarcella, R.C. and Brunak, J. (1981) On speaking politely in a second language, *IJSL*, **27**: 59–75.

Scarcella, R.C. and Higa, C. (1981) 'Input, negotiation, and age differences in second language acquisition', *Language Learning*, **31**(2): 409–35.

Scarcella, R.C. and Krashen, S.D. (eds) (1980) *Research in Second Language Acquisition: selected papers of the Los Angeles Second Language Acquisition Research Forum*. Rowley, Mass.: Newbury House.

Scarcella, R.C., Andersen, E. and Krashen, S. (eds) (1986) *Developing Communicative Competence*. New York: Harper & Row.

Schank, R. and Ableson, R. (1977) *Scripts, Plans, Goals and Understanding*. Hillsdale, NY: Lawrence Erlbaum.

Schegloff, E.A. (1982) 'Discourse as an interactional achievement', in Tannen, D. (ed.).

Schmidt, R. (1977) 'Sociolinguistic variation and language transfer in phonology', *Working Papers in Bilingualism*, **12**: 79–95.

Schmidt, M. (1980) 'Co-ordinate structures and language universals in interlanguage, *Language Learning*, **30**: (2).

Schmidt, R. (1983) 'Interaction, acculturation and the acquisition of communicative competence: a case study of an adult', in Wolfson, N. and Judd, E. (eds).

Schumann, J. (1978a) *The Pidginization Process: a model for second language acquisition*. Rowley, Mass.: Newbury House.

Schumann, J. (1978b) 'Second language acquisition: the pidginization hypothesis', in Hatch, E. (ed.), *Second Language Acquisition: a book of readings*. Rowley, Mass.: Newbury House.

Scollon, R. (1976) *Conversations with a One Year Old*. University of Hawaii.

Scollon, R. and Scollon, S. (1981) *Narrative, Literacy and Face in Interethnic Communication*. Norwood, NY: Ablex.

Selinker, L. (1972) 'Interlanguage', *IRAL*, **10**: 201–231. Reprinted in Richards, C. (ed.), *Error Analysis*. London: Longmans.

Selinker, L. (1984) *The Current State of IL Studies: An Attempted Critical Summary*. In Davies *et al.* (eds), pp. 332–43.

Selinker, L. and Douglas, D. (1985) 'Wrestling with context in interlanguage theory', *Applied Linguistics*, **6**(2): 190–204.

Shenkein, J. (ed.) (1978) *Studies in the Organization of Conversational Interaction*. New York: Academic Press.

Simons, H. and Murphy, S. (1986) 'Spoken language strategies and language acquisition', in Cook-Gumperz, J. (ed.), *The Social Construction of Literacy*. Cambridge: Cambridge University Press.

Sinclair, J. and Coulthard, M. (1975) *Towards an Analysis of Discourse*. Oxford: Oxford University Press.

Skehan, P. (1984a) 'On the non-magical nature of second and foreign language learning', *Polyglot*, **5**(1).

Skehan, P. (1984b) 'Issues in the testing of English for specific purposes', *Language Testing*, **1**(2): 202–20.

Smith, L.E. (ed.) (1983) *Readings in English as an International Language*. Oxford: Pergamon Press.

Southgate, V., Arnold, H. and Johnson, S. (1981) *Extending Beginning Reading*. London: Heinemann Educational.

Stern, H. (1983) *Fundamental Concepts of Language Teaching*. Oxford: Oxford University Press.

Sutcliffe, D. (1982) *British Black English*. Oxford: Blackwell.

Swan, M. (1985) 'A critical look at the communicative approach (2)', *ELTJ*, **39**(2): 76–7.

Tajfel, H. (1981) In Tajfel, H. (ed.), *Human Groups and Social Categories*, pp. 17–40. Cambridge: Cambridge University Press.

Tanaka, S. and Kawade, S. (1982) 'Politeness strategies and second language acquisition', *Studies in Second Language Acquisition*, **5**(1): 18–33.

Tannen, D. (1979) 'What's in a frame?: surface evidence for underlying expectations', in Freedle, R.O. (ed.).

Tannen, D. (1981) 'The machine-gun question: an example of conversational style', *Journal of Pragmatics*, **4**.

Tannen, D. (1982) *Analyzing Discourse: text and talk*. Georgetown University Press.

Tarone, E. (1977) 'Conscious communication strategies in interlanguage: a progress report', in Brown, H., Yorio, C. and Crymes, R. (eds), *Teaching and Learning English as a Second Language, TESOL*, **77**, 194–203.

Tarone, E. (1979) 'Interlanguage as chameleon', *Language Learning*, **29**(1): 181–92.

Tarone, E. (1982) 'Systematicity and attention in interlanguage', *Language Learning*, **32**(1): 69–84.

Tarone, E. (1983) 'On the variability of interlanguage systems', *Applied Linguistics*, **4**(2): 142–63.

Tarone, E. (1985) 'Variability in interlanguage use: a study of style-shifting in morphology and syntax', *Language Learning*, **35**(3).

Tarone, E. and Yule, G. (1983) 'Communication strategies in East–West interactions', in Smith, L. (ed.), *Readings in English as an International Language*. Oxford: Oxford University Press.

Thakerar, J.N., Giles, H. and Cheshire, J. (1982) 'Psychological and linguistic parameters of speech accommodation theory', in Fraser C. and Scherer K.R. (eds), *Advances in the Social Psychology of Language*, pp. 205–55. Cambridge: Cambridge University Press.

Thomas, J. (1983) 'Cross-cultural pragmatic failure', *Applied Linguistics*, 4(2): 91–112.

Traugott, E. (1974) 'Exploration in linguistic elaboration: language change, language acquisition and the genesis of spatio-temporal relations; in Anderson, J. and Jones, C. (eds), *Historical Linguistics 1*. Amsterdam: North Holland.

Trevise, A. and Noyau, C. (1984) 'Adult Spanish speakers and the acquisition of French negation forms: individual variation and linguistic awareness', in Andersen, R.W. (ed.), *Second Languages*. Rowley, Mass.: Newbury House.

Troike, R. (1967) 'Receptive competence, productive competence and performance', *Georgetown Round Table Meeting on Linguistics and Language Studies*, **20**. 63–9.

Varadi, T. (1973) 'Strategies of target language learner communication: Message adjustment'. Paper presented VI Conference of the Romanian–English Linguistic Project in Timisoara.

Varonis, E.M. and Gass, S. (1985) 'Non-native/non-native conversations: a model for negotiation of meaning', *Applied Linguistics*, **6**(1): 71–90.

Weir, C.J. (1983) 'Identifying the language problems of overseas students in tertiary education in the United Kingdom'. Unpublished PhD thesis, University of London.

Wells, G. *et al*. (1981) *Learning Through Interaction: the case study language development*. Cambridge: Cambridge University Press.

Wells, G. (1985) *Language Development in the Pre-school Years*. Cambridge: Cambridge University Press.

Wetherell, M. (1982) 'Cross-cultural studies of minimal groups: implications for the social identity theory of intergroup relations', in Tajfel, H. (ed.), *Social Identity and Intergroup Relations*. Cambridge: Cambridge University Press.

Widdowson, H.G. (1975) 'The significance of simplification', *Studies in Second Language Acquisition*, University of Indiana Linguistics Club, **1**(1).

Widdowson, H. (1979) 'Rules and procedures in discourse analysis', in Myers, T. (ed.), *The Development of Conversation and Discourse*. Edinburgh: Edinburgh University Press.

Widdowson, H. (1983) *Learning Purpose and Language Use*. Oxford: Oxford University Press.

Widdowson, H. (1984) *Explorations in Applied Linguistics, 2*. Oxford: Oxford University Press.

Winitz, H. (ed.) (1981) *The Comprehension Approach to Foreign Language Instruction*. Rowley, Mass.: Newbury House.

Winograd, T. (1972) *Understanding Natural Language*. New York: Academic Press.

Wode, (1976) 'Four early stages in the development of L1 negation', *Journal of Child Language*, **4**: 84–102.

Wode, H. (1978) 'Free vs bound forms in three types of language acquisition', *Interlanguage Studies Bulletin*, **3**: 6–22.

Wode, H. (1981) *Learning a Second Language*. Tübingen: Gunter Narr.

Wolfson, N. (1976) 'Speech events and natural speech: some implications for sociolinguistic methodology', *Language in Society*, **5**: 189–209.

Wolfson, N. and Judd, E. (1983) *Sociolinguistics and Second Language Acquisition*. Rowley, Mass.: Newbury House.

Wright, F. (1984) A sociolinguistic study of passivization among black adolescents in Britain. Unpublished PhD thesis, University of Birmingham.

Wuthnow, R. (1984) 'The critical theory of Jürgen Habermas', in Wuthnow, R. *et al*. (eds) pp. 179–239.

Wuthnow, R., Hunter, J., Bergesen, A. and Kurzweil, E. (eds) *Cultural Analysis*. London: Routledge & Kegan Paul.

Yule, G. and Tarone, E. (forthcoming) 'Eliciting the performance of strategic competence', in Scarcella, R. *et al*. (eds.) *Developing Communicative Competence in a Second Language*. Rowley, Mass.: Newbury House.

Zuengler, J. (1982) 'Applying accommodation theory to variable performance data in L2', *Studies in Second Language Acquisition*, **4**(2): 181–92.

Index

n refers to a note at the end of an article

Accommodation theory, 37, 50, 200, 201
Accuracy vs fluency, 161, 180, 185, 193
Acquisitional order, 15–17, 68, 76, 153–54, 198
Acquisition vs learning, 97n, 180, 181, 197–98
Acts of identity theory, 50
Analysis of Variance (ANOVA), 46
Analytic strategies, 106
Applications of SLA research, 159–60, 193–94
Approximative strategies, 105–106
Articulation rate, 123
Attention to speech (*see* Variation, stylistic)
Authentic communication, 189

Backsliding, 51, 53, 114, 180, 191
Bangalore Project, 185, 186
Basilect, 52
British black speech, 149–50
Broken English, 56n

Casual style (*see* Variation, stylistic)
Categorical language use, 8, 13, 31, 183
Channel capacity, 70, 113, 120ff
Classroom interaction (*see* Interaction)
Classroom research, 209ff
Classroom roles (*see* Pedagogic issues)
Classroom SLA, 11–12, 68–69, 73–74, 79, 83–84, 90–95
Code-switching, 147
Collocation, 169–70
Communication/compensatory strategies (*see* Interlanguage)
Communicative competence (*see* Competence)
Communicative pressure, 190
Competence
  capability, 198–99, 202
  communicative, 3, 18ff, 131, 196
  differential, 149–50

discourse, 19, 196
dual, 198
linguistic, 3, 4ff, 19, 102, 131, 149–50, 196
multiple, 61–62, 65, 200
receptive, 156, 161
relationship to language use, 130–31
scale, 151ff
sociolinguistic, 19, 147, 196
strategic, 19, 131, 147, 196 (*see also* Interaction, strategies)
unitary, 197
Context
  classroom, 210
  domains of, 7, 11–12, 68
  ideology and, 21–23
  interaction and, 19–21, 134–35, 172ff
  language acquisition and, 26–28
  language change and, 23–26
  linguistic, 7, 14–15, 45–46, 129, 130, 182
  situational, 4–5, 6–9, 17–18, 31, 36–41, 135, 165–66, 172ff, 180–81
  social, 22, 54–55, 129–31, 135–36
Contextualization cues, 20, 24
Convergent speech behaviour (*see* Accommodation theory)
Critical sociolinguistics, 21, 25–26, 148n
Culture specific knowledge (*see* Schema)

Development vs acquisition, 120, 126n
Discourse
  domains, 114, 162, 200, 203–204
  planned, 162, 191
  unplanned, 146, 162, 191
  variation and, 39–40, 181–82
Discourse management, 24
Diffusion model, 17
Divergent speech behaviour (*see* Accommodation theory)

English for Specific Purposes (ESP), 162, 200, 204

Environmental weight, 184, 187, 189
Error-correction, 191, 211
European Science Foundation (ESF)
    Project, 133–34, 148n

Formal vs informal contexts of learning (*see*
    Classroom SLA; Naturalistic SLA)
Form–function relationships, 183, 187
Formulaic speech, 13, 69, 91–92, 113, 120,
    121, 122
Fossilization, 184

Gatekeeping interactions, 129, 136, 139,
    147
Grammaticality judgement tasks, 39, 42

Holophrastic learning, 81, 86

Implicational order, 76
Implicational scaling (*see* Research
    methodology)
Impression management, 34
Indexicality, 51
Information processing model (*see* Speech
    processing)
Input, 3, 79, 159
    vs interaction, 210
Instruction
    effect on acquisition, 68–69, 79–80,
        178–79, 185ff, 192
    nature of, 83–84, 211
    reading, 165ff
Interaction
    classroom (types of), 191, 211
    presuppositions and, 138–39, 144
    reading and, 172–77
    SLA and, 26–28, 143–44, 146–47,
        190–92
    short-term vs long-term goals in, 147
    strategies of, 139–43, 144–46
    three-phase, 191–92
Interactional sociolinguistics, 19–21, 32,
    130
Inter-ethnic communication, 133, 136,
    138ff, 144ff
Interlanguage (*see also* Variation)
    approaches for describing, 67
    continuum (*see* Variation, stylistic)
    developmental continua, 82
    explanations of, 53–54, 63

'metaphors' of, 60–61
social context and, 54–55
strategies of, 27, 69–70, 100ff, 113,
    120–21, 130
types of rule, 13
Interlingual strategies (*see* Linguistic
    strategies)
Interpretative frame, 24

J-S performance analysis, 75

Knowledge vs control, 63, 68, 70, 113, 120,
    122–23, 204

Language change (*see* Variation)
Language choice, 5–6, 22
Language proficiency, 206
Language teaching materials, 188–90
    focused, 188
    role of, 191
    unfocused, 189
Language tests
    communicative, 195–96
    data elicitation in SLA research and, 206
    integrative, 195
    psychometric, 195
    reliability, 205
    sampling behaviour and, 195–97
    theoretical framework for, 196
    validity, 205
Language transfer
    variation and, 37–38, 43, 181
Length of runs, 123
Linguistic competence (*see* Competence)
Linguistic strategies, 106–107
London-Lund corpus, 79
Long-term memory, 202

Macro vs micro sociolinguistic approaches,
    7, 69
Materials development (*see* Pedagogic
    issues)
Memory (*see* Long-term memory; Short-
    term memory)
Miscue analysis (*see* Reading aloud)
Monitor Model, 36, 180, 181, 192, 193,
    197–98
Morpheme orders, 85, 97n, 127n, 179
Motivation
    integrative, 201

instrumental, 201

Naturalistic SLA, 11–12, 87
Negation, 50–51, 69, 85–88, 89–95, 179, 201
Negotiation of meaning, 26–28, 192
Non-systematic variation (*see* Variation, free variation)

Obligatory contexts, 15, 42–43, 76
Observer Paradox, 55, 199

Patois, 130, 149, 150ff
Pause/time ratio, 123
Pedagogic issues (*see* Section Five)
    classroom interaction, 173ff, 190–92
    classroom roles, 174
    reading skills, 160, 161, 165–78
    materials development, 160, 162, 188–90
    syllabus design, 162, 185–88
    testing, 162, 195ff
Pedaogogic efficiency, 163
Pedagogic relevancy, 163, 179ff
Performance, 31, 32, 63, 67
Politeness strategy, 52–53
Processing constraints, 123ff

Questions
    learners', 174
    teachers', 173

Rate of acquisition, 192–3
Reading in a L2
    context of reading, 165–66, 172–77
    learner factors, 168, 174
    miscue analysis, 166
    methods, 168
    strategies, 168
    teacher factors, 172–77
    text factors, 168–71, 173
Reading tests, 166
Referential communication in a L2, 100ff
Research methodology (*see* Section Two)
    baseline data, 43–44, 107–108
    cross-sectional, 10, 15, 33
    elicitation task, 35–36, 62, 75, 89, 90–91, 108, 110, 134, 149, 179–80, 180–81, 206

ethnographic, 136–37
experimental, 33, 35–46
heremeneutic vs nomothetic, 57n
implicational scaling, 11, 16, 76–79, 82n, 151ff
longitudinal, 27, 50, 113–14, 134, 167
qualitative methods, 44–46
quantitative methods, 4, 46
triangulation, 135
Route vs rate of SLA, 12, 73–74 (*see also* Acquisitional order; Rate of acquisition)
Routines and patterns (*see* Formulaic speech)

Schema, 23–24, 171–72, 177
Sentence schemata, 117
Short-term memory, 162, 202
Skill-getting vs skill-using, 180
Social network, 129, 154–55
Sociolinguistic models, 47ff
Spatial prepositions, 68, 74, 76–82
Speaking rate, 123
Speech community of L2 learner, 37–38
Speech planning, 199, 202, 203–204 (*see also* Discourse, planned/ unplanned)
Stereotypes, 52
Strategies (*see also* Interlanguage, strategies)
    application of, 107
    taxonomies of, 102–107
Style-shifting (*see* Variation)
Syllabus
    design (*see* Pedagogic issues)
    learner, 186
    parallel, 188
    process, 185
    product, 185
    spiral 188
Systematic variation (*see* Variation, stylistic)

Teachers' questions, 173–74
Temporal variables, 113, 120, 123–25
Translation tasks, 179
Types of learner, 131

Universal grammar, 34
U-shaped development, 122, 125

Variability perspective on SLA, 183–84
Variation (in SLA)
  diachronic, 9, 18
  free variation, 6, 9, 17, 73, 113ff, 182–83
  gender and, 155
  interactional, 15, 28, 32, 34, 49, 50–54
  intratextual (reading aloud), 165–66,
    168–72
  language change and, 9–11, 17
  language choice and, 5–6, 136
  language forms and, 41–42, 182, 186–87
  multiple causes of, 63–64
  normative pressures and, 184, 190
  relationship between extra- and
    intralinguistic, 182
  scope of, 65–66
  studies of, 180–83
  stylistic, 8, 14, 17–18, 28–29, 31, 32, 34,
    36–41, 47–50, 61–62, 162, 181–82,
    200–201
  synchronic, 9, 18
  systematic variation, 6
  task and, 39–41
  teacher-induced, 172–77
  topic and, 38–39
Vernacular style (see Variation, stylistic)

West Indian community (British), 149
White noise experiments, 47–48, 56n